Professor Bernard L. Ramm is well known to readers of theology and biblical studies. He received a Ph.D. from the University of Southern California, and pursued postdoctoral studies at the University of Basel (where he studied with Karl Barth) and the Near Eastern School of Theology in Beirut. At present, he serves as Professor of Christian Theology at the American Baptist Seminary of the West in Berkeley, California. Included in Dr. Ramm's extensive writing credits are *Protestant Biblical Evidences, A Handbook of Contemporary Theology,* and *The God Who Makes a Difference.*

An Evangelical
Christology

Books by Bernard L. Ramm
Christian View of Science and Scripture
Hermeneutics
Protestant Biblical Interpretation
The Evangelical Heritage
The Devil and Seven Wormwoods
After Fundamentalism: The Future
  of Evangelical Theology
The Christian Appeal to Reason
An Evangelical Christology:
  Ecumenic and Historic

An Evangelical Christology

Ecumenic & Historic

BERNARD L. RAMM

Thomas Nelson Publishers
Nashville • *Camden* • *New York*

Published in Nashville, Tennessee, by Thomas
Nelson, Inc., Publishers and distributed in Canada
by Lawson Falle, Ltd., Cambridge, Ontario.

Printed in the United States of America.

Scripture quotations noted are from the Revised
Standard Version of the Bible, copyrighted 1946,
1972, © 1971, 1973.

ISBN 0-8407-7518-0

Prologue

There are so many facets to Christology that it would take an encyclopedia of Christology to do them all justice. Experts of subdivisions in Christology lament that the literature is beyond them. Doctoral dissertations of the present have grown out of footnotes of dissertations in the past. Therefore we must severely prescribe our limits.

First of all this is a generalist treatise. It is of the nature of a program in Christology. As such it also serves as an introduction to Christology. Second, we have also written a tract for the times. The historic Christology of the Christian church is being discredited from many sides. Most of these discreditors are members of a Christian communion who own up to the name of Christian. The debate is then of supreme importance. It is a debate about which compass or which chart the church shall follow in its course through this world.

Very much is said of Bultmann in the following, almost as if his opinions were the only ones influencing New Testament scholarship. We have done this because Bultmann stands at the center of a distinctive mood in New Testament studies. Those who do not follow him in all points nevertheless reflect some of his basic presuppositions. It is in this sense that we have let Bultmann stand for a class of New Testament scholars. Further, his position is presented so consistently that he becomes an ideal foil for contrasting ideas. It has been affirmed that the Bultmannian program has come to an end. The program of an extreme historical scepticism combined with an existentialist theology has come apart. That may well be, and if it has that is good news. But apparently that good news has not yet evangelized enough New Testament scholars.

Although we write about Christology as if it were one thing we real-

An Evangelical Christology

ize that the New Testament has many Christologies. Nor is it obvious how the Christology of Colossians can be harmonized with the Christology of Hebrews. The richness of the witness to Christ in the New Testament must not be underestimated nor evened out in the name of a uniform Christology. We use the word Christology in the singular for sake of convenience and to indicate an ecumenical and historical tradition.

Finally, those readers who are unfamiliar with the vocabulary and personalities of biblical and theological studies may want to read Chapters 9 and 10, as a technical survey of modern trends.

Contents

Contents

Introduction

HISTORIC OR ECUMENIC CHRISTOLOGY

In a very thorough (but now dated) article on Christology, P. Schaff and D. S. Schaff sum up ecumenical Christology (which we call historic Christology) as that Christology believed by the Greek, Latin, and evangelical Protestant churches.*

(1) There is a true incarnation of the Logos, the second person of the Godhead. This is an actual assumption of the whole human nature— body, soul, and spirit—into an abiding union with the divine personality of the eternal Logos, so that they constitute, from the moment of the supernatural conception, one undivided life.

(2) There is a distinction between nature and person, in which nature denotes the totality of powers and qualities which constitute a being; while person is the ego, the self-conscious, self-asserting and acting subject.

(3) The God-man is the result of the incarnation. Christ is not a double being, nor a compound being, nor a middle being, but he is the one Person of the Lord Jesus Christ.

(4) In the incarnation there is not qualification or diminution of either the Godhead or the humanity of Christ, but each retains its own integrity.

(5) It is a genuine hypostatic union, which is a real, supernatural, personal, and inseparable union.

---

* "Christology," *The New Schaff-Herzog, Encyclopedia of Religious Knowledge*, Vol. 3, 54-55. I am condensing the seven points of the authors.

(6) The whole work of Christ is to be attributed to his person and not to the one or the other nature exclusively.

(7) Jesus Christ exists only in an incarnation, and in this sense there is no Jesus of Nazareth possessing an independent life of his own (the *Anhupostasia* and *Enhupostasia*).

THE DOCUMENTS OF HISTORIC CHRISTOLOGY

THE APOSTLES' CREED

I believe in God the Father Almighty, Maker of heaven and earth,

And in Jesus Christ his only Son our Lord; who was conceived by the Holy Ghost, born of the Virgin Mary, suffered under Pontius Pilate, was crucified, dead, and buried; he descended into hell; the third day he rose again from the dead; he ascended into heaven, and sitteth on the right hand of God the Father Almighty; from thence he shall come to judge the quick and the dead.

I believe in the Holy Ghost; the holy catholic Church; the communion of saints; the forgiveness of sins; the resurrection of the body; and the life everlasting. Amen.

THE NICENE CREED

We believe in God the Father Almighty, Maker of heaven and earth, and of all things visible and invisible;

And in one Lord Jesus Christ, the only-begotten Son of God, begotten of the Father before all worlds, God of God, Light of Light, Very God of Very God, begotten, not made, being of one substance with the Father by whom all things were made; who for us men, and for our salvation, came down from heaven, and was incarnate by the Holy Spirit of the Virgin Mary, and was made man, and was crucified also for us under Pontius Pilate. He suffered and was buried, and the third day he rose again according to the Scriptures, and ascended into heaven, and sitteth on the right hand of the Father. And he shall come again with glory to judge both the quick and the dead, whose kingdom shall have no end.

And we believe in the Holy Spirit, the Lord and Giver of Life, who proceedeth from the Father and the Son, who with the Father and the

Son together is worshipped and glorified, who spoke by the prophets. And we believe one holy catholic and apostolic Church. We acknowledge one baptism for the remission of sins. And we look for the resurrection of the dead, and the life of the world to come. Amen.

THE DEFINITION OF CHALCEDON

Therefore, following the holy Fathers, we all with one accord teach men to acknowledge one and the same Son, our Lord Jesus Christ, at once complete in Godhead and complete in manhood, truly God and truly man, consisting also of a reasonable soul and body; of one substance [*homoousios*] with the Father as regards his Godhead, and at the same time of one substance with us as regards his manhood; like us in all respects, apart from sin; as regards his Godhead, begotten of the Father before the ages, but yet as regards his manhood begotten, for us men and for our salvation, of Mary the Virgin, the God-bearer [*theotokos*]; one and the same Christ, Son, Lord, Only-begotten, recognized in two natures, without confusion, without change, without division, without separation; the distinction of natures being in no way annulled by the union, but rather the characteristics of each nature being preserved and coming together to form one person and subsistence [*hupostasis*], not as parted or separated into two persons, but one and the same Son and Only-begotten God the Word, Lord Jesus Christ; even as the prophets from earliest times spoke of him, and our Lord Jesus Christ himself taught us, and the creed of the Fathers has handed down to us.

THE ATHANASIAN CREED

It is necessary, however, to eternal salvation that he should also faithfully believe in the Incarnation of our Lord Jesus Christ. Now the right faith is that we should believe and confess that our Lord Jesus Christ, the Son of God, is equally both God and man.

He is God from the Father's substance, begotten before time; and he is man from his mother's substance, born in time. Perfect God, perfect man composed of a rational soul and human flesh, equal to the Father in respect of his divinity, less than the Father in respect of his humanity.

Who, although he is God and man, is nevertheless not two but one Christ. He is one, however, not by the transformation of his divinity

11

into flesh, but by the taking up of his humanity into God; one certainly not by confusion of substance, but by oneness of person. For just as rational soul and flesh are a single man, so God and man are a single Christ.

Who suffered for our salvation, descended to hell, rose from the dead, ascended to heaven, sat down at the Father's right hand, whence he will come to judge living and dead: at whose coming all men will rise again with their bodies, and will render an account of their deeds; and those who have behaved well will go to eternal life, those who have behaved badly to eternal fire.

This is the Catholic faith. Unless a man believes it faithfully and steadfastly, he will not be able to be saved.

THE SECOND HELVETIC CONFESSION

There are in one and the same Jesus Christ our Lord, two natures, the divine and the human nature; and we say that these two are so conjoined or united that they are not swallowed up, confounded, or mingled together, but rather united or joined together in one person, the properties of each nature being safe and remaining still; so that we do worship one Christ our Lord and not two; I say, one, true God and man; as touching his divine nature, of the same substance with the Father, and as touching his human nature, of the same substance with us, and "like unto us in all things, sin only excepted."

THE AUGSBURG CONFESSION

The Word, that is, the Son of God, took unto him man's nature in the womb of the blessed Virgin Mary, so that there are two natures, the divine and the human, inseparably joined together in unity of person; one Christ, true God and true man: who was born of the Virgin Mary, truly suffered, was crucified, dead and buried.

THE THIRTY-NINE ARTICLES OF RELIGION

The Son, which is the Word of the Father, begotten from everlasting of the Father, the very and eternal God, and of one substance with the Father, took man's nature in the womb of the blessed Virgin, of her substance; and so that two whole and perfect natures, that is to say, the Godhead and Manhood, were joined together in one person, never to be divided, whereof is one Christ, very God and very man; who truly suffered, was crucified, dead and buried.

THE WESTMINSTER CONFESSION OF FAITH

The Son of God, the second Person in the Trinity, being very and eternal God, of one substance, and equal with the Father, did, when the fullness of time was come, take upon him man's nature, with all the essential properties and common infirmities thereof, yet without sin; being conceived by the power of the Holy Ghost, in the womb of the Virgin Mary, of her substance. So that two whole, perfect and distinct natures, the Godhead and the manhood, were inseparably joined together in one person, without conversion, composition, or confusion. Which person is very God and very man, yet one Christ, the only Mediator between God and man.

THE THEOLOGICAL DECLARATION OF BARMEN

Jesus Christ, as he is attested for us in Holy Scripture, is the one Word of God which we have to hear and which we have to trust and obey in life and death...As Jesus Christ is God's assurance of the forgiveness of all our sins, so in the same way and with the same seriousness he is also God's mighty claim upon our whole life. Through him befalls us a joyful deliverance from the godless fetters of this world for a free, grateful service to his creatures...We reject the false doctrine, as though there were areas of our life in which we would not belong to Jesus Christ, but to other lords...The Christian Church is the congregation of the brethren in which Jesus Christ acts presently as the Lord in Word and sacrament through the Holy Spirit.

THE WORLD COUNCIL OF CHURCHES

A fellowship of churches which confess the Lord Jesus as God and Saviour according to the Scriptures and therefore seek to fulfill together their common callings to the glory of the one God, Father, Son and Holy Spirit.

In order to establish peace or communion between sinful human beings and Himself, as well as to fashion them into a fraternal community, God determined to intervene in human history in a way both new and definitive. For He sent His Son, clothed in our flesh, in order that through this Son He might snatch men from the power of darkness and of Satan (cf. Col 1:13; Acts 10:38) and that in this Son He might reconcile the world to Himself (cf. 2 Cor 5:19). Through Him, God made all orders of existence. God further appointed Him heir of all things, so that in the Son He might restore them all (cf. Eph 1:10).

For Jesus Christ was sent into the world as a real Mediator between God and men. Since He is God, all divine fullness dwells bodily in Him (Col 2:9). According to His human nature, He is the new Adam, made head of a renewed humanity, and full of grace and of truth (Jn 1:14). Therefore the Son of God walked the ways of a true Incarnation that He might make men sharers in the divine nature. He became poor for our sakes, though He had been rich, in order that His poverty might enrich us (2 Cor 8:9). The Son of Man came not that He might be served, but that He might be a servant, and give His life as a ransom for the many—that is, for all (cf. Mk 10:45).

The sainted Fathers of the Church firmly proclaim that what was not taken up by Christ was not healed. Now, what He took up was our entire human nature such as it is found among us in our misery and poverty, though without our sin (cf. Heb 4:15; 9:28). For Christ said concerning Himself, whom the Father made holy and sent into the world (cf. Jn 10:36): "The Spirit of the Lord is upon me because he anointed me; to bring good news to the poor he sent me, to heal the broken-hearted, to proclaim to the captives release, and sight to the blind" (Lk 4:18). And again: "The Son of Man came to seek and to save what was lost" (Lk 19:10).

But what was once preached by the Lord, or what once wrought in Him for the saving of the human race, must be proclaimed and spread abroad to the ends of the earth (Acts 1:8), beginning from Jerusalem (cf. Lk 24:47). Thus, what He once accomplished for the salvation of all may in the course of time come to achieve its effect in all.

14

1

Christology at the Center

The Christian faith is based upon the person and work of Jesus Christ. Christology is the reflective and systematic study of the person and work of Jesus Christ. The concept of a Christology is unique to Christianity. The notion of such a person as Jesus Christ is unique, namely that in virtue of an incarnation he bears within himself at the same time the divine and the human. That requires much explanation. The concept of the work of Christ is also unique. That the world is redeemed by a very few unique and unusual events (e.g., a vicarious death, a bodily resurrection) is unique in the history of religions. It is unique in a third way in that the exploration of the significance of the person and work of Christ leads to extended historical, linguistic, literary, and theological topics.

Jesus Christ is called a teacher in the New Testament (TDNT: 2, 148ff.). However he was a unique teacher in that his teaching cannot be separated from his person. Some philosopher other than Plato could have argued for the immortality of the soul; and some mathematical genius besides Einstein could have proposed the theory of relativity. However Jesus' teaching is so joined to who he was that his teaching falls to the ground if he is separated from his teaching.

THE IMPORTANCE OF CHRISTOLOGY

Evangelical Christology is a continuation of historic Christology. It is the Christology stated in The Apostle's Creed, refined in the Nicean-Constantinople Creed, elaborated in the Chalcedonian Creed, and finally summed up in the Creed of Athanasius (see Skard: 1960).

Belief in historic Christology does not mean that every line of a creed is beyond criticism, nor that the original creeds resolve all problems, nor that the creeds end Christological reflection. It is the belief that the creeds reflect in their way the materials found here and there in the New Testament. To believe in the Christology of these creeds is also to say that one believes in the Christology of the New Testament.

Further, evangelical Christology is in harmony with the Christology that prevailed in subsequent history after the creeds. There is essential agreement among the Roman Catholic theologians, the Eastern Orthodox theologians, and the theologians of the Reformation of the sixteenth century. Although Luther and Calvin made some different emphases in their Christologies, they were one in affirming the Christology of the creeds. One can find historic Christology woven into all the great confessions of the sixteenth and seventeenth centuries.

It was Schleiermacher who launched a critical attack upon historic Christology, and since then it has been losing ground. Theologians and New Testament scholars who hold to it are a minority. Many alternative Christologies have been set forth in place of historic Christology. However if there is a change in Christological doctrine, a change is mandated in all other doctrines. Christology is so central to Christian theology that to alter Christology is to alter all else. W. Elert (1960, 291), a prominent Lutheran theologian, stated it as follows:

> Without the Christological affirmation there is no doctrine of God himself, no doctrine of the Holy Spirit, and no doctrine of the Trinity. Christology builds the presupposition for the doctrine of creation, for the doctrine of divine providence, for the doctrine of election, for the doctrine of justification and for the doctrine of the church and its sacraments.

If there is a change of Christology then there must be a change in all the doctrines which Elert mentions. If a person chooses Bultmann's or Tillich's Christology he must also make the corresponding shifts in the whole range of theological topics.

If there is a major shift in Christology there must also be a major shift in one's doctrine of the church. According to the New Testament and historic Christology, Christ is Lord, Savior, and Foundation of the church. In his *Christology* Dietrich Bonhoeffer says that all the liberal theologians from Schleiermacher to Ritschl who abandoned historic Christology must in principle abandon the historic doctrine of the church. He presses the point even harder. To abandon historic Christology is to abandon the concept of heresy. But if there is no heresy it follows logically that there is no truth.

Although not putting it so bluntly, Wolfhart Pannenberg also argues that if we abandon historic Christology we must so cut back our other doctrines to the point that there is no Christianity left in our theology.

It is not only the doctrine of the church that is involved deeply in Christology but also Christian experience. There are two ways in which Jesus Christ can be present in his church and to the believer: (i) as the Son of God risen from the dead he is at the right hand of the Father but in virtue of his deity and the Holy Spirit he is mystically present on earth; or (ii) as not the Son of God and as not risen from the dead he can be present only in the sense of the remembered Christ—remembered in preaching and teaching. It is only on the grounds of historic Christology that Christ can be truly (but mystically or secretly) present to the believer. Again to follow Bonhoeffer (1966, 49ff.), Christ is present in the Word, in the Sacrament, and in the Community. The Christian experience of Christ according to historic Christology is with the present mystical Christ.

When historic Christology is denied, Christ is not really present in the church or in the sermon or to the Christian. It is true that liberal theologians and existential theologians (like Bultmann) will speak of Christ being present in the message or in the kerygma, but that is but another way of speaking of Christ remembered. Christian experience in such a context is the person's response to the sermon, not to the living Christ.

Modern church people may claim to have come to terms with modern science, modern philosophy, and modern biblical criticism and therefore can no longer believe in historic Christology. But has this person truly reckoned with the price one must pay for the rejection of historic Christology? The presence of the mystical Christ is lost, and with it the kind of experience that only the encounter with Christ our contemporary (Kierkegaard) can yield. Faith is in the present, living Lord Jesus. To speak of faith in a dead Christ is impossible (Heim: 1959, 177ff.). A Christian cannot have a personal relationship with a totally human Jesus who died and never rose from the dead. There can be an "I-thou" relationship only between the living believer and the living Christ.

Both Tillich and Bultmann admit that no such personal relationship is possible in terms of their theology. The change in Christology radically changes the nature of Christian experience. R. Prenter bears down hard on this point (1960, 274). Peter's confession, "you are the Christ, the Son of the living God," is the norm of all confession of Christ. "[Peter's] answer, which did not speak *of* Jesus in the third person, but in the second person *to* him, is *the Christological confession*" (italics are his). Then Prenter says that it must be the same today. But we can say "you are the Christ" today only if Christ is the living Christ. If there is no living Christ we may have opinions about Christ (*Christusanschauung, Auffassungen*), but we have no experience of the living Christ. A change in Christology radically alters what is meant by "the experience of Jesus."

If historic Christology is rejected then the mission of the church becomes ambiguous. The Great Commission is based on the affirmations of historic Christology. If a denomination in its missionary work eliminates, directly or implicitly, the Great Commission, the vacuum created by such a decision is filled with much lesser activities. Such activities have virtues of their own, such as medical work, education in agriculture, or the development of schools. All are noble tasks. But such noble and humanitarian goals have their own implicit Christology which in turn cannot rival the clear call of the Great Commission and the historic Christology upon which it rests.

In the following we shall make our case for a Christology that we think is biblical, ecumenical Christology, and is in turn the current evangelical Christology. It is not an easy matter to defend historic Christology in the contemporary church. The temperament of the times is against it. The drift in theology and in New Testament criticism is strongly away from historic Christology. In the next section we shall review in a summary way why this is the case.

THE ATTACK UPON HISTORIC CHRISTOLOGY

Even though historic Christology has had such a sustained acceptance in the church it has had difficulty in sustaining itself the past two hundred years. The attack upon it is well documented and has not let up. Berkouwer (1954) has a chapter on "crisis in the doctrine of two natures," and Pannenberg (1968) has a section on "the impasse on the doctrine of the two natures." The book *The Myth of God Incarnate* (Hick: 1977) gives the impression that it wants to drive the final nail in the doctrine of the two natures. A brief review of the reasons this attack began and continues is proper at this point even though many of these matters will be discussed in more detail later on.

(1) It has been asserted that the Gospels are not substantial history, that when the criteria of scientific history are applied to the Gospels not much survives, nor is it possible to construct a valid biography of Jesus from the Gospels. Further the amount of material about Jesus outside the New Testament is so small as to be almost worthless.

It is true that Arthur Drews (1865-1935) did deny that Jesus ever lived. Recently the German scholar, G. A. Wells, affirmed the same (cf. Marshall: 1977, 14ff.). There is almost universal agreement that Jesus lived, that he was a remarkable spiritual personality, that he stands at the beginning of the Christian movement in history, and that he was put to death by Pontius Pilate. However, from such slim materials no meaningful Christology can be constructed.

(2) The critics of the Gospels have applied various critical methods to the study of the Gospels. They have concluded that most of the materials in the Gospels are the products of elaboration, patching up, editorializing, and theologizing. If the Gospels are seen as having this character, then there is an end to historic Christology. Historic Christology is built on the general authenticity of the Gospels, and if that historical authenticity is undermined so is historic Christology.

(3) Modern mentality is the product of many past forces and personalities. Some of these trends include: scepticism in philosophy (Kant, Hume); the development of scientific writing of history; the birth of psychology, sociology, and anthropology; the growth of the sciences; and the spilling over of these into technology and education that effects the masses. Granted that the very notion of "modern mentality" is a loose one, those who have it do not believe the sort of things found in the Gospels. They do not believe that leprosy can be cleansed by a word, or that a storm can be stilled by a command, or that God can become incarnate.

It is presumed that the supernatural elements in the Gospels are the results of mistakes or elaborations, or by some other process lost to us. It could have been that the manner in which Jesus helped somebody was transmuted into a miracle. Or some passing remark of Jesus could have later been elaborated into a high Christological claim. Or the early church converted the obscure events after the crucifixion into stories of the resurrection appearances.

(4) Theologians and biblical scholars do not do their work isolated from larger contexts of consideration. Such scholars always have in mind some larger view of the universe which has some bearing on their limited projects. We know that there are two versions of the theory of evolution. There is the very limited or restricted one which

19

limits its attention to the production of life on this earth. It is concerned with the ordering and dating of the strata of the earth and the attempt to interpret the fossil record. The larger theory of evolution could be called the cosmic theory of evolution. This presumes that the story told of cosmic evolution from the original Big Bang is the most comprehensive vision of things. And the human race finds its interpretation by fitting itself into this cosmic ordering of things.

In a debate in England sparked by the publication of *The Myth of God Incarnate*, those who defended the incarnation as a religious myth were challenged by those who defended the historic Christology of the church. The debate was moderated by a very competent British philosopher, Basil Mitchell. Speaking to the "mythographers" (as Mitchell labeled the deniers of historic Christology) he accused them of taking such an evolutionary view in their understanding of things that they had to reject the incarnation because of its incompatability with the theory of a philosophical or cosmic evolution (see Stott: 1979, 30).

To the degree that Christian theologians and New Testament scholars are influenced by the myth of evolution, to that the same degree they find it difficult to defend historic Christology. The Christian meaning of humankind contained in historic Christology and the meaning of man derived from the myth of evolution can only collide with each other.

(5) A famous biblical scholar of the nineteenth century proposed the thesis that the creeds of the early church were not attempts to reproduce simple biblical teaching but were thoroughly permeated with Greek philosophical or metaphysical concepts (Edwin Hatch, *The Influence of Greek Ideas and Usages on the Christian Church*). In the twentieth century the same thesis was applied to the production of the Gospels, their Christologies, and eventually the many other parts of the New Testament.

If this is the case it creates a major difficulty for those who believe in historic Christology. If the New Testament and the creeds of later centuries are so saturated with this Hellenistic vocabulary, then the New Testament and the creeds lose much of the traditional authority. Later we shall raise this very question again. That Hellenism exerted a great influence in the church is manifest in the New Testament being written in Greek and not the Aramaic of Jesus and his disciples. But we shall deny that the whole of Christology as it historically developed is thereby corrupted. If the bishops of the early church did make such a philosophical shift and substitution in vocabulary, then the great creeds lose most of their authority.

(6) There is a tyranny of truth in the New Testament. God has honored the name of only one man whereby we can be saved (Acts 4:12). Further no person comes to the Father except through the Son (John 14:6). This is in direct conflict with so much modern mentality—religious or secular. It was during the Enlightenment that in religion the supreme virtue was reckoned to be tolerance and the supreme vice to be bigotry. This was set out so dramatically in Lessing's famous play, *Nathan the Wise*. John Hick's essay, "Jesus and World Religions" (in Hick: 1977) is a recent, prose version of Lessing's basic thesis. Historic Christology cannot but collide with the mentality of the Enlightenment in its toleration for all religious opinions.

(7) Both modern philosophy and modern science have moved away from attempting to create grand philosophical schemes. Philosophy in particular has given up the goal of writing out a description of the universe as a whole. The analytic or linguistic school has greatly narrowed the scope of philosophy. A. R. Lacey's *A Dictionary of Philosophy* concentrates on logical and mathematical concepts and is symptomatic of the current status of philosophy. Existentialism also flees from creating a grand metaphysical system and limits itself to the view of reality as seen through the grid of the human person (*Dasein*). On a pragmatic level the lay person is also a person of much restricted vision, living from home to job, from school to family, from world news to professional sports.

Historic Christology comes in direct conflict with this kind of mentality. It has a doctrine of creation and a doctrine of world history as well as a doctrine of man. It claims to speak of eternity-past, present time, and eternity-future. In its cosmic scope it spans the ages and the spaces. To be a Christian is to step out of the narrow confines of vision that characterize so much of our philosophy, science, and the patterns of our daily living.

(8) The long-range effect of the moral philosophy of Kant has had its influence on Christology. In his *Critique of Practical Reason* (1969 ed.) Kant interpreted religion as primarily ethics. It gave rise to what has been called "ethical theology." Certainly other factors were at work too, such as an ethical interpretation of the kingdom of God. The tendency has been to shift theology away from dogmatic concerns to ethical issues. This is seen in the earlier part of this century in the emergence of the social gospel and in the latter part of this century in the ethics of the theology of hope and its related political theology (i.e., theology with a pronounced concern for social ethics at its very center). This has meant that Christology with its great concern for the-

ology is out of harmony with Christianity understood as ethics. Neo-orthodoxy's return to concern for dogmatics may have for a time slowed down the drive to interpret the Christian faith primarily as concern for ethical issues, but it never stopped the trend.

(9) Modern psychology has also created problems for historic Christology. Part of the task of psychology has been to look at the older psychological terminology of our language and subject it to criticism. There are new definitions of person, personality, and self-consciousness. Such new definitions involve tensions with the older terms used in historic Christology. A. Gilg (1966, 105-06) lists sixty-nine terms (in Greek) of historic Christology, many of which are psychological in nature and have come under reassessment in modern psychology.

It has also been urged that modern psychology makes it very difficult to imagine the nature of a person's self-consciousness who is alleged to be both God and man. Others have raised questions about Jesus' sexual life and sexual fantasies.

The concept that God comes into this world by the incarnation and appears as a historical figure crashes into all our human self-sufficiencies. It is an offense to our sense of the natural order, to our sense of scientific history, to our sense of our intellectual competence, and to our sense of our moral worth. *It is therefore of necessity that Christology and the human mind*—wherever and whenever—*clash* (Prenter: 1960). It is not a matter of being an unfortunate clash; *it is a necessity*. Rather than Christians shying away from the collision they should say: *that too is part of our Christology*. One cannot hold to historic Christology and in turn expect to have peace in the world. Of necessity there cannot be peace. Therefore any person who stands with historic Christology in the twentieth century must expect the confrontations of human self-sufficiency, for it is a clash in academics as well as morality.*

METHODOLOGICAL QUESTIONS

In any work in Christology there are certain questions of method

---

* Emil Brunner knew that decisions in Christology were not made solely on the basis of the interpretations of the texts. He claims too many theologians have surrendered to the scientific and positivistic mentality so prevalent in our contemporary culture. If this mentality is questioned the challenger is branded a barbarian. But, as Brunner concludes, it is impossible to merge the supremacy of science with Christianity. *The Mediator*, 119, fn. 1.

which are matters of choice. Each writer on Christology must make these methodological decisions, for they are guides for his entire work. Six of these important and related decisions are listed here.

(1) Which has the priority in Christology: the work of Christ or the person of Christ? It is Bultmann in modern times who has argued most vigorously that Christology should be limited to the benefits of Christ (the work of Christ) and not be bothered with Christological speculations (the person of Christ). His favorite text is a citation of Melanchthon, the coworker with Luther at Wittenberg. In protest against the kind of theological speculation characteristic of the medieval theologians, Melanchthon said that to really know Christ is to know his benefits and not to speculate about the natures of Christ or the mode of the incarnation. This enables Bultmann and his followers to greatly restrict their scope in Christology and avoid the difficult problems which attend historic Christology.

Berkouwer has taken up this challenge and argues for the priority of the study of the person of Christ over the work of Christ (1954, Ch. 6). To begin, Bultmann's interpretation of Melanchthon is suspect. Melanchthon was not de-emphasizing historic Christology nor the creeds of the church. He was focusing his protest against scholastic scholarship, which Luther had also criticized very sharply.

Berkouwer is right in affirming that it is the person of Christ that gives the work of Christ its dignity, its worth, and its importance. When the author of Hebrews speaks of Christ offering himself to God by an "eternal Spirit," the very point being made is that it is the unusual person of Christ that gives his death its saving worth (Heb. 9:14). This is also reflected in Philippians 2:5-11. The reason Christ is given a name above all names is that he was the Son of God in the flesh who was obedient, who suffered, and who died the death on the cross. The reason Jesus Christ is the Lamb of God who can take away the sins of the world (John 1:29) is that he is the incarnate Logos (John 1:14).

In Bultmann's theology, dogmatic assertions are replaced by existential prescripts. This means that theology is not about the relationships that obtain among God, man, and creation, and which are "out there" and true. Rather theology is about the existential quality of our lives, and hence theology gives us the prescripts or rules or guides for authentic Christian existence. For theology understood in this fashion, all Bultmann needs is the work of Christ (really, his existential benefits).

To an adherent of historic Christology this is not only a sad reduction in Christology but also a sad reduction of the benefits of Christ. A reductionist Christology has reductionist benefits.

In a reductionist Christology there must come a great loss in sacramental theology, for the sacraments as historically understood are based on historic Christology. There is the loss of the life everlasting and the resurrection from the dead; that is, the traditional Christian hope is emasculated. Another loss is that of *Christus praesens* which refers to the personal communion of every believer with Christ and to the presence of Christ in Christian assemblies.

(2) Does Christological investigation start with the earthly life of Jesus and from that attempt to determine what might be special about Jesus (*von unten*—Christology from below); or does Christology start with the eternal Son and follow his career from pre-existence to incarnation (*von oben*—Christology from above)? Most New Testament scholars prefer the *von unten* approach. Pannenberg (1968, 33ff.), though a theologian, is a strong defender of Christology from below, and his reasons are the same as the New Testament scholars. His position is that modern man will not accept the affirmation of a developed Christology such as is found in the Chalcedonian Definition. We are all locked in history and therefore must start in history. This means that the life of Jesus in the Gospels must be studied and from that study we learn what else can be said of Jesus.

In his preaching and in his theology (*Evangelical Theology*, 3 vols.), Thielicke follows the same route but for different reasons. As human beings we cannot understand high Christological affirmations at first encounter. There is an abstraction to them which we cannot translate into life. However when the Gospels are read and it is seen how Jesus meets various people and talks with them, we may then have a very concrete picture of what coming to Jesus Christ means. For evangelistic reasons *von unten* is the proper procedure.

W. Elert (1960, 291-93) is critical of the *von oben* approach because it became too closely connected with official Roman Catholic dogma. He sides with Luther who was critical of that approach but not sceptical. We must follow the *von unten* approach because the basis of all Christology is the report of the earthly life of Jesus in the Gospels and in the Epistles of the New Testament. If there is any truth in Jesus it can be found out only by carefully sifting the New Testament documents in a critical fashion. However the question must be asked: does the New Testament truly contribute anything to the discussion? The New Testament keeps an open stance on the issue. It is the situation that determines which method is used. Elert himself concedes that John 1:1-14 follows the *von oben* approach. There is also *von oben* Christology in

Philippians 2:5-11. On the other hand, the Synoptic Gospels and the sermons in the book of Acts follow a *von unten* approach. If the New Testament may start with either, the issue must be kept open.

Further, it is not difficult to imagine situations where the *von oben* approach is better. In a debate with a Muslim concerning Mohammed or Jesus it could well be that the *von oben* approach would be the more effective. The same may be the case in a debate with a learned Hindu or Buddhist. A culture shift could force the *von oben* approach over the *von unten*. As obvious as it may appear in the present context of studies to stress the priority of the *von unten* method, we ought with the New Testament not presume that it must always be this way.

(3) The most important decision in a method of approach to Christology hinges on the following issue: has critical methodology in New Testament studies become so technically sophisticated that only New Testament experts can write about Christology, or do the issues in Christology inevitably spill over into a comprehensive view of history and basic philosophical commitment?

Some books written by New Testament scholars ignore completely any reference to any issues outside the confines of critical New Testament research. Other books as R. Fuller's *The Foundations of New Testament Christology* do give some attention to Christology in the confessional life of the church. Theologians like Kasper (*Jesus the Christ*), Berkouwer (*The Person of Christ*), and Aldwinckle (*More Than Man*) recognize critical issues but write mainly on the larger issues of Christology, especially in church tradition.

It is a point that will be argued at many places in the following exposition so we will make it here for the first time: *the issues in Christology involve so many disciplines and decisions that the final assessment is a combined philosophical and theological decision.* By *philosophical* is not meant any particular philosophy but that the decision is a complex one involving the whole range of a person's thought and presuppositions. A *theological* decision without being informed by current New Testament studies is not a responsible assessment; nor is the assessment of the critical scholar who would ignore the inevitable philosophical, theological, and historical presuppositions in Christology.

(4) Another decision with far reaching implications, and which again forms much of the following exposition, can be stated analytically as follows:

The historic thesis: Granted the complexity of the Synoptic problem and other critical considerations, nonetheless, the starting point in the interpretation of Gospels is that they are historically authentic materials describing what Jesus said, what he did, as well as his fate on the cross and his resurrection from the dead.

The radical thesis: The point of beginning is to presume that the Gospels are primarily the creations of the early church communities and their scribes in which they reflect their own trials and experiences, and working backwards from that some of the authentic sayings and deeds of Jesus may be recovered.

This decision for one or the other governs all the work one does in Christology, and it ought to be obvious that historic Christology fosters the first thesis.

(5) At stake in the previous decision is our approach to the methodology of understanding history. It is proposed that people of the first Christian century would accept as historical all sorts of unusual phenomena without hesitation. On the other hand since the Enlightenment, the historian is sceptical of all historical data on principle and rejects outright all supernatural tales. This is proposed as a radical difference in historical consciousness. It is not a matter of accepting or rejecting things piecemeal, but it is an entire and radical difference in mentality. Thus the writer of the book of Acts mentions common historical matters but also miraculous events and interventions all in the same breath. This means that his historical consciousness is radically different from a modern historian who would never write such a mixture of events (cf. Hahn: 1966, 8ff.).

On the other hand it is argued that the gap in historical consciousness (*Geschichtsbewusstsein*) is not all that great between ancient and modern historians. The writings of Hebert Butterfield (1979) on biblical history would be a case in point. Historic Christology is obviously built on the assumption that, whatever differences there might be in historical consciousness between the writers of the Gospels and the modern period, it did not prevent them from giving us authentic historical materials about Jesus Christ. Similar opinions can be found in Martin Hengel's (1980) *Acts and the History of Earliest Christianity*.

In conclusion let us state as clearly as possible the current crisis in Christology. If the radical critic is right, namely that the Gospels are church creations with great elaboration of materials and deeply colored all the way through with mythological materials, then historic Christology with all its topics is dead. Such concepts as the pre-existence of Christ, incarnation, the virgin birth, sinless life, atoning sacrifice, bodily resurrection, ascension to heaven, and second coming are empty of meaning. All the great discussions about the deity of Christ, the nature of the incarnation, and the universal significance of Christ may have been learned, interesting, and vital in their times, but in reality there was no substance to them. From this perspective historic Christology was built upon many mistakes. The history of historic Christology from the perspective of the radical critic must appear as many dreary centuries in which the same fundamental mistakes were continuously repeated. At best we can be kind and tolerant to our forerunners in Christology, confessing that if we lived in their times we would not have been wiser. But the only Christology remaining to us today is the technical, piecemeal, analytic, and dissective work of New Testament specialists.

Or, historic Christology still has the right to focus on the person of Christ. Granted previous generations overlooked many of the problems connected with the Synoptic problem; nevertheless, the Gospels remain as authentic historical witnesses which form the bedrock of historic Christology.

2

Creeds and Christology

THE APOSTLES' AND NICEAN-CONSTANTINOPLE CREEDS

In discussing Christology there is some choice in the order of topics. Currently there is much emphasis upon the newer critical methods of New Testament scholarship which developed since World War II. However we have chosen to first look at the historical developments.

The amount of Christological materials produced by the church Fathers is enormous. In his first large volume on the Christology of this period Aloys Grillmeier (1975) projects two more in order to finish the task of tracing out Christological thought in the first seven Christian centuries. Our purpose is not to cover any of that ground, for that is a study for experts in Patristics. We shall limit our discussion to the famous creedal statements because in subsequent historical developments of Christology it is the creeds that are most readily picked up. Further, in that these creeds and the controversies around them have been rehearsed so many times we shall treat them briefly.*

THE APOSTLES' CREED

As far as Christology is concerned the following observations may be made about this confession:

(1) It is a confessional statement, a soteriological affirmation. The

---

* The most thorough work on the subject is J. N. D. Kelly, *Early Christian Creeds*, third edition. There is also much detailed material on the opinions of the individual fathers in Jaroslav Pelikan, *The Christian Tradition: The Emergence of the Catholic Tradition (100-600)* Vol. I.

creed does have a long history (cf. Schaff: 1897, II: 52-55). It arose out of the practice of baptism in which the candidate made his confession. Therefore it is neither abstract nor theologically technical. It does indicate that original formulations about the meaning of Jesus Christ grew out of the ministry of the church and not out of theological reflection, which is a point to remember when later creeds assumed the status of church law.

(2) It presumes the historical authenticity of the four Gospels. For whatever the reasons were, the early church did not reflect critically upon the Gospels. On this subject Bettenson (1963, 26-29) lists the writings of Papias, Irenaeus, and the Muratorian Canon as containing reflections on the origins of the Gospels. At this period in the church the Gospels were accepted at face value, and that is why in current critical studies the opinions of the early church fathers are not deemed important.

(3) It confesses Jesus as "God's Son and our Lord," which is a strong Christological affirmation but not as yet precise enough to settle the disputes that arose later in the church.

(4) It also specifies what we call "the career" of Jesus. He was conceived of the Holy Ghost and born of the virgin Mary, He was crucified, buried, and risen from the dead. He did ascend to the right hand of God. The point is that the confession of Christ in the creeds is not limited to affirmations about our Lord's deity or humanity or the nature of the incarnation. In modern language they also confess the work of Christ. The salvific action of Christ is no less confessional than his person.

THE NICENE CREED

It was Arius (250-336) of Alexandria who placed the church in its first great Christological debate. In two brief letters Arius declared that Jesus Christ is not the eternal, unbegotten, uncreated Son of God, rather he is the first and most glorious of God's creation and therefore yet a creature (see Hardy: 1954, III: 329-34). Athanasius (296-373) responded to the challenge and defended what we have called here historic Christology. *On the Incarnation of the Word* by Athanasius is one of the classics of Christian theology (see Hardy: 1954, III: 41-110). It was the emperor Constantine who called the contestants and their parties to Nicea, a small town near Constantinople, to reach a decision and so keep peace in the empire (325).

The result of this council was the Creed of Nicea. But such matters are complicated since a later document is now traditionally known as the Creed of Nicea. A document was read at the Council of Chalcedon as the Creed of Nicea, which has also been called the Nicean-Constantinople Creed. Kelly (1972) traces out this complex story. Our remarks center on the tradition of 325.

(1) In every way the creed affirmed the deity of Christ so that no ambiguity could remain. The text reads: "We believe...in one Lord Jesus Christ, the only-begotten Son of God, Begotten of the Father before all ages. Light of Light, true God of true God, begotten not made, of one substance with the Father, through whom all things were made."

(2) In order to state the deity of Christ in such a way that it could not be evaded by the Arians, the creed said that Christ was of the same substance (*homoousios*) as the Father. Although the Arians could admit that Christ had a similar substance (*homoiousios*) they could not agree to the ascription of the same substance to Christ. The term *homoousios* was controversial in the church. It was objected that it was not a biblical word. It has been charged that it is a philosophical term, but Kasper (1976, 176ff.) claims that it was not used in a philosophical sense. After a century of discussion the term won its way in the creed since nobody could suggest a better one.

(3) It has become so customary in this century to assert that the creed has been too heavily influenced by Greek substance philosophical terms that the biblical elements in the creed have been overlooked. That God is Light is a truth to be found in both Testaments. Therefore to call Christ Light of Light is to make a clear affirmation of his deity on biblical grounds. In John 17:3 it speaks of the true God. This word *true* is then picked up and said of Christ. If the word applies to God the Father it also applies to God the Son.

(4) The creed affirms the incarnation and the humanity of Christ. However it said nothing about how the humanity and deity were related in Christ and therefore left a problem unsolved. It took the Definition of Chalcedon to attempt a statement of the relationship of the deity and humanity.

With the Apostles' Creed it likewise mentions the career of Christ. Again we make the point that Christology is not only saying something of the deity and humanity of Christ. It must say something of the career or work of Christ. It also means that heresy is also involved in denying something of the career of Christ, such as his saving death or his bodily resurrection.

(5) It is again in line with the Apostles' Creed in being a confession

about salvation. The real issue at Nicea was: *who can truly save us?* The deity of Christ was affirmed out of concerns of salvation. It was a conference of bishops from churches rather than academicians. The incarnation was for us and our salvation. Too much literature in Christology focuses on Nicea as if it were a debate about Greek philosophical terms. There was debate about words, but the center of the debate was a great soteriological concern; namely, *only God can truly save us.*

There is historical interest in the manner in which the AD 325 version was amended in the AD 381 version. However the most controversial matter in the amending of the creed has been the *filioque* (Latin: "and the Son"). Arianism had broken out in Spain in the sixth century and it was felt necessary to put yet another phrase in the creed to reject thoroughly Arianism (Third Council of Toledo, AD 589). The Holy Spirit is said to have proceeded from the Father *and the Son.* The Holy Spirit can proceed from the Father only if the Father is truly God. If the Holy Spirit also proceeds from the Son then the Son is as much God as the Father is. If that is the case Arianism is an impossible position.

This addition did not please the Eastern church. It was Photius (810-895) who vigorously attacked it. It was the major doctrinal difference between the East and the West in their formal division in 1054. The Eastern church attacked it for two basic reasons: (i) Once an ecumenical council has expressed itself in written form it is wrong to add to its written decrees; and (ii) the *filioque* creates a distortion in the historic understanding of the doctrine of the Trinity.

Protestants (cf. Pusey: 1876 and Barth: 1936-69, I/1: 536ff.) have vigorously defended the *filioque* as a protection of the role of Christology in Christian theology. With the *filioque* never can the center of Christian theology move from the person of Christ to the Holy Spirit. This is a serious tendency in the theology of Pentecostalism and the modern charismatic movement.

In a surprising way Thielicke (1974-82, 2: 181-83) takes a strong position in favor of the *filioque*. The denial of the *filioque* by the Eastern church is symptomatic of other things wrong with its theology. Eastern Orthodox theology loses a Christocentric faith for a God-centered mysticism. Its mysticism borders on pantheism. It also devaluates historical revelation and the real meaning of the cross. Although on the surface it may appear to be a battle over one word, in reality it is a matter of important theological substance.

CHALCEDON

The Nicene Creed affirmed that Jesus was a man, that he was God, and that he was God incarnate. But it did not speculate on the manner of the incarnation or the problems an incarnation might raise. The result was that a number of speculations were made about the nature of the incarnation. To clarify the issues Emperor Marcian called a council at Chalcedon (another small town near Constantinople). This council met in 451 and promulgated the Chalcedonian Creed (Hardy: 1954, 371-74) or the Chalcedonian Symbol. It became the official creed of the church with respect to the incarnation, which has been called two-nature Christology or Chalcedonian Christology. The council specified that its point of departure was the Nicene Creed, which is more popularly known as the Nicean-Constantinople Creed. It was not intended to replace that creed but to expand on the doctrine of the incarnation. This means that the Nicene Creed is still the fundamental confession of the church and not Chalcedon.

The bishops at Chalcedon did not intend to add something new to Christology but to clarify that which the church already believed. As at Nicea, the bishops were not learned theologians. Grillmeier (1975, 543ff.) says that there was not one distinguished theologian in the group. This means that the bishops were pastors in the church seeking to say something for pastoral concerns. Further, their use of language was not meant to be technical in a philosophical sense but practical for pastoral concerns; namely the confessional material of baptismal candidates (Grillmeier: 1975, 374 n.q).

In a summary way the creed or Definition said the following: (i) Jesus Christ on his divine side is God undiminished; (ii) Jesus Christ on his human side is man undiminished; (iii) he was sinless in his life; (iv) he was born of the virgin Mary; (v) there were two natures in the incarnation; (vi) in the union of the two natures there is no confusion, no change, no division, and no separation—the famous four adverbs; (vii) the union of the two natures in no manner compromises either nature; (viii) there is the one person of the Lord Jesus Christ.

This "two nature" Christology has been under severe attack since the middle of the nineteenth century and the attack continues unabated. The major objections to the creed are: (i) it is not biblical for nothing like the creed can be found in the New Testament; (ii) it is a case of Greek substance philosophy intruding into Christian theology and confusing the Christian gospel; (iii) it represents a nest of psychological problems created by two natures existing in the common territory of one body and one consciousness; and (iv) it stated the problem but did not resolve it. In defense of Chalcedon we respond to each of these attacks.

(1) The issues raised and debated at Chalcedon were not problems unique to the church in the fifth century; they are within the New Testament itself (contra Stroup: 1978, 52-64). More and more theologians and New Testament scholars are granting this (see Macquarrie: 1979, 68-72). For example the deity of Christ is affirmed in John 1:1 (to be discussed in detail later) and the incarnation affirmed in John 1:14. How do we understand how God the Son, of John 1:1, appears in history as the man Jesus Christ, of John 1:14ff.? That issue is at the center of the discussion of Chalcedon. Or what kind of person is the One who is at the same time in the form of God and the form of a servant (Phil. 2:5-11)? Colossians 2:9 affirms that God dwelt bodily in Jesus Christ. That too raises the fundamental questions of Chalcedon. It is not maintained that the New Testament reflects the language of Chalcedon but rather the kinds of issues Chalcedon spoke to are to be found already on the pages of the New Testament.

(2) It is not accepted by all scholars that Greek substance philosophy and its terms corrupted patristic Christology. It has been Hatch and Harnack who made much of this. In reply to Harnack and others Macquarrie (1979, 72) writes:

> But we should bear in mind another point, overlooked by Harnack and many other critics of the alleged Hellenizing of the Gospel. Just as Christianity took over from Jewish thought terms such as Messiah and profoundly changed their meaning in the new Christian context, so it was with terms borrowed from Greek philosophy. Christian doctrines were not conformed to the mould of already existing terminologies, but terms already available were adopted into Christian discourse and given new meanings.
>
> . . . .
>
> If it would be irresponsible to repudiate Chalcedon, it would be equally irresponsible to take it over thoughtlessly or to think that it excuses us from the task that must be taken up by every generation of Christians, the task of exploring and proclaiming anew the mystery of God in Christ.

It cannot be shown that the meaning of the terms used at Chalcedon had the same meaning that they had in Greek philosophy. It has been said a number of times that the terms used at Chalcedon were pressed into special service for the purpose of the Definition and must be understood in that context. Grillmeier made an important point when he said that the men of the council were not professional theologians but bishops with pastoral concerns (cf. also Macquarrie: 1979). The study of the word essence (*ousia*) shows that it was a term with a number of meanings and cannot be taken as an unambiguous technical term. All confessional materials manifest the same phenomena of the use of terms which have both popular and technical meanings.

Further, those who defend Chalcedon have said repeatedly that whatever words were used that are also to be found in Greek philosophical writings were used in a special way in Christological discussion. The sense in which the terms are to be understood is determined by the issues discussed and not Aristotle's meaning given to such terms. The Fathers certainly entertained no crude notion of the mixing of physical substances yet that crude interpretation is forced upon them. Conversely, it is not uncommon to find those who reject the language of Chalcedon state their Christology in terms of some recent philosophical language which in a hundred years will also be dated. In our particular situation we are on firm ground because the issues of Chalcedon are already found in the New Testament. Though we may reject the "substance philosophy" of Chalcedon the issues raised in the New Testament remain unaffected.

(3) If a theologian believes that an incarnation is impossible or that it is dated mythology then any defensive statements of Chalcedon will make no impression. If one accepts the incarnation of God in Christ then he already has the scriptural affirmation that it is a mystery (1 Tim. 3:15-16).

Philosophers are very testy about any appeal to mystery. They suspect it is an easy way out for a difficult problem. Mystery in Scripture is of another order. A mystery is a disclosure of God so that it derives from God and not from human speculation. Mystery means we do not have all the data we need for satisfactory clarification of the problem. Although the theologian may begin his treatment of mystery with some very clear ideas, the deeper he gets into the mystery he discovers the depth of the mystery and that by its very nature the mystery drifts out of focus. The incarnation can be understood up to a point or else it would be nonsense to affirm it. But because it is an event that happens from the divine initiative there is that aspect of it not available to human understanding. It cannot be totally clarified. It has a mysterious dimension human rationality can never relieve (cf. Brunner: 1947, 332).

35

(4) The Definition is a great affirmation of the incarnation. But it also has a regulatory function, or some have called it the negative function. In its regulatory function it tells us what ought not to be said in Christology. That is, whatever one says of Christ cannot be said contrary to the Definition of Chalcedon. It stands as the limit of Christological speculation; not the complete clarification of the incarnation.

(5) There is a sense in which the creed states the problem but does not solve it. Why should that be a criticism of the creed? The accurate statement of a problem is already on the way to its clarification. It could be argued that in stating the problem it also set limits on attempts to clarify the incarnation. If a theologian expects Chalcedon to totally clarify the incarnation he expects the wrong thing. Therefore we find no case made against Chalcedon by the remark that it states the problem but does not solve it.

(6) There was also the passion at Chalcedon to preserve the psychological unity of Jesus Christ. It affirmed that the two natures were in the one Lord Jesus Christ. Before modern psychology the bishops sensed that the incarnation could not create a psychological oddity of two "persons" living in one body. Hence to preserve the psychological unity, the sanity as it were, of the incarnate One, they affirmed that the incarnation was the one person of the Lord Jesus Christ.

(7) The creed is not the end of reflection on Christology. It is affirmed by such defenders of incarnational theology as Kasper, Berkouwer, Aldwinckle, and Grillmeier that Chalcedon was never intended to be the last word on Christology. The debate among the Lutheran and Reformed theologians at the time of the Reformation showed that there were yet issues about the incarnation to be settled. Further the development of kenotic Christology in subsequent centuries opened up another set of problems in Christology. And the development of modern psychology yet another group of them.

An excellent survey of the current status of Chalcedon is that of John Macquarrie (1979: 68-72). He takes up three major objections to the Definition (that the two-nature theory is incomprehensible, that it is too metaphysical, and that it uses too much Greek vocabulary), and he shows how none of them constitute a major objection to Chalcedon.

The most comprehensible book in English on the Definition of Chalcedon is that of R. V. Sellers (*The Council of Chalcedon: A Historical and Doctrinal Survey*). He regrets that his work was already going through the printing process when A. Grillmeier and H. Brach's massive symposium came to his hands (*Das Konzil von Chalkedon: Geschichte und Gegenwart*, 3 vols.). It would be well to state Seller's conclusion as he finished his masterful survey of Chalcedon:

> So we conclude that in the Chalcedonian definition of her faith concerning the Person of her Lord, the Church possesses a treasure of inestimable worth—the work of an age which deliberately embarked on the task of attempting to offer an answer to the Christological problem—which she can hand down to succeeding generations of believers, as they themselves are confronted with the same problem. The form of the doctrine may vary as new thought-forms arise, but the content will remain. For, express it as we may, fundamental to the Christian faith is the confession that Jesus Christ is no mere man, but God himself living a human life, and sharing its experiences as the Saviour of the world; and, once this is accepted, there comes, itself the result of Christological inquiry, the affirmation that in his one Person are to be seen in closest union both Godhead in its supreme act of condescension and manhood in the height of its perfection. (p. 350).

THE ATHANASIAN CREED

It is not known who composed the *Athanasian Creed*, but because it sounds so much like Athanasius' thought it has been attributed to him. The creed is in two parts. Articles 1-28 state the classical view of the Trinity. Articles 29-41 summarize the Christology of the patristic church. The most thorough and positive approval of the creed was made by J. N. D. Kelly, *The Athanasian Creed*.

To rehearse the creed would overlap our discussion of Chalcedon almost line for line. Kelly's opinion is that it stands as a kind of great monument to the development of Christology in the early church, and the views of such a famous patristic scholar are to be taken seriously.

(1) The creed has had a difficult time in the past two centuries because of its damnatory clauses. For example it reads in article 2: "Unless a man keeps it in its entirety inviolate [the Catholic faith], he will assuredly perish eternally." It concludes in article 42: "This is the Catholic faith. Unless a man believes it faithfully and steadfastly, he will not be able to be saved." Another reason for its poor reception recently is its strict forensic style in contrast to a more confessional or doxological style.

Kelly comes to the defense of the creed on the grounds that it must be seen in the context of the early church and not in terms of modern sensitivities. For example, the early church took a hard line on the absolute truth of the Christian faith and was not impressed by the fact of the exclusion principle in such a stand; in contrast theologians today feel very sensitive about damning the non-Christian world as lost. Kelly argues that seen in its own context the creed is a magnificent theological document.

(2) The creed places Christology in the context of the doctrine of the trinity. This is a topic almost uniformly omitted in modern discussions of the trinity. The doctrine of the trinity emerged out of the Christological debate. Athanasius of Egypt is most distinguished for his defense of the deity of Christ, and it washis position which won out at the Council of Nicea (325). In the discussion Athanasius saw that the doctrine of the Holy Spirit posed similar questions as did the doctrine of Christ. This appears first in the correspondence between Athanasius and Bishop Serapion also of Egypt. In this correspondence Athanasius indicated to Serapion that all the fundamental questions of the deity of Christ were also applicable to the Holy Spirit. If the result of the reflection is that the Holy Spirit is as much deity or God as Jesus Christ was, then the pieces of the doctrine of the trinity are moved into place. It was therefore necessary to properly relate the Father, and the Son, and the Holy Spirit. Hence out of this reflection the resolution was found in the doctrine of the trinity. That is why theologians through the centuries have said that the doctrine of the trinity is the logical outgrowth of the doctrine of Christology.

(3) The Christology of the creed is important on two scores: (i) it states in a brief, clear, and lucid manner the sum of ecumenical Christology to the time of its composition; (ii) it includes the career of Jesus—as we have called it. We are not saved by the person of the God-man *per se*, but by the God-man who suffers, who dies, who rises from the dead, who sits at the right hand of the Father, and who will come again.

3

The Deity of Christ

THE HISTORIC AFFIRMATION

In that our method is to treat Christology in a historical development, the modern critical issues will be discussed in the later chapters. There is no question that New Testament scholars are divided as to how much of the Gospels is authentic material and how much is mythological or hellenistic material imported into the Gospels. The problem is also present in the study of the New Testament letters. Granted we cannot hold onto the simplistic notions of the composition of the Gospels of earlier centuries, but we do take the Gospels and Epistles as authentic sources for the development of our Christology.

The affirmation of the deity of Christ has been the central assertion of historic Christology. The creeds affirmed it; the medieval theologians affirmed it; the Reformers affirmed it; and most of the Protestant confessions of the sixteenth and seventeenth centuries affirmed it.

Some clarification of terms is in order. Historically the expressions "the divinity of Christ" and the "deity of Christ" were used as synonyms. Liddon's great defense of the deity of Christ is titled: *The Divinity of our Lord and Saviour Jesus Christ* (1875). However in the debates of the twentieth-century liberal theologians were willing to speak of the divinity of Jesus but not his deity. Hence the expressions pulled apart, and the expression "the deity of Christ" meant exclusively historic Christology.

There was a small minor report at the time of the Reformation. The Socinians in Poland with the Racovin Cathechism of 1605 challenged the orthodox tradition. There was also the earlier case of Michael Servetus (1511-53) who challenged Calvin's Geneva and the doctrine of the trinity. As will be mentioned later, there were differences in Christology between the Swiss Reformers and the Lutheran theologians.

The deity of Christ began to be systematically denied at the time of the Enlightenment. It was challenged in its historical form by the theologians of modernism with an effort to restate what is meant by the divine in Jesus. Nonetheless the faith in the deity of Christ is an unbroken tradition. It is still the official faith of the Eastern Orthodox churches, the Roman Catholic church, and wherever Protestant churches are true to their historic confessions. Further, most of the emerging churches of the nineteenth and twentieth centuries (e.g., Pentecostals and Nazarenes) affirm the deity of Christ. It is a doctrine that has never lacked for distinguished defenders.

DIRECT AFFIRMATIONS OF THE DEITY OF CHRIST

In the literature of Christology one encounters flat denials of the deity of Christ and equally flat affirmations. Our concern is whether or not a case can be made for the deity of Christ that has scholarly integrity. We believe that such a case can be made.

(1)There are two basic stances about the New Testament and its Christology. There are the evolutionists who believe that the Christ of New Testament Christology evolved from an original, historical Jesus who is radically different from the later Jesus of Christological speculation. There are the developmentalists who believe that from a primitive Christological core the high Christology of the New Testament developed. This means that the later Christology is the result of the logical implications of the original core of Christology. Such is the stance of I. H. Marshall (1976, 123) and C. F. D. Moule (1977, 142ff.), and the one we adopt.

(2) Appeal can be made to specific texts which according to our best knowledge of the Greek of the New Testament affirm the deity of Christ. Two scholars who have collected and expounded such texts are Oscar Cullmann (1959, ch. 11) and Arthur Wainwright (1962). These men appeal to such texts as Romans 9:5, Hebrews 1:8, John 1:1, John 1:18, John 20:28, Titus 2:13, 2 Peter 1:11, 2 Thessalonians 1:12, Colossians 2:2, John 17:3, 1 John 5:20, James 1:1, 1 Corinthians 8:6, Colossians 1:15, 2 Peter 1:1, Revelation 12:19, and Acts 20:28. Both scholars admit that all of these verses are not equally supportive of the diety of Christ, for some verses argue the case clearer than others.

(3) There are some odd cases that, once discarded as witnesses for the deity of Christ, have been reinstated by some scholars. John 1:1c has been considered a clear affirmation of the deity of the Christ over against the Arians. The E. C. Collwel Rule has affirmed the historic interpretation of the verse. The best manuscripts read *God* in John 1:18 and not *Son*. The latest critical editions of the New Testament read *God* as the authentic text, but the Revised Standard Version goes contrary to the manuscripts and reads *Son*.

In the King James Version Romans 9:5 reads as an affirmation of the deity of Christ. Many modern translations put a period after Christ and make the second part of the verse a pious exclamation. However, such scholars as Wainwright (1962, 312), Cullmann (1959, 64ff.), Metzger (1970, 520ff.), and Cranfield (1979: II, 464-70) believe that the punctuation of the King James Version is correct, and if so the verse attributes deity to Christ.

Some scholars have taken Thomas' words "my Lord and my God" (John 20:21) as a pious, uncensored outburst. But there are those like Cullmann, Wainwright, and R. Brown (1970: 1026, 1046ff.) who take it as a valid theological observation of Thomas.

According to G. C. Berkouwer (1954, 155-92) the witness of the New Testament to the deity of Christ is massive. The only way in which the evidence can be evaded is to affirm that the deity of Christ is a projection upon the person of Jesus by the early church. John Knox (1967) explains such evidence on the theory that the early church explained the divine action of God in Jesus by mistakenly attributing divinity to Jesus—a theme which colors his entire book (*The Humanity and Divinity of Christ*). That is not an exegesis of the texts but an exegesis of the whole New Testament in one lump.

Berkouwer is aware of such efforts to negate the deity of Christ as taught by the individual verses. However he points out something that Liddon had done in the nineteenth century in his book on the deity of Christ. There is an abundance of indirect evidence for the deity of Christ. Even if the direct appellations of deity to Christ are overstatements, the indirect evidence is not, such as the worship Jesus received, his authority to forgive sins, his preexistence, and his claim to have power in himself to perform miracles.

There are ways of denying that such texts teach the deity of Christ. Some scholars have said that as close as the verses come to that, they do not bestow upon Christ the identical deity of God the Father. Others may state that such texts are mythological in origin and therefore cannot be taken as literal assertions. Or in Knox's opinion the recognition of a divine action in Jesus was stretched too far and made into an affirmation of deity. Or the texts may be admitted to teach the deity of Christ but that does not make it true.

Despite all this scepticism a persuasive, responsible exegetical case can be made from the New Testament that it does as a matter of fact teach the deity of Christ.

INDIRECT EVIDENCE

By the very nature of the incarnation it follows that there are not only direct affirmations of the deity of Christ but also items which indirectly suggest that deity. As indirect evidence these are not compelling, but along with the texts teaching the deity of Christ the evidence is a powerful pointer.

AUTHORITY

There is general agreement that Jesus impressed his contemporaries by the authority he expressed in his teaching and deeds. This is one item that shines through even after the critical assessment of the gospel texts. The classic text expressing the authority of Christ is Matthew 7:28-29. Hebrews 1:1-2 is also important in this connection as it sets the revelation which came through the Son as superior to that which came through the prophets.

The prophets did speak with a sense of divine authority. As bearers of the Word of God they stand as unique persons in the history of world religions. Prophets are more than gurus or teachers. The frequent expression "thus says the Lord" is both a witness of the origin of their message and its authority.

However the authority of Jesus Christ in teaching is a measure higher than that of the prophets. It must also be attributed to the works that he did. He taught with immediate, underived authority. He did on occasion appeal to the authority of the Old Testament but that too was already the Word of God in Israel.

Such an authoritative manner of speaking and acting has always been regarded in the church as the logical counterpart to the incarnation. The incarnation cannot be deduced from the authority of Christ, but in the light of the incarnation such authoritative acting and speaking logically follows.

THE SABBATH

Our Lord's teaching about the Sabbath is indirect evidence of his deity. The reason for this is partly theological, for Sabbath-keeping is part of the Ten Words of Exodus 20, and partly historical. When Israel was carried away from Palestine she developed a new kind of religious life. This centered on the rabbi, the synagogue, the law (Torah), and the festivals. Central to this new kind of piety and cultic life was the development of a high view of the Sabbath with its meticulous rules. For Jesus to counter the Jewish interpretation of the Sabbath was to clash with the Jews at the most sensitive and important point. Raymond Brown argues that these clashes cannot be post-resurrection inventions of the early church but bear the marks of historical authenticity (1970, p. 215ff., Vol. 29).

In some instances our Lord broke with the current Sabbath interpretation for humanitarian reasons; in others for theological reasons. It is the latter that is most important. For Jesus to give an authoritative interpretation of the Sabbath, which originated in the Ten Commandments, is virtually to teach with the identical authority of God. He speaks with the same authority as the One who originally gave the law (cf. Mark 2:28, Luke 6:5). It constitutes indirect evidence for his deity.

Our Lord's claim that he works in continuity with the Father and performs the same divine functions is indirect evidence of his deity. The clearest passage on this point is John 5. Because Jesus healed a man on the Sabbath the Jews persecuted him. Jesus' defense is that his Father worked through all the Old Testament period including the Sabbaths and now at this point (*heos arti*) Jesus is working. If the Lord did not break the Sabbath working through all the Sabbaths of the Old Testament neither does Jesus break the Sabbath in healing a man. Commentators on this passage have observed that Jesus was talking to Jews who were theologically sophisticated enough to see the implications of his words. If what Jesus said is true, he is "making himself equal with God" (John 5:14).

At this point, from the human perspective, there is only one thing for Jesus to do. He ought to deny the charge and give some reason why he healed the man on a Sabbath day. This he does not do. He says that the Jews were right. He is equal with God. In the verses that follow Jesus specifies the kind of things only God can do but yet that he can do. Hence he is equal with the Father. Jesus can give new spiritual life; he can raise the dead; he can exercise final judgment; and he can receive worship. Nowhere else in the New Testament is such a strong case made for the deity of Christ as in this passage.

The only possible way of undercutting the evidence of this chapter is to assign it to some unknown church scribe who wrote later in the first century with the express purpose of embellishing the church's picture of Jesus.

AN ARGUMENT FROM SILENCE

When people in the New Testament worship Christ and he does not rebuff them this is indirect evidence of his deity. The prohibition against idolatry in the Old Testament includes the worship of other people. In the New Testament Paul includes the worship of mere mortals as part of the idolatry sin generates (Rom. 1:23). Also illustrating the Jewish antipathy for the worship of man was Paul's strong refusal to receive idolatrous worship at Lystra (Acts 14:8-18). Therefore for Christ to receive openly acts indicated by the Jewish method of bowing low or actually falling prostrate on the ground was to receive an act of divine worship. In his article on *proskuno* "to worship," Heinrich Greeven shows that the Jews reserved such worship only for God even though variations may be found among the Greeks (TDNT, 6:763ff.). This makes it all the more impressive that Jesus was worshiped and he did not refuse the worship.

C. F. D. Moule (1977, 175-76) does not believe that the usual word for worship (*proskunein*) means the worship of God in every case. It may mean the manner in which one man responds to another man. Hence the use of this word for the worship of Christ in the New Testament does not mean that he was honored as God. L. G. Parkhurst counters and says that in context (Matt. 28:16-20) the act of worship can only mean the worship of God. He sums it up by saying that "the early Palestinian tradition does indicate worship of the risen Lord, as well as its justification" (p. 180). ("Matthew 28:16-20 Reconsidered," *The Expository Times*, 90: 179-180. March 1979).

THE SUMMONS TO FAITH

In that Jesus summons men to faith in himself (or that the apostles point to Christ as one to be believed in) this is indirect evidence for his deity, for in Israel only God is trusted as the Lord and the Savior. In John 14:1 Jesus makes faith in his person identical to faith in God.

Christ is presented as the object of faith in the New Testament in such a way that God is believed in the Old Testament especially as Israel's Creator, Lord, and Redeemer (cf. 1 Cor. 15:3-7, 1 Cor. 12:3, Acts 16:31, Rom. 10:9-10).

A MIRACLE WORKER

The ability to perform miracles from his own sovereign will is another indirect evidence for the deity of Christ. The prophets of the Old Testament and the apostles of the New could not perform the miraculous on their own but were totally dependent upon God. Jesus is presented in the Gospels as acting freely, personally, and sovereignly in the performance of miracles.

These miracles of Christ have been a point of intense controversy especially since the day of David Hume and his sceptical views about miracles. Fortunately we have a very excellent historical survey in Colin Brown's work, *Miracles and the Critical Mind*. Miracles have been rejected for a number of reasons. According to David Hume a miracle by its very nature cannot be authentically reported. According to others miracle stories abound in the literature of the ancient world so that the New Testament simply reflects the world in which it was written. Others insist that the kind of universe that we know exists in virtue of advances in modern science is a universe that has no room for the miraculous. So according to many current New Testament critics miracles stories are the innocent inventions of the early church, in its efforts to enhance the stature of Jesus, or were devised to meet some sort of crisis in the early church.

On the other hand there are stalwart Christians who believe otherwise. James Kallas argues that the saving work of Christ must be more than a quiet theological revolution. There is conflict between Jesus and evil powers, and miracles show that the kingdom of God has come not only in word but also in power. The famous Dutch Calvinist, Abrahman Kuyper, argued that salvation involves not only the human soul and body but also the structure of the cosmos. To eliminate miracles from the life of Christ is to reduce the gospel to subjective feelings. As the Christian puts together the whole schema of the faith and its theology, miracles are part and parcel of this schema (Brown: 1984). There is a connection between the world of the spirit and the world of matter, and miracles reveal that connection. Otherwise the gospel is reduced to merely inward spiritual blessings and is not an event of cosmic proportions. For example, the outstanding Roman Catholic scholar, Walter Kasper, says that miracles anticipate the future kingdom of God in its eschatological establishment.

The gospel of John has its own theology of miracles (cf. Brown: 1966, 1970). John does not use the word miracle but the word sign. A sign is a pointer. As such in John's gospel the miracles have a Christological importance in pointing out who Jesus Christ is. K. Rengstorf, in a long discussion of signs in John's gospel (TDNT, 7: 200-68), notes that the element of compassion is not totally missing in John's miracle accounts, but the miracles are still more directed to their theological function of pointing out the divine nature of Jesus' authority and message.

R. Aldwinckle (1976, ch. 11) asks whether miracles can function as confirmations of the claims of Jesus Christ or not. This is a much better way of posing the question than asking the theoretical question whether miracles are possible.

Aldwinckle's approach to miracles is based on the modern concept of interfacing. The biblical picture of reality is not that of a dualism in which the physical and the spiritual stand in isolation with reference to each other. The physical and the spiritual interface each other, which means that there may be smooth transitions from one to the other. One example of such interfacing is the sacraments, for in both baptism and communion there are physical elements and spiritual meanings and powers blended into one ritual. The prayer which requests that our daily bread be supplied is another instance in which the physical (bread) and the divine providence which supplies it blend together in the petition. According to Aldwinckle miracles are but another example of interfacing, and as such miracles attest to spiritual realities.

In W. Kasper's (1976, II, ch. 3) discussion of Jesus' miracles he takes the same basic stance as Aldwinckle; namely, that God as Creator automatically joins together the physical and the spiritual. Kasper holds to a mediating position. The miracles are so thick in the life of Jesus they cannot be denied. But biblical criticism has pointed out certain things we must reckon with such as the temptation seen in the Gospels to elaborate miracles. Further he eliminates all the natural miracles. His rationale for miracles is that they have an eschatological character. Miracles are *signa prognostica*. He therefore believes that, when properly understood and carefully guarded in interpretation, it is right (against Bultmann) to assume that Jesus did perform miracles.

THE PRE-EXISTENCE OF CHRIST

It has been standard teaching in historic Christology that the Logos, the Son, existed before the incarnation. That the Son so existed before the incarnation has been called the pre-existence of Christ. F. B. Craddock (1968) has summed up the present discussion. He lists the following texts which have been used in support of the doctrine: John 1:1, 14, 8:58, 17:5, 1 Corinthians 8:6, 10:4, 2 Corinthians 8:9. Philippians 2:6-7, Colossians 1:15, 16a, 17, Hebrews 1:2, 11:26, Revelation 22:16. Craddock says that the term first occurs in Justyn Martyr's *Dialogue with Trypho* (*ca.* AD 160).

Although the pre-existence of Christ has been a standard concept in the history of Christology in recent years, it has been attacked or interpreted in an unexpected way. (i) It was a method common to that cultural epoch to indicate how important a person was by declaring his pre-existence in a life before his earthly one. (ii) The expression means that God always had Jesus in mind from all eternity for his role in the kingdom of God. In other words Jesus was not an afterthought in the mind of God but as one might put it a primal decision of God. (iii) Finally, it has been explained as a myth. The notion of pre-existence was one of the current mythological concepts, and the early church picked it up for use in its Christology.

In reply to these alternate interpretations it can be said that the pre-existence of Christ is part of the earliest Christian tradition and is understood literally rather than mythologically. For example, in *The Son of God* M. Hengel (1976, 66ff.) argues for the pre-existence of Christ on the grounds that it comes very early in Christian thought and is certainly not that of an inflated mythological concept. It is a concept even earlier than the virgin birth and must therefore be a Jewish rather than a Hellenistic concept. He finds that the belief in the exaltation of Christ directs the Jewish mind back to the origin of all things. Hence pre-existence is part of the protology ("first things") or the theology of beginnings (see also Little: 1934).

The notion of myth will occur repeatedly in the following pages. In anticipation it can be indicated here how Bultmann has actually inflated the concept of myth. In Bultmann's employment of the term in his interpretation of the New Testament, virtually every doctrine of historic Christology is designated as a myth. One must suspect a methodology which results in such an overkill.

Other theologians defend the pre-existence of Christ on the basis that it is not one isolated doctrine or a foreign piece improperly introduced into theology. Rather the pre-existence of Christ is part of the total drama of redemption, and to eliminate it is to create a hole in the fabric of Christology (Berkouwer: 1954).

The concept of pre-existence prevents us from interpreting Jesus as another one of the great religious leaders who appear from time to time in world history. Rather the pre-existence of Christ reveals that he is God and has come into this world by his sovereign choice, and he is therefore not the product of any people, any special time period, or any cultural situation (Elert: 1960).

Finally, it may be argued that the denial of the pre-existence of Christ is the manifestation of a deeper theological error. Antiochene theology is a theology that maximizes the humanity of Christ to the detriment of his deity. In his mature, theological reflections contained in *The Evangelical Faith* (3 vols.) Helmut Thielicke indicts those who deny the pre-existence of Christ as Antiochenes. Such a doctrine cannot be assimilated to a Christology that is Antiochene at heart. He therefore wrote some strong lines in defense of the pre-existence of Christ (Ibid.: II, 264).

> Nevertheless, no matter how we may speak of pre-existence, and no matter how dubious many of our reflections on it may be, the thesis at issue, namely, that Christ's reality is not restricted to his historical existence, but includes the "yesterday, today, and for ever," is still an essential element in Christian theology.

4

The Incarnation of God in Christ

THE NEW TESTAMENT INCARNATIONAL WITNESS

The incarnation of God in Christ has been the affirmation of the great ecumenical creeds. It is a cardinal doctrine in historic Christology. There has been a "cloud of witnesses," of great theologians, who have defended it. But first we must see it in proper perspective. The Nicene Creed said that the purpose of the incarnation was for us and our salvation. This has always been the conviction behind the affirmation of the incarnation from Athanasius, to Augustine, to Luther, to Calvin, and to such moderns as Berkouwer, Barth, and Brunner. The incarnation is not an academic matter as if it were about a debate with no living or serious consequences. Nor is it merely a matter of academic jousting as if whoever was winner was really immaterial. It is an affirmation which speaks to the kind of Savior the world needs, and without this kind of Savior there is no salvation.

At the time of the Enlightenment in the eighteenth century the deity of Christ and the incarnation came under attack. During the nineteenth century the attack was enhanced radically, and a whole series of so-called "lives of Christ" were produced. But a real turning point in the methodology of Christological research was initiated by W. Bousset. In his famous book *Kyrios Christos* (1913) he attempted to explain the person of Christ by a detailed study of contemporary literature in order to show how Christology emerged out of the sociological mix of the first Christian century. In other words Christology is not a matter of the careful interpretation of New Testament passages but rather a ransacking of the religious and philosophical concepts of the times in order to root out the meaning of New Testament words or concepts as they were understood in the first century. Hence he founded the "History of Religions" school of research. It took a period of time before this became established among New Testament scholars, but since the pioneering days of R. Bultmann it has become standard practice along with other methods of criticism, such as form criticism and redaction criticism.

Of course there is a valid point in all of this criticism, for even the older textbooks on hermeneutics spoke of the *usus loquendi* ("what did the word mean in the popular conversation or literature of the time?"). But the presuppositions of this methodology can be pressed too far.

In a very provocative book James D. G. Dunn (*Christology in the Making: A New Testament Inquiry into the Origins of the Doctrine of the Incarnation,* 1980) takes up the traditional texts which have been appealed to in support of the incarnation and shows by his methodology that these are not incarnational texts (save for a few texts in John's gospel).

This means that all those biblical appeals made in the past by both Roman Catholic and Protestant scholars for the incarnation are invalid because they were not informed by the contemporary religious and philosophical literature of the first century.

The kindest evaluation that can be made of Dunn's book is that he takes the minimum assessment of a text for its Christological witness. Only on other grounds could we ever return to these texts and exact more from them. The sharpest thing that can be said is that the New Testament is only allowed to say what current studies of the first century allow it to say. The New Testament has no inherent right of its own to break fresh ground and, for example, affirm an incarnation. The most distressing thing about Dunn's book is that once one has read two or three instances of his disarming a traditional incarnational text, one can easily anticipate what treatment the other texts are going to receive. Once the methodology is so systematically adopted then it follows that the exegesis of the texts is predetermined.

Of course to establish the incarnation of God in Christ by an appeal to the traditional texts, with the thoroughness attributed to Dunn, could only be done with a book the same size. We shall have to be content with a suggested pattern for the defense of the doctrine.

(1) R. Bultmann endeavored to interpret much of the content of the New Testament by a general appeal to the current terminology that was prevalent in the culture in which the New Testament was written, and more particularly to define much of it as myth. Hence the incarna-

tion is so reinterpreted. The result is such a glut of attempts to define a myth that the efforts to define it have multiplied out of hand!

At one end of the spectrum is Bultmann's position that a myth by its very nature cannot be believed by modern man. At the other end is C. S. Lewis who claimed that he had spent a lifetime of scholarly research which was concerned with myth. His assessment is that Bultmann does not really know what a myth is. According to Lewis a myth can break out into history. The myth that humankind is eventually rescued from its fate by the incarnation of the gods breaks out into history in the singular incarnation of God in Jesus Christ.

We know that the New Testament, as its authors understood the term, is strongly opposed to myth. And it is difficult to see such a simple, analytic line as John 1:14 ("And the Word became flesh") as a mythological statement. It has been correctly said that all the issues thrashed out in the Definition of Chalcedon are implicit in this verse.

(2) The church traditionally has seen 2 Corinthians 8:9 as a metaphorical way of speaking of the incarnation. The rich person Christ, in turn gives up his wealth and becomes poor. Then in return we poor people, sinners, become rich in the salvation of Christ. In recent interpretation of the verse the meaning is shifted away from the incarnation to a statement of a more ethical nature. But the traditional interpretation of this verse was based on a true instinct about the incarnational meaning of the text.

(3) Biblical interpretation, as with all other interpretation, does not compel a person to accept a given interpretation. The options are open, whereas in science, at least on the theoretical level, experimentation will eliminate the spurious options. There are a great number of texts that the exegetes in the church historically have taken as incarnational passages. And in some instances the language is very strong (e.g., John 1:14, Col. 2:9, 1 Tim. 3:16, Heb. 2:14, Phil. 2:5-11, Heb. 5:7). Recent commentators have attempted to circumvent the strong incarnational implications of these texts so that they read otherwise. We would raise an *ad hominem* observation and ask what there is about current New Testament scholarship that wishes to reverse the historic interpretation of these verses.

(4) Another series of texts do not specifically state an incarnation but make sense only if an incarnation is assumed. These verses speak of the Father sending the Son into the world or of the Son coming into the world. The three basic verbs used are *apostello*, *pempo*, and *erchomai*. Such expressions would make no sense if applied to ordinary per-

sons, but when applied to Christ they presume an incarnation.

(5) It is customary to believe that Old and New Testament experts are in the best position to know the meaning of Holy Scripture, and it seems odd if that assumption is challenged. There is a very small but strong body of literature which declares that novelists or people in literature are more reliable than the technical scholars. They come to the text with very different assumptions and perspectives. With reference to the incarnation we have in mind such persons as T. S. Eliot, Dorothy Sayers, and C. S. Lewis. With further research a good many more names could be added such as G. K. Chesterton and Flannery O'Connor. They do not see the incarnation as a logical conundrum or an impossible claim. They see the incarnation as the wonder of wonders, the drama of all dramas, the one Great Myth that has broken into history (for the creed mentions Pontius Pilate, a person known and datable outside the Scriptures). Hence as some of the biblical experts are like centipedes who have lost the rhythmic control of their legs through oversubtle introspection, it is left to people of literature to see the truth as it really is.

Critical mentality is so very different. Such a mentality focuses its attention upon problems, difficulties, and imponderables. It desires a religion which has no mystery, no supernatural, and nothing transcendental. Therefore the incarnation is not a magnificent drama to be affirmed in joy but a doctrine too imponderable to believe.

Certainly we are not dealing with a difference of intelligence or learning, for those who marvel at the incarnation carry heavy academic credentials (Eliot, Lewis, Sayers, Williams). It is a modernized, secularized, positivistic mentality which has lost the capacity to wonder. It reflects the human effort to reduce a three dimensional universe into one of two dimensions.

THE POSSIBILITY OF AN INCARNATION

It is assumed that the incarnation did not pose a problem to Christians who lived in a pre-critical, pre-historical, and pre-scientific period. However to twentieth-century thinkers the incarnation does propose serious questions. It may be a logical puzzle, for the finite cannot bear the infinite; God cannot be limited to a man by an incarnation. Or it may be said that the concept of an incarnation is a myth which a modern thinker cannot believe. Such views are not held outside the church alone, for some professing Christian scholars within the church hold to them. For example, Reinhold Niebuhr (1948, II:60-61) objects to the incarnation as historically understood, for to him it is an impossibility. God could not be incarnate in one man. It is the over-riding thesis in the book edited by John Hick (1977) that the incarnation is nothing but a first-century myth.

THE IMAGE OF GOD

If there has been any traditional explanation of the possibility of an incarnation it would be that humankind is made in the image of God. In the very act of the creation the possibility of a future incarnation was made possible. If humankind is produced in the image of God then there is some of that image in God. Hence God can become incarnate. In recent times it has been Rahner (1978) who has done the most to rehabilitate this notion with a theological anthropology inspired by the philosophy of Heidegger.

John Meyendorff's *Christ in Eastern Christian Thought* indicates that the Christology of the Eastern Church is committed to making its anthropology (doctrine of man) the proposed basis of an incarnation. In this the Eastern theologians naturally come close to the view of the Roman Catholic theologian, Karl Rahner (see Macquarrie: 1976, 36-39).

FATHER-SON

Russell Aldwinckle (1976, 161) believes that there is an eternal Father-Son relationship in God. This is not a theological assumption but something one finds in reading the New Testament. The relationship of Jesus Christ to his heavenly Father is of the order of a Father-Son relationship. The New Testament (and the creeds) push this back into something in the very nature of God. The incarnation is then founded on this eternal Father-Son relationship in God. Hence it is not a *deus ex machina* for man's salvation. It is in the very order of things. The breaking out of the Father-Son relationship in the incarnation is manifesting something eternally inherent in the nature of God.

THE SOURCE OF DOCTRINE

Two Lutheran theologians approach the problem from a very different perspective (see H. Thielicke: 1974-82 and D. Bonhoeffer: 1966).

To them it is impossible to have a true and saving knowledge of God without an incarnation. This conviction stems from Luther's view of the incarnation, where he used the concept of God sunk deep in the flesh. It is only in an incarnation that God can be truly known. All else must be of the order of speculation, even if theological speculation. In Bonhoeffer's thought (1966, 41-60) Christ is present in the Christian community, in the preached Word, in the sacraments, and in the fellowship of the community. But this is possible only because there has been an incarnation.

Even stronger than Thielicke's and Bonhoeffer's words are those of G. Wingren (1960, ch. 16). In passing Wingren is complaining of Barth's Christology, which makes too radical a division of the two natures. It is Luther's doctrine of the incarnation (*theorom communicatio idiomatum*) which is the true doctrine, for it illuminates the whole range of Christian theology. It is at the cross that Luther found the key to all the great Christian concepts, for it is at the cross that the total God-man suffers and dies. There we learn what majesty really is. Only in the incarnation do we really know anything about God. Is an incarnation possible? We must reply that nothing is possible in Christian theology without the incarnation.

In commenting on the possibility of an incarnation Barth writes as if he had just read Niebuhr's assertion of its impossibility (*Church Dogmatics*, IV/1, 184). Barth's stance is that God and God alone knows whether God can become incarnate. Therefore our judgment can only be after the fact. The fact is that God did become incarnate. He concludes: "And if that was His will, who can question His right to make possible this impossibility? Is He not supremely right to exercise his Mercy in this way?" Later in his career Barth again turned to the possibility of an incarnation. He had been accused of having too strong a doctrine of God as the Totally Other (than man). This would appear to make an incarnation impossible. He returned to the subject in a small book, *The Humanity of God*. The incarnation is possible because through Jesus Christ we learn of the eternal humanity in God. In this eternal humanity God is therefore the potential of the incarnation. In Jesus Christ the potential becomes actual (cf. John Thompson, *Christ in Perspective*, ch. 8).

In Barth's theology he virtually comes to the same conclusion as Luther, Bonhoeffer, and Thielicke: *after the incarnation the only real, significant, and saving knowledge of God is in Jesus Christ as God the Son incarnate.* It is not that there is no true knowledge of God in the Old

Testament or even in the current Jewish faith which still rests on the Old Testament. Now that we know God in the flesh, God in the cross, and God in the resurrection, all else has become preliminary (though not trivialized).

KENOTIC CHRISTOLOGY

The words *kenosis* and *kenotic* derive from the Greek verb in Philippians 2:7 which speaks of Christ emptying himself to become in the form of a servant (*kenoo*). The simple meaning of the verb is "to empty" (TDNT, 3: 661), hence it is the context of the verb which must supply its meaning. Closely connected to it is the "humbled himself" clause of verse 8. Historically the text has been understood as a commentary on the incarnation. In order for the pre-existent Son of God to become man he had to in some radical sense limit himself, "pull himself in" so that he could become incarnate. Hence some kenotic assumption has always been part of historic Christology.

However since the Reformation a distinct kind of Christology has been developed which has been called *kenotic*. An older valuable summary of kenotic Christology is to be found in A. B. Bruce, *The Humiliation of Christ* (1881, ch. 4), and a more recent study is that of D. G. Dawe, *The Form of a Servant: A Historical Analysis of the Kenotic Motif* (1963). It is not our purpose to review this history but to point out how a kenotic Christology is proposed to help relieve certain pressures in Christology.

To declare that God became man is an enormous assertion theologically and philosophically. One of the ways of lessening the demands on our reason is to assert that there was a major lessening of deity in the incarnation. We can assume that in the incarnation God the Son divested himself of the natural attributes of God, such as omnipresence, omnipotence, and omniscience. But the spiritual or personal attributes of love, justice, and holiness were retained. Among the gains of such a view of the divine self-limitation would be that it relieves much of the pressure in understanding the mental life of Jesus.

For those who make the concrete proposal of the split of the attributes into the natural and the spiritual so that the incarnate God had only the spiritual attributes of God, D. Baillie (1948, 94ff.) has some strong lines. It is inconceivable that God could so "fission" himself into two parts. In a long note on the subject Barth voices his objection to kenotic Christology. Unless it is the total God incarnate in Christ the redemptive work of Christ is undermined (1936-69, IV/1 181ff.).

OMNISCIENCE

A number of kenotic theories were developed in England in the past two centuries and have been reviewed by J. S. Lawton (1947) and V. Taylor (1958).

One of these centered around the growth of biblical criticism in England in the nineteenth century. Jesus made statements about the authors of Old Testament books (e.g., Moses, David, and Isaiah). If he were God incarnate and could neither err nor mislead, his word must be taken as settling these matters in biblical criticism.

In a famous essay in *Lux Mundi* Bishop Charles Gore (1889) set out to resolve this dilemma by appealing to a kenotic Christology. In the incarnation there was a kenosis—an emptying—of divine omniscience. On all factual matters Jesus knew no more than the average Jew of his time. This means that Jesus did not know any more about who wrote the books of the Old Testament than Peter, James, and John. Therefore his opinions on the authorship of Old Testament books are not binding, and Old Testament scholars are free to continue their work in biblical criticism. But by advocating a kenotic Christology he kept faith with the historic doctrine of the incarnation.

Both C. J. Ellicott (1891) and J. S. Lawton (1947) challenged this view. Ellicott argued that the sinlessness of Jesus meant that Jesus would never deceive anybody at any point. Therefore what he said about Old Testament authorship must be taken as truth or else we impute sin to Jesus. Lawton collected all the verses in the Scriptures which speak to the range of Jesus' knowledge. He lists all the verses about Old Testament authorship and about events in the Old Testament. He notes the verses in which it is affirmed that Jesus knows what is going on in somebody else's mind; verses which represent Jesus as surprised at some knowledge or learning something by observation; verses in which Christ asks a question as if he didn't know the answer; verses which imply Jesus can grow in knowledge; verses in which Jesus professes ignorance; verses which imply that Jesus had supernatural knowledge; and verses which represent Jesus as knowing the future. Lawton's book is a major attack on liberal theology and its Christology, and it states that in review of this evidence none of the verses militate against Jesus knowing the authorship of Old Testament books. In a word he endorses Ellicott's thesis.

Of course this is no issue to modern New Testament scholars who view the incarnation as a myth. Most of that which is attributed to Jesus was not said by Jesus at all but by later church scribes. But to those who hold to the incarnation the issue is still meaningful.

(1) Some think that Gore is right. In all mundane matters Jesus knew no more than other Jews (see L. Hodgson: 1951, 26).

(2) A number of evangelicals agree with Ellicott and Lawton that on all matters Christ spoke with inerrant assertions, and therefore his opinions on Old Testament matters are binding.

(3) It can be argued that both of the above views oversimplify the issue. The number of instances in which the New Testament either cites the Old Testament or in some other way alludes to it must run over two thousand (collated in the appendix to the twenty-sixth edition of Nestle's *Greek New Testament*). There is no uniform, consistent manner in which the New Testament uses the Old Testament but a great plurality of ways. Hence how the New Testament uses the Old Testament must be determined by each instance. This also applies to how Jesus used the Old Testament. Gore's view founders on the fact that at times Jesus cites the Old Testament as the very word of God; the second view founders in the flexibility of the New Testament's use of the Old and prevents any monolithic version of the New Testament's use of the Old.

Jesus' Self-Consciousness

Another group of kenotic theories centered in the problem of the self-consciousness of Jesus as posed by the modern developments in psychology. How could a God (by definition, possessing consciousness) indwell a man (by definition, possessing a consciousness) without creating some sort of psychological oddity? One manner of resolving or at least lessening this problem was to presume such a *kenosis* of the divine in Christ so that the human consciousness could develop normally.

Lawton is certainly right in warning that such psychological speculations can lead to nowhere if not heresy. The burden of the Chalcedon Definition was to express the limits of Christology and not attempt to give answers about the consciousness of Jesus. Nicholas of Cusa of the late Middle Ages taught a doctrine of learned ignorance—*docta ignoranta*. And this is one of those places in Christology that it is well to invoke the *docta ignoranta*.

There can be no question that there was a *kenosis* for the incarnation to take place. And the reminder must be sounded: whatever we say of God incarnate in Christ we must be true to the formula of very God of very God and very man of very man. Scripture itself calls the incarnation a mystery (2 Tim. 3:15-16), and it would be well to observe the affirmation in talking of the divine *kenosis*.

Historic Christology has always taught a kenosis in the incarnation if for no other reason than the text of Philippians 2:5-11 asserts it. There is no debate about this point. With reference to the kinds of problems raised by kenotic theories the explanation has been in terms of the divine restraint. In order for the human nature to grow and develop from babyhood to adulthood the divine nature held itself back to permit this to be a natural and authentic development. Again in the spirit of the Definition of Chalcedon, historic Christology does not attempt to explain the mystery of the incarnation but to make assertions which protect its authenticity. Hence the historic doctrine of the divine restraint of the divine nature does nothing to clarify the matter of the consciousness of Jesus Christ; it is only an affirmation that no matter what we say we cannot compromise the authenticity of the humanity of Christ.

THE INCOGNITO

It was Kierkegaard who remarked (in so many words) that no Israelite would see Jesus walking down the street of some Palestinian town and say, "There goes God incarnate!" To the contrary the deity in Christ was too deeply hidden for this to happen. This is known as the *incognito* of Christ, and Kierkegaard's thought on this has influenced thinkers like Brunner and Barth.

It is this version of the *incognito* that led Barth to say that ordinary historical research would reveal Jesus to be but a rabbi from Nazareth or that the most important time in the life of Christ for Christology was the forty days of our Lord's post-resurrection appearances when the *incognito* was removed. This is behind Brunner's (1947, 308) remark that "the real event of Christ [the incarnation]...cannot be perceived as an historical event at all." Brunner also says that the believer must stay by the *incognito* and its paradoxical nature even if unbelievers charge believers with irrationality (1947, 331-32).

That there was a large measure of the *incognito* or concealment in the incarnation has never been denied in historic Christology. The self-emptying of Christ (the *kenosis*) does result in the state of humiliation of Christ. However it is Berkouwer's (1954, ch. 13) contention that the doctrine of *incognito* in Kierkegaard, Barth, and Brunner is more extreme than the evidence of the New Testament allows.

To begin with (i) there is no complete denial of Kierkegaard's statement that there is an extreme hiding or concealment of the deity of Christ in his earthly life; and (ii) it is also evident from Peter's confession that an illumination was necessary for a person to see in Jesus Christ more than another man (Matt. 16:13-20). On the other hand there is biblical evidence that the hidden glory of Christ did radiate from time to time, indicating that he was more than a man.

First, there is the witness of John's gospel which focuses on two points: the glory of Christ and the theology of signs. In the great affirmation of the incarnation in John 1:14, John also mentions that the disciples saw the glory of the incarnate one. The glory theme is also expressed in John 2:11, 11:4, 40 and 17:5, 22, 24. In this manifestation of glory the *incognito* was temporarily or momentarily lifted. Secondly, it is a well-known fact of John's gospel that it carries within it a theology of signs. The miracles are signs which point to God and/or Christ and/or the in-breaking of the kingdom of God. The signs are then again temporary alleviations of the *incognito*.

This also must be carried over to the miracles in the Synoptic Gospels. The sign-miracle is not totally opaque. Nor is it beyond equivocation. But it is an event in which some Israelite could come to faith in Christ. If the *incognito* were total this could never happen.

We have treated the transfiguration of Christ at some length at another place (Ramm: 1963, p. 37ff). To most critics it is a misplaced resurrection account. However that is not the case; the transfiguration was a remarkable suspension of the *incognito*. It is treated in 2 Peter 1:16-18 as a "dress rehearsal" of the glory of Christ manifest at his return.

Berkouwer makes one other point of significance about the extreme doctrine of the *incognito*. If Kierkegaard and followers are right, there is no guilt assigned to those who rejected Christ. There would be guilt only if the Israelite saw some sign, token, or evidence that Jesus was more than another Jew. There is no guilt involved if one Jew rejects the outlandish views or claims of another Jew. Equally so there would be no merit in faith for it would be but a most fortunate guess. But our Lord is very severe in his judgment upon those who did have a chance to see beyond the *incognito* and did not believe (cf. Matt. 11:20-24).

PERSONAL OR IMPERSONAL HUMANITY

One of the most difficult parts of historic Christology is the discussion over *enhupostasia* and *anhupostasia*. It is a discussion meaningful only to those who accept the doctrine of the incarnation. To clarify it is difficult because if Jesus is a man, he is a person; if he is God, he is a person; hence the incarnation would present us with the oddity of two persons in one body. How do we escape that dilemma? The terms *enhupostasia* and *anhupostasia* stand for attempted solutions.

Leontius of Byzantium (sixth century) reasoned that if Jesus were a man, he must also be a person. The oddity of two persons in one body is alleviated by saying that the human person was included in the person of the Logos (*enhupostasia*, meaning in-personed). The personal life of Jesus in his manhood lived "within" the personhood of the Logos.

The other solution was to affirm the full humanity of Christ but affirm that the humanity had not yet come to personhood, hence, *anhupostasia* (or impersonal). There is no second person to create the oddity of two persons in one body.

Both positions contain strength. Certainly the full humanity of our Lord must be maintained lest the incarnation is undermined. And by all means the affirmation of one Lord Jesus Christ must be maintained, which speaks against any psychological oddity in the incarnation.

The discussion over *enhupostasis* and *anhupostasis* has taken an unexpected turn in the twentieth century. It is based on the ever-growing conviction that the full humanity of Jesus Christ must be retained (which is probably pressure from the development of psychology in the twentieth century). Theologians are saying that both affirmations are true, for each makes a valid point. (See Berkouwer [1954, ch. 12], Baillie [1948, 85-93], and Thompson [1978].)

Enhupostasis seeks to emphasize the undiminished humanity of Christ. *Anhupostasis* emphasizes the uniqueness of Christ in the incarnation, for there would have been no Jesus of Nazareth if there had not been an incarnation. (Pannenberg [1968, 337ff.] is an exception and does not agree with this resolution of the problem.)

THE INCARNATION AND THE EUCHARIST

The Lutheran Reformation may be conveniently dated in 1521 when Luther refused to recant from his writings at the Diet of Worms. The

Swiss Reformation may be dated in 1523 when the cathedral in Zurich accepted the reforms suggested by Zwingli. In the following years it became apparent that there were significant differences between the Lutherans and the Swiss over the nature of the Eucharist. To assess what these differences might be and what harmony might be achieved, a conference was called at the German town of Marburg in 1529. This has become known as the Marburg Colloquy. Luther and Melanchthon represented the Lutherans while Zwingli, Bucer, and Oecolampadius represented the Swiss, or as later known, the Reformed. The difficulty at the Colloquy came with the fifteenth and last article, which concludes as follows:

> And although at present we cannot agree whether the true body and the true blood of Christ be corporeally present in the bread and wine, yet each party is to show to the other Christian love as far as conscience permits, and both parties should fervently pray to Almighty God that by his Spirit he may strengthen us in the true understanding. Amen (Schaff: 1897, I: 212, fn. 1).

Although the Lutheran theologians rejected the Roman Catholic view of the real presence of Jesus in the Eucharist by its doctrine of transubstantiation, they did teach their own view of real presence. Zwingli was more of a mind that the Eucharist was a church celebration which did not require a doctrine of the real presence. Luther believed that the differences were much deeper than that of the interpretation of the words of the Eucharist. Two radically different views of creation and redemption were being debated. It is in this context that Luther's famous words to Zwingli must be understood: "You have a different spirit" (*Ihr habt einen andern Geist*).

Out of this division developed a major difference in Christology between the Lutheran and the Reformed theologians.* The debate centers around the concept of *communicatio idiomatum*; that is, to what degree does the human nature of Christ share in the divine nature? The Lutheran view is that God is sunk so deep in the flesh in the incarnation that properties of the divine nature may be imparted to the human nature. On this basis Christ is present in all the eucharistic services in Lutheran churches. Whoever partakes of the bread and wine partakes of the whole Christ.

---

* For a current view of the matter from the Lutheran side see Ian D. Kingston-Siggins, *Martin Luther's Doctrine of Christ* (Yale Univ. Press, 1970). For the Reformed view see E. David Willis, *Calvin's Catholic Christology* (E. J. Brill, 1966).

Calvin's view is known as the extra-Calvinisticum which Willis (1966, 23) traces to its first usage in Theodore Thumm. The Latin expression is *etiam extra carnem*—"even so [Christ exists] outside of flesh." Christ was not totally "enclosed" in the flesh in the incarnation but ruled with the Father even when incarnate. The debate goes on today. T. F. Torrance (1969) argues that the Lutheran concept of space is wrong, and that the Reformed position is in harmony with current views of space. The Lutherans (see Bonhoeffer: 1966 and Thielicke: 1974-82) have reasoned that the Reformed view of creation was defective, for in denying realism in sacramental theology it denies that this world is God's creation through which he can convey grace.

The issue returns again to the nature of Christ's presence in the Lord's Supper. In the Lutheran view the Lord's Supper offers to the believer the whole Christ in all his deity and humanity. In that the human nature shares some of the omnipresence of the divine nature, the human nature is potentially everywhere. This is known as the ubiquity of the body of Christ. There is for Lutheran theologians no other Christ but the whole Christ (cf. Althaus: 1966, ch. 15).

Calvin on the other hand intentionally taught the Christology of Chalcedon. However in the incarnation, the Son of God did not give up his role of co-ruling with the Father. Hence there was yet the ministry of Christ outside of (*extra*) the human nature of Jesus. In John 3:13 (KJV) the Son of Man is on earth and in heaven at the same time.

Calvin reasoned further that in the ascension the body of Christ was transported to heaven to the right hand of the Father. To Calvin a body meant a total human body. The body of Christ cannot be eucharistic wine and bread. To say that Christ is bodily present in bread and wine is to distort completely the notion of a body. To call the wine and the bread the "eucharistic body" will not do. The body of Christ is at the right hand of the Father. For Calvin Christ is present in the eucharist spiritually via the Holy Spirit.

In reading the learned arguments on both sides one could wish both were true (e.g., Bonhoeffer: 1966, 49-60). Certainly every Christian would want the whole Christ. Although Barth is in the Reformed tradition he moves in the Lutheran direction in defending the notion that we must always have the whole Christ.

Another aspect of the debate between Lutheran and Reformed dogmatics is the Lutheran interpretation of Philippians 2:5-11. The traditional interpretation is that the passage outlines the career of Christ from his pre-incarnate glory, to his incarnation, to his death on the cross, and then to his resurrection and exaltation. The Lutheran interpretation limits the range of the text to the earthly life of Christ. It asserts that the meaning of the text is the state of humiliation of Christ—the deep humiliation of Christ. Though the Son of God is incarnate he nevertheless lived a life of complete humiliation and did not use his prerogatives of deity to help him along or blind others with the radiance of his inner glory. It is, again, God sunk deep in the flesh.

This also manifests itself in the Reformed and Lutheran differences over the two states (humiliation/glorification). The Lutheran theologians understand the humiliation of Christ to be the state of humiliation in his earthly life followed by his glorification. The Reformed theologians interpret the humiliation in the context of the act of incarnation.

These Lutheran and Reformed differences constitute two radically different kinds of theology (see Wingren: 1960). The *communicatio idiomatum* is not only about the nature of the incarnation and the nature of the Lord's Supper. It is also a profound doctrine of the two states of Christ and the proper understanding of the true majesty of Christ.

It is neither our intention nor in the range of our ability to resolve these Lutheran-Reformed differences which have persisted through the last four centuries. It is part of our fractured sinful existence that even at deepest points of Christian theology our minds can be most divided. However that which does unite the two traditions is the great affirmation of the incarnation.

5

The Virgin Birth

THE OPTIONS

In historic Christology the birth narratives of Matthew and Luke are valid traditions which inform the Christian church about the specific details of the birth of John the Baptist and Jesus. Since Strauss' writings in the nineteenth century the birth narratives have been puzzling problems of myth and legend (cf. Duling: 1979, 179ff.), and this is not much different from where many critical scholars stand today.

Where did these materials come from? What purpose did the birth narratives serve in the early church? How were they appended to the stories of Jesus circulating in the early church? Although this kind of questioning is as old as Strauss, it took on new life in New Testament studies since World War II.

Raymond Brown (1977) has written an encyclopedic book on the birth narratives (*The Birth of the Messiah*). It provides us with a comprehensive review of the problems. Some of the options in the interpretation of the birth narratives are:

(1) According to historic Christology these materials were preserved by relatives and friends (neighbors?) of John the Baptist and Jesus. In historic and evangelical thought part of the doctrine of the incarnation is also tied to the notion of special revelation and inspiration. Incarnation, virgin birth, revelation, and inspiration are all one piece. If God comes incarnate into the world there is also provision made for recording that event. This does not deny the part that played in setting out the final form of these narratives by their authors, but it does deny that the accounts are pure (but innocent) fabrications which took place in the infant church. One of the features of the narratives that

points to their historical rootedness is their fidelity to the kind of life and piety we would expect to find in the Judean hill country (cf. J. G. Machen: 1932).

(2) Another opinion about the birth narratives and the virgin birth is that they reflect the manner in which important people were exalted at that time. To exalt a great general or emperor was to declare that he was born of a virgin. Hence the early church sought to exalt Jesus by this method. Although most New Testament critics take the virgin birth as but one of the typical myths about Jesus, hence unbelievable today, Thomas Boslooper (1962) takes this version of the virgin birth story in a very positive way. Applying the myth of a virgin birth to Jesus by the early church was its way of exalting Jesus and the incarnation. Thielicke (1974-82: II. ch. 29) has similar thoughts about the virgin birth.

(3) In *The Mediator* (1947) and other places Emil Brunner interprets the virgin birth as an attempt to give a biological explanation of the incarnation. He accepts the incarnation but rejects the virgin birth. He does not believe that Jesus could have had a complete human nature if he were born without a father.

(4) R. Brown (1977) offers an unusual theory. He believes that the Roman Catholic Church is right in holding to the virgin birth, but it is wrong in believing that the birth narratives are authentic historic documents. Rather the narratives are later church reflections in which the attempt is made to picture the historical situation around a virgin birth. Brown says that this does not deny that there are historical elements in these narratives; rather they should be seen in the light of redaction criticism as one of the means by which the early church rounded out its Christology. While appreciating redaction criticism he does admit to its limitations (p. 38). To be fair to Brown it should be said that he sees these birth narratives as inspired and a witness to the great theological reflections of the Christians of the early church. These are not to be regarded as just more material begging for a critical assessment.

(5) Most New Testament scholars (especially under the influence of Bultmann) agree with Strauss that the virgin birth is a myth and the kind of myth common in the first Christian century.

Can anything be learned historically from the birth narratives themselves? Luke mentions that many have attempted to write a history of Jesus (Luke 1:1), but most scholars now consider that a bit of rhetoric common to documents of that time. However it has been suggested that somebody as experienced as Matthew was in working with documents could have kept notes. Luke does mention that Mary kept these events in her heart (Luke 2:19, 51). Mary could have been the source of much of the birth narratives, for she does appear in the book of Acts (1:14). Brown is dubious of this, but at least he admits that Mary is the link between the birth narratives and the early church.

What possible sources were Elizabeth, her household, Zechariah, Simeon, and Anna? They flutter before our eyes as possibilities, and that is the most that can be said. John does tantalize with mention that Mary's sister stood with her at the cross (John 19:25), for if Mary were a confidant with her sister there would be another possible source of the birth narratives.

At yet another historical level are the "brothers and sisters" of Jesus (Mark 6:3 mentions James, Joses, Judas, and Simon; Matt. 13:55 mentions James, Joseph, Simon, and Judas. Acts 1:14 speaks of the brothers of Jesus as does John 7:5). One of the interpretive presumptions of the book of Jude is that Jude is the Lord's brother.

At still another historical remove are the large number of converts in Jerusalem as recorded in the book of Acts (three thousand in Acts 2:51; five thousand in Acts 4:4; a host of priests in Acts 6:7). One theory is that the material came from the disciples of John the Baptist. The growth of followers of John the Baptist and their persistence is witnessed by the events of Acts 19. This time after Pentecost Paul finds as far away as Ephesus a group of followers of John the Baptist.

While the above notations are not sufficient in themselves to give an adequate historical account of the birth narratives, they should at least temper the assumption that all the materials are creations of the early church. I. H. Marshall (1978, 46ff.) has reviewed the theories of the origins of the birth materials in Luke and says that at the present time the problem is insoluble. Although now an older work, J. G. Machen's *The Virgin Birth* (1932, chs. 4, 5, 6) maintains the historical integrity of the first two chapters of Luke in the sense that they faithfully represent that which took place and are not a later fabrication in the early Christian communities.

THE PARADOXICAL STATUS OF THE VIRGIN BIRTH

It is generally agreed that the only clear passages on the virgin birth of Christ are Matthew 1:18-25 and Luke 1:26-28. Older theologians appealed to verses in the Old Testament which they thought implied a virgin birth (e.g., Jer. 31:22). Today it is held that the interpretation of such texts is not based on solid exegesis. A number of verses in the New Testament besides those mentioned above have been cited (cf. Brown: 1977, p. 518ff.). It is also judged that these verses do not explicitly teach the virgin birth.

In his discussion of the virgin birth Barth (1936-69, I/1, 172ff.) points out the paradoxical status of the virgin birth. On the one hand the New Testament witness to the virgin birth is small; on the other hand the virgin birth has had a sustained role in the confessional literature of the church. Barth asks the question why a doctrine with such limited witness in the New Testament has had such a large citation in the history of the church.

His solution is that the church saw in such a small window an unexpected great witness to the incarnation. The Apostles' Creed is the Christian faith cut to the bone. The Latin text has only seventy-five words. Yet it mentions the virgin birth. Philip Schaff lists eleven of the creeds which built up to the Apostles' Creed and nine of them mention the virgin birth (*Creeds of Christendom*, II, 53). It must be something about the rationale for the virgin birth which explains the paradox.

How is this paradox to be explained? Why was the virgin birth so central from the earliest days of the second century (on this cf. Machen: 1932, ch. 1)? What was its dogmatic importance? The leading options are:

(1) The virgin birth became important as it was a means for the early Christian churches to exalt the person of Christ. As Boslooper (1962) shows, it was customary to exalt great public figures by saying that they were born of a virgin. Brown (1976, 531) is skeptical of this explanation, for he doubts if the common people of Judea would know of such notions. Further, Machen (1932) has worked so diligently to show the local Palestinian and Judean coloring of the infancy narratives.

(2) The *raison d'etre* has been argued from the analogy with Melchisedek. In that he had no mother or father (Heb. 7:3), so some say Jesus was born of a virgin to be like Melchisedek. However the analogy was so artificial it could not maintain itself.

(3) The most common theological justification for the importance of the virgin birth is that it cuts Jesus off from the original sin of the race and so makes it possible for him to be the Savior. The earliest mention of this kind of argument is in Ambrose (see von Campenhausen: 1962,

61) during the fourth century. Mary was born free from sin in order that her Son might be sinless. The difficulty with this explanation is that it can be found nowhere in the New Testament. It is said that the child will be holy (Luke 1:35), but that could well be without being sinless.

(4) Barth and others connect the virgin birth with the incarnation. Barth sees in the virgin birth a sign of the incarnation. Barth understands Isaiah 7:14 very literally; the promise of God-with-us (Emmanuel) is signified by the virgin birth.

To sustain this position Barth works out a theory of bracketing. Unless the life of Christ is bracketed at the beginning and at the end we would never be sure of the incarnation. There are enough legends and stories of the gods appearing as men that some means must be used to set the incarnation over against them. The bracket at the beginning of the life of Christ is the virgin birth; and at the end of the life of Christ there is the bracket of the resurrection.

Barth also believes that the virgin birth of Christ is a word about divine grace and human helplessness. The exclusion of the father in the virgin birth is the sign of the exclusion of all human effort in salvation. It is in this key that Werner Elert (1960, 310) picks up his understanding of the virgin birth. It is a clear word of grace in salvation. The virgin birth both reveals and protects the sovereign grace of God in human salvation. In support of his position Elert appeals to John 1:13. There is a disputed reading of the text. If it is read in the plural, it refers to all of the children of God being born from the free grace of God; if it is read in the singular, then it is a reference to the birth of Christ, and in that case only a virgin birth could meet the demands of the text. Elert appeals to some very early church fathers as reading the text in the singular and therefore its earliest form, with some support of modern textual critics.*

Otto Weber (1962, II: 119-21) is another theologian who centers the meaning of the virgin birth in the doctrine of the incarnation. He does not view the birth narratives as a patchwork created by the early church scribes but rather as profound theological witnesses. The meaning of the virgin birth is that Jesus Christ comes into this world initiating a new creation. The Savior cannot belong to the history of

---

* In *A Textual Commentary on the Greek New Testament* (1970) Bruce Metzger shows why modern scholarship prefers the plural reading of the text, hence the text is not a commentary on the virgin birth (p. 196f.).

death. Weber makes use of the distinction between two German words: *Herkunft* and *Ursprung*. The virgin birth is not a chatty story of the immediate ancestry of Jesus (*Herkunft*) but of the ultimate origin of Jesus (*Ursprung*). The birth narrative is not an attempt to show who Jesus and his relatives are but to show that he has his origin in the purposes of God. In short, the virgin birth is the theological explanation of the origin of Jesus.

Regin Prenter (1960, 407-10) also defends the virgin birth in an incarnational context, but goes a little different route. To him the virgin birth is the absolute, necessary connection between the eternal Logos and the man, Jesus. The Ebionite heresy denies the eternal Logos in Jesus; the virgin birth affirms it. The Docetic heresy denies the real humanity of Jesus; the virgin birth affirms that. Hence the virgin birth refutes both heresies at once and preserves a true incarnation.

Prenter states that there is a necessary and inevitable conflict between historical judgments (*Wahrscheinlichkeitsberechnung*) and dogmatic assertions. The virgin birth is a necessary affirmation to protect the incarnation. There is a necessary *conflict* between critical scholars and theologians, but it is not a *contradiction*. The virgin birth is a matter of dogmatics, and it is affirmed or denied on dogmatic bases. In dogmatic differences we have *conflicts* but not necessarily *contradictions*.

(5) T. F. O'Meara defends the virgin birth as a valid doctrine of the Roman Catholic church ("Introduction," in Oberman: 1971). Any decision about the virgin birth will contain four elements: (i) a due regard for the current status of New Testament criticism; (ii) the faith of the church in its continuity through the centuries; (iii) the mind of the present Christian community; and (iv) guidance from the Holy Spirit. A decision about the virgin birth cannot be a simple historical judgment because the documentary issues are too complex; nor can it be a simple theological affirmation. The documents do have a historical core. In view of the four criteria the church is then on good ground in affirming belief in the virgin birth.

Those who accept historic Christology do assert that there is a connection between the virgin birth and the incarnation. These birth narratives are not free creations of the early church scribes with no historical connectives. Further, the virgin birth is part of a complex of doctrines where each doctrine supports the rationale of the other.

TYPICAL OBJECTIONS TO THE VIRGIN BIRTH

In the past hundred years and more the virgin birth has been denied from within the Christian community. It is necessary to look at some of the objections as they are posed by scholars who claim to be members of some Christian communion.

(1) It has been said that the virgin birth must be something at the edge of Christian faith, for apart from the stories in Matthew and Luke, it is unknown in the rest of the New Testament.

It is agreed that the evidence is limited. It is also agreed that the virgin birth is never part of the "gospel" or Christian kerygma as it is stated in the texts of the New Testament. It is still necessary to note that it is a major critical and theological decision to either underrate or eliminate the virgin birth from serious theological reflection. Further, when it is said that the rest of the New Testament is silent about the virgin birth, another criterion is being added to such an assessment. That other criterion is that the virgin birth was unknown or if known was considered of no importance. We are faced here with the well-known argument from silence. Logically this is a precarious approach. All we ask is that those who underrate the virgin birth from the silence of the rest of the New Testament (outside Matthew and Luke) should at least recognize that the argument from silence is, from the standpoint of logic, precarious.

D. Edwards (1943, ch. 3) has made an interesting comparison between the virgin birth and the Lord's Supper. There is more specific material about the virgin birth than there is about the Lord's Supper. If something is to be judged for importance by the sheer count of verses, then if the virgin birth is discounted so must the Lord's Supper be discounted. But who would ever assess the theological weight of the Lord's Supper in terms of the counting of verses? No theologian as yet has been able to establish how much material any given concept must have in its scriptural witness to be seriously considered in theology. To the other side, there are many extensive discussions in the Old Testament that have very little theological importance. It is the weight of the concept itself that measures its importance, and in the methodology of historic Christology the virgin birth weighs heavily.

(2) The virgin birth has been rejected on the grounds that it is contrary to our knowledge of biological science and human reproduction.

No doubt we live in an epoch of human history where the miraculous and the supernatural is rejected. However the criticism made against the Christian faith, that it breaks with the consistency or regularity of nature making science impossible, is not true. Christian theology has been a strong supporter of the uniformity of nature. In defining a miracle Augustine argued so eloquently back in the Patristic period that only as nature goes its orderly way could a miracle ever be detected. It would be destructive to the Christian faith to interpret nature as sporadic or unpredictable. At the point of the constancy or uniformity of nature there is no debate between the Christian and the scientific community.

The issue of the virgin birth in this context is the collision of philosophies or world views. In the Christian scheme of things the virgin birth is part of the great supernatural scheme of redemption. Evangelicals who know their science believe in the virgin birth on the higher ground of divine revelation and the divine redemption of the world through Jesus Christ. If the virgin birth were not part of this grand drama of the ages it could then be very well seen as a piece of dated folklore.

(3) It is affirmed that the virgin birth is out of place, theologically speaking, because it requires both a mother and a father to produce a human being.

This is a hard one to assess. Certainly the creeds affirmed the full humanity of Christ and in our language the authentic personhood of Christ. It has not been until recent times that a conflict was seen between being born of a virgin and being a complete human being. Certainly there was a tacit assumption in historic theology that even though being born of a virgin "God saw to it" that Jesus was an authentic person. It is to be correctly assumed, in our opinion, that in stressing the full humanity of Christ the creeds also intended to assure his personhood and its authenticity.

Further, at the present state of psychological studies, and at the present state of our knowledge of genetics (DNA, RNA,etc.), it is to be questioned if we can dogmatize about what it takes to make a person. For example, does a cloned frog lack froghood because it lacks a father? Until we know more of human personality and human genetics the above objection ought to be held in abeyance.

The British patristic scholar, H. E. W. Turner (1956, 12-17), has written a judicious article on the virgin birth, surveying much history and material in a short space. He reviews the Barth-Brunner debate and thinks Barth is in the right, and he makes two other points of worth in the article. He challenges the notion that the virgin birth is an explanation of the incarnation. He sees the incarnation and the virgin birth as two mutually related doctrines. Turner affirms that the virgin birth and the incarnation are not involved in circular dependence: That is, we believe in the virgin birth because we believe in the incarnation, and we believe in the incarnation because we believe in the virgin birth. This means that scholars have to interact with both claims, with each having its own integrity. From the perspective of historic Christology this is consistent.

Secondly, he expresses the worry that if the virgin birth can be discarded as unessential to Christian theology other doctrines will follow. It was for this very reason that the fundamentalists made such a stir about the virgin birth. It was not that the virgin birth was to be exaggerated beyond its just proportions, but rejection of the virgin birth uniformly involved rejection of other great Christian doctrines. Hence the virgin birth became a kind of fever thermometer in assessing the state of someone's theology.

In summary historic Christology affirms the virgin birth for the following reasons: (i) In that inspiration, revelation, redemption, and incarnation are of one piece it follows that in the providence of God a record was provided for the birth narratives; (ii) that the inspection of the documents shows the probability of the existence of a historical core to these birth narratives so that they cannot be viewed as totally the product of early church scribes; (iii) that the church from the earliest of times believed the virgin birth part of the doctrine of the incarnation and therefore part of vital church confession; and (iv) that the virgin birth is not part of Christian gospel or kerygma but part of a healthy dogma.

To return to the typical terms of O. Weber, the issue is over the status of the virgin birth as *Herkunft* or as *Ursprung*. Current New Testament scholarship understands the birth narratives as the attempt of the early church to explain the immediate origins of Jesus, hence the virgin birth rises no higher than *Herkunft*. According to historic Christology the virgin birth is part of the drama of redemption and incarnation, and therefore it says something enormously important about the origin of Jesus Christ. Hence the virgin birth is about the *Ursprung* of Jesus—the *assumptio carnis* (the event of the incarnation).

6

The Humanity of Christ

THE COMMON ASSUMPTION

It is the uniform witness of the Gospels that Jesus Christ was a man among men. He was born in Palestine, lived in Palestine, and was put to death under Pontius Pilate. There is no hint that he was in any manner less than a person. Further, there is nothing in the rest of the New Testament to contradict the picture of Jesus in the Gospels and his full humanity. The bodily humanity of Christ is challenged only in later church history and that for philosophical reasons.

The clearest expression of the humanity of Christ in terms close to theological expression is to be found in Philippians 2:5-11. As previously mentioned this passage has been, and is, the subject of much debate (cf. Martin: 1967). Nonetheless the passage reflects so directly the humanity of Christ it must be examined.

There are three expressions in the Philippian passage that speak to the humanity of Christ: (i) he was in the *form* of a servant; (ii) he was in the *likeness* of men; and (iii) he was in the *appearance* of a man. Each one of the Greek words (*morphē, homoīoma, schēma*) has been the subject of intense research. In that "form of a servant" parallels "form of God" it means that the humanity of Christ was genuine, authentic humanity. J. Schneider takes *likeness* to mean: "He truly became man, not merely in outward appearance, but in thought and feelings. He who was in the full image of God became the full image of man" (TDNT, 5: 197). *Schēma* refers to something of public appearance and at minimum means the complete normal appearance of Jesus in his daily routine. Looking at all the words together the following may be said of the humanity of Christ:

(1) Christ had a full, complete, undiminished humanity (as the creeds all insisted upon).

(2) Jesus was a man in his own right. He was not general man or universal man but was a particular man existing in his own right as a particular man.

(3) Jesus lived as his contemporaries lived. There was nothing supranormal in the conduct of his life. He appeared to his contemporaries as any other Jew would.

The common assumption of the full humanity of Christ has also been argued by an inspection of the gospel records. It is noted that Jesus hungered, thirsted, and tired; that he had such emotions as love, anger, impatience, and pity. The final and certain touch is his death on the cross. These experiences of Jesus have been set out enough times and need not be repeated.

The creeds further emphasize the undiminished humanity of Christ. Nicea briefly indicates that Christ was made man, but both the Chalcedonian Definition and the Creed of Athanasius spell out the full humanity of our Lord in greater detail.

In the seventh century it was debated whether our Lord had one will (only the divine) or two wills (a divine and a human will). Those who argued for the first were called *monothelites*; those who argued for the second, *dyothelites*. In a solidly written statement the Third Council of Constantinople (681) argued for the dyothelite position. It did so on the grounds that if Jesus were truly man he must have a will. To deprive him of his will would be to curtail his humanity. As odd as the psychology of the debate might seem to us, it nevertheless emphasizes how strong the church felt that it must maintain the full humanity of our Lord.

It is then the common assumption of the New Testament, of the great Christological confessions, and of all who stand in the tradition of historic Christology that the human nature of Jesus Christ was a complete, undiminished human nature; and that the experiences of Jesus were genuinely human and in no manner made less than human in view of the incarnation.

The New Testament says even more. It indicates that the human nature of Christ is the nature to which all the redeemed will be conformed. Christ is the last and therefore eschatological Adam (1 Cor. 15:42-50). In Romans 8:29 Paul states that all the redeemed shall be made in conformity to the image of God's dear Son. In 2 Corinthians 3:18 Paul writes that we shall all be changed from glory to glory—

degree to degree—until we conform to the image of Jesus Christ.

It is from this juncture that Barth constructs his view of man. In the light of these texts we know what human nature is. Without Jesus Christ we cannot comprehend our own humanity. We cannot determine the true option among the many options. In the humanity of Jesus Christ God has revealed what it is to be a true person. Hence a Christian anthropology can be constructed only from a Christology.

There is some confirmation of Barth's position from P. Rhinelander's (1973) *Is Man Incomprehensible to Man?* The more we know about the human situation the more mysterious it becomes, and the less we understand. Although Rhinelander does not end with total agnosticism, it is difficult to see that even his understanding of man (man the creative inventor) breaks the deadlock.

THE NORMAL HUMANITY OF CHRIST

There is no question that those who believe in historic Christology carry with their belief some profound problems. These problems are the inevitable consequences of affirming an incarnation. In the previous discussion the normal humanity of Christ has been presumed, but it is necessary to say something special about it. Historic Christology wills to maintain that the humanity of Jesus Christ was normal humanity. To phrase it in popular language, the deity of Christ did not so crowd the humanity of Christ that the humanity of Christ was less than normal. This is the reason behind *enhupostasis*. This expression means "in a person." It intends to say that in the incarnation Jesus Christ was a real person as a human being but that this person had his life in the context of the Logos. We cannot imagine the interior life of God incarnate nor do we need to. There are just two points to be reckoned with: (i) everywhere in the Gospels Jesus appears as an ordinary human being functioning totally as such a being. There was nothing unnatural about his life as one might suspect in an incarnation; and (ii) a valid doctrine of the incarnation demands a normal human nature for the incarnate One.

It is only in Luke's gospel that anything is said about the life of Jesus from birth to his public baptism (Luke 2:40, 52). These texts suggest that Jesus was a remarkable child, but there is no hint that there was anything which today we would call abnormal. It is only in the speculative apocryphal Gospels where such materials may be found.

There is also the unusual incident of Jesus talking with the rabbis at age twelve (Luke 2:41-51). This did suggest that Jesus was a precocious child, but a precocious child (from a Latin word meaning "early ripened fruit") is rare but not abnormal. There is a suggestion of a divine consciousness in Jesus in the expression "Father's house" (Luke 2:49). But again there is nothing in the text suggesting the abnormal.

As far as the public ministry of Christ is concerned Christ appears everywhere as a normal person. Jesus eats like other men, sleeps like other men, tires like other men, hungers like other men, registers emotions like other men, is tempted like other men, and dies like all men do. The only significant material in the New Testament outside of the Gospels about the personal life of Jesus is contained in the epistle to the Hebrews, which will be a subject of later comment.

Although John's gospel presents us with an exalted Christ even in his earthly life, nevertheless some of the deepest natural and human aspects of Jesus' life are contained in John's gospel. In John 11:5 it is recorded that Jesus loved Martha, Mary, and Lazarus. Here is an instance when we are told Jesus loved particular people. That is exactly what a normal person does. Jesus as a normal person can love particular people who are named in the text. Later on in the same chapter Jesus is confronted with the death of Lazarus. In John 11:33 and 11:38 it is recorded that Jesus was deeply moved in his spirit and troubled. John uses language here which indicates maximum inward stress. This again shows that at the time of death Jesus manifests emotions that normal people do on such occasions.

Elert's discussion (1960, 294) of the normal humanity of Jesus is based on Paul's statement (Gal. 4:4) that Christ was born of a woman under the law. Christ was born under the law of what we must do (*Müssens*) and what we ought to do (*Sollens*). He was born under the laws of space (he lived in a certain geographical area) and of time (he lived in a given historical epoch). He was under the laws of biology, for he hungered and thirsted. He also lived under the laws of psychology, for he could be angry, he could love, he could cry, and he could be filled with anxiety (Gethsemane). Christ also lived according to the moral "Ought" of his call. He lived under the law of the Decalog, and he lived under the cultic law in keeping the Passover.

In speaking of an incarnation we are in a boundary land where two universes overlap. There is no analogy in our experience of an incarnation. There is no handbook on how incarnations occur. The incarnation is a mystery in that the human mind understands it to a degree then it drifts out of range of our powers of conception. Historic Christology has one major concern at this point. It is to affirm that the humanity of the incarnate One was a normal humanity. The human nature of the incarnate One was not made strange nor unbalanced nor distorted in virtue of an incarnation.

The impression given in *The Myth of the God Incarnate* (Hick: 1977) is that if a doctrine of the incarnation could be propounded which created no significant problems it might be believed. It was Kierkegaard who best in the history of theology spelled out in detail the many ways that an incarnation is a maximum shock to the human mind. It cuts across our comfortable lines of rationality; it is rude to our notion of historical possibility; it makes us stutter over our scientific world-picture; it agitates our religious sensitivities; and it cuts across our logic. An incarnation that did not stir up a nest of vexing problems would not be an incarnation. A bland incarnation voids the term of its meaning. (See Baelz in Sykes: 1972, 34.)

THE SINLESSNESS OF CHRIST

The New Testament does not present Christ as living a quiet, detached life. To the contrary! He was often in clash with his contemporaries, and the Gospels record temptation at its highest level at the beginning and at the end of the public career of Christ. Bonhoeffer wrote provocatively on this point:

> He was not the perfectly good man. He was continually engaged in struggle. He did things which outwardly sometimes looked like sin. He was angry, he was harsh to his mother, he evaded his enemies, he broke the law of his people, he stirred up revolt against the rules and the religious men of his country. He entered man's sinful existence past recognition (*Christology*, p. 112).

Yet it is the uniform witness of the New Testament that in it all Jesus did not sin. He is always presented as the sinless Savior. But the sinlessness of Jesus is most controversial today. Some of the issues can be surfaced by means of pointed questions.

SINFUL OR SINLESS

Did Jesus Christ assume a sinful or sinless human nature in the incarnation (Rom. 8:3)? The majority opinion has been that Jesus Christ took sinless human nature in the incarnation in order to be the Savior.

C. E. B. Cranfield (1979, I: 379-82) has examined the possible ways of interpreting Romans 8:3 and stays close to the traditional understanding. However he does put it in the same context of Philippians 2:5-11, making it part of a great Christological confession and not as a sheer isolated moral miracle.

However there has been a minority report which interprets Romans 8:3 to mean that Christ took actual sinful human nature in order to come to where we are in order to save us.* That Jesus took actual sinful nature to save us was taught by the great Reformed scholar of the nineteenth century, A. Kuyper and by K. Barth in the twentieth century. It is not affirmation that Jesus sinned, for part of his redeeming work was to overcome sin in his own experience, even though having a sinful nature.

The issue is starkly stated as follows: if Christ is to truly save us he must be born sinless in order to be the spotless Lamb of God; if Christ is to truly save us he must become one of us right down to assuming our sinful nature.

One can see the logic in both interpretations, but J. Schneider has stoutly defended the correct interpretation of Romans 8:3, which affirms that Christ took sinless human nature (TDNT, 5: 195-96). Paul purposely did not say that Christ took sinful flesh (*en sarki hamartias*), for then he would need a Savior. Paul's expression was intended to convey two ideas: Christ really took genuine human nature, and the human nature he took was sinless. Only as a sinless Savior could he conquer sin and death.

GENUINE TEMPTATIONS

If we affirm that Jesus Christ is God-incarnate how is it possible that his temptations were genuine?

There is certainly a strong paradoxical situation. The Gospels and the Epistles state it clearly that Jesus Christ underwent severe experiences of temptation, but the same Gospels and Epistles affirm the incarnation. How can an incarnate God suffer temptation? Could he in the experience of temptation actually sin? If he cannot, is the meaning

---

* The minority report has been traced historically by A. B. Bruce, *The Humiliation of Christ* (Hodder and Stoughton, 1881), 266ff.; D. C. MacIntosh, *The Doctrine of the Person of Christ* (Charles Scribner's Sons, 1931), 277ff.; and by Wolfhart Pannenberg, *Jesus—God and Man* (Westminster, 1968), 362.

of temptation undermined? Was it impossible for Jesus to have sinned (the so-called "metaphysical" impossibility); or was it a moral impossibility? W. Kasper (1976, 92) says that Chalcedon left this to a matter of choice, and therefore it is a matter of options, as delineated below, for theologians. And if theological complications were not enough, there are more problems raised about Jesus and temptation by modern knowledge of pyschology and psychiatry. This will be a matter of later comment.

(1) It has been affirmed that *metaphysically* (i.e., by the very nature of the incarnation) that Jesus could not sin. If Jesus could sin, both the doctrine of the incarnation and the doctrine of salvation would be undermined.

(2) It has been affirmed that it was a *moral impossibility* for Jesus to have sinned. Origen said that Christ's love for his Father was so great that the Son could not sin against that love (cf. Pannenberg: 1977, 356). Berkouwer (1954) shies away from the notion of metaphysical impossibility to moral impossibility. It was Christ's moral power stemming from the Father-Son relationship that kept him from sinning. Our own view would be similar to that of Origen and Berkouwer.

(3) It has been affirmed that it was morally necessary for Jesus to have the possibility of sinning. The usual argument for this position is that temptation is real only if it can be affirmed and acted upon. A variation of this view is that it is impossible to be a genuine human being and not sin.

We think the real problem here is the failure to press more deeply into the nature of temptation. If it is asserted that temptation is real only if one can sin, then that leads to the odd conclusion that sinners are the experts on temptation. But the church has instinctively and correctly refused to take counsel on temptation from sinners. Rather, it has turned to the saints for such counsel. The sinners are those who yielded to temptation; and saints are those who have resisted because they understand it well enough to defeat it. This means that wisdom about temptation does not rest upon having yielded to temptation and thereby having sinned. The essence of temptation rests elsewhere. To be tempted is to enter the gravitational field of seduction, for temptation is but a species of seduction. The essence of seduction in temptation is to present the evil as a good. By entering this gravitational field of seduction the sinner (by definition) yields; the saint (by definition) does not yield. The essence of temptation is then how the tempted person manages the gravitational pull of seduction and not whether or not such a person may sin. If this is the nature of temptation then a sinless person who is at the same time genuinely human (and capable of entering realistically into such a gravitational field) can have genuine temptations without yielding to sin.

It is our contention that the temptations of Christ were real. He did enter the gravitational field of seduction. He did feel the full psychological, moral, and spiritual force of temptation. The very nature of an incarnation with a full humanity of the incarnate One mandates this. Therefore the temptations of Christ were authentic, genuine, and real.

NEW TESTAMENT TEXTS

What does the New Testament mean by declaring the sinlessness of Jesus (2 Cor. 5:21; Heb. 4:14, 7:25; 1 Pet. 2:22; 1 John 3:5; Acts 3:14; John 8:46)? In what sense, then, is Jesus sinless? The options are as follows:

(1) It is an empirical judgment. Jesus was never heard to say something that was sinful or do anything that was sinful. His public record is clear.

This interpretation is inadequate for a number of reasons. The most important is that this is not what the New Testament really says. It is a *totality* judgment which includes the private life as well as the public life. The sinlessness of Jesus is not such a mundane thing as nobody ever caught him with his hand in the till. Further, as an empirical claim it could never be verified. If nothing else, it is a declarative statement of divine revelation and not an induction from the life of Jesus.

(2) It is an affirmation of intent and not an affirmation of moral perfection. Advocates of this view will affirm that Jesus could sin and most likely did. His sinlessness is an affirmation that he was completely dedicated to the will of his Father, or that he always willed the good, or that he always acted out of love, or that he always acted as the man for other men.

There are two difficulties with this view. First, it is not what the New Testament texts affirm. It is something far more profound and radical than the sinlessness of right intention. Second, it is possible that a great number of human beings have been sinless in the sense of having right intentions (e.g., Job). But if great numbers of people can be called sinless in view of the rightness of their intentions, the unique claim of the sinlessness of Jesus is lost.

It has been contended that the gospel records themselves reveal instances where Jesus sinned (such as losing his temper as recorded in Matthew 23). R. Aldwinckle (1972, 199ff.) has viewed such allegations and offered a substantial refutation. It has also been argued that Jesus classified himself as a sinner when he said only God was good (Mark 10:18). In a finely reasoned essay B. B. Warfield (1929, 97-148) shows that this is not the case at all. The remark was part of Jesus' strategy to reach the rich young ruler and had nothing to do with the moral status of Jesus.

(3) It is impossible to live in this world and not sin, and this must be true of Jesus. Accordingly his sinlessness must be defined in some other manner. The contention here is that persons are so embedded in the life of their society that they cannot help but share in its corporate sinfulness. Jesus as a member of a sinful society therefore shares corporately in the sins of that society. J. Knox (1967, 69) has stated this as clearly as anybody (cf. also N. Pittenger: 1970, 55). To Knox sin is not only personal in that a person steals, lies, or murders. It is also social because in that the very way society is put together there cannot help but be sin in the total structure of society. Further, this is in the very fabric of society in a thousand subtle ways. So every person is a contributor to this endemic nature of sin in that he or she lives and cooperates with the society; but each of us is also victim of these sins in the fabric of our society. Therefore a definition of the sinlessness of Christ cannot avoid the conclusion that to live in a sinful society is in some measure to partake of its sins.

It is not a new thesis that a whole society may be sinful to a pervasive degree. Both Claus Westermann (*Creation*, 1974) and Helmut Thielicke (*How the World Began*, 1965) have commented on the sinful societies of Genesis 4-11. The reality of corporate sin is very important in the Old Testament. But Knox and Pittenger are saying more than this. They are affirming that every society has its "sinful structures," and that to live in such a society involves to some measure cooperating with those sinful structures and hence sinning. For example, a person may have objected to slavery in pre-Civil War days in America and yet bought something in a store made by slave labor. Jesus lived in a society with sinful structures, and because he participated in it (wore its clothes and shoes, ate its food, participated in its commerce, and agreed with its civil law, etc., etc.), he to some measure sinned. That is the claim. Does it hold?

At the present time it is difficult to make a law on the matter even if it can be defended in a general way. The War Trials after World War II were a nest of legal ambiguities.* Here exactly was an effort to assign guilt in view of the sinful structures of society. Who was to be charged as guilty and who was exempt became very arbitrary; and what ought the penalty to be? It is our contention at the present time that the concept of sin and guilt through participation in the sinful structures of society has not as yet been adequately evaluated by legal experts and by ethicists. If the thesis can be substantiated then theologians must rethink the nature of our Lord's identification with sinners. In either case we must be careful about forcing a modern ethical opinion on an ancient text.

Pittenger redefines sin in view of his process theology. The older notion of sin as transgression of the divine law is rejected. The new moral standard is identified with whatever it means to be human, and the new definition of sin is to deviate from what it means to be human. The golden rule of this morality is to do all things for love and from love. Jesus is sinless (according to Pittenger) in the sense that he did attempt to do all things from and for love. It ought to be obvious that this is more a philosophical and theological judgment rather than an exegetical one from the data of Scripture.

However Pittenger does raise another important point. He says theologians have (historically) underplayed the sexuality of Jesus rather than coming to terms with it as part of the valid humanity of Christ (Ibid., 60ff.). The result is a typically asexual concept of Jesus seen most clearly in Christian art. In reply to this we would grant that if Jesus' body followed the laws of physiological development, then his psyche followed the laws of psycho-sexual development. If sexual fantasies are part of our normal sexual maturing then we need not deny them to Jesus. But we are limited in such speculations by the uniqueness of the incarnation. We need to invoke again at this point Nicolas of Cusa's learned ignorance—*docta ignoranta.*

(4) R. Williams (1974, 4-8) has examined carefully Hebrews 4:15 ("without sin") and come to another version of the sinlessness of Christ. He reviews both the interpretation of Hebrews 4:15 and modern debates over the sinlessness of Jesus. His basic notion is that for Jesus to be truly our compassionate Savior he must suffer sin as we do. Part of his saviorhood is his struggle with sin and victory over it. In a

---

* Cf. George Bailley, *Germans* (Avon Books, 1972), for Bailley's observations where he wrote from the privileged place of being an official translator at the trials.

word he grew into a *state* of sinlessness. Therefore at the end of his life, when he is to offer himself as both priest and victim he achieved sinlessness. Hebrews 4:15 is then a statement about Jesus' accomplishment at the end of his life marked by his complete obedience to the will of the Father to suffer death on the cross.

(5) Pannenberg (1968, 362ff.) believes that the church's affirmation of the sinlessness of Jesus is based on his resurrection from the dead. Brunner's (1947, 227) position is similar. To him it is a post-Easter theological judgment of the church in light of the incarnation and not an empirical judgment.

(6) There is a growing concensus that the affirmation of the sinlessness of Jesus is a claim that he is qualified to be the Savior of the world. It is not an abstract sinlessness. Bonhoeffer (1966, 112ff.) sets it out in the context of Jesus' struggles, his temptations, his assailants, and his victories. There is nothing that Jesus ever said or did which would disqualify him as the Lamb of God. (For a complete discussion cf. Berkouwer: 1954, ch. 10.)

The affirmation of the sinlessness of Christ is an affirmation that could originate only from the Father to the disciples. It is not affirmation isolated from the saviorhood of Christ. It could be called the moral foundation of the atonement.

An indirect affirmation of the sinlessness of Christ is to be found in Christ's authority to forgive sin. This is certainly one of the most radical elements in the Gospels. The radical character of it is that the Jewish tradition in which Jesus stood held such a high view of the holiness of God. In this context he proclaims forgiveness of sins. Would he be so bold to do that if he himself were not free from the charges of other men?

The best thoughts on this subject in our opinion have been written by H. Vogel (1952, 665-66). The sinlessness of Christ is not basically a matter of moral perfection; it is a matter of holiness. Jesus Christ is our Savior for us. To be our Savior, our Substitute, and Representative he dedicates himself completely to that task. His sinlessness is not a statement about Christ-in-himself but of Christ-for-us. He is therefore holy in order to be fully qualified to be for us Lord, Savior, and Redeemer. And so as we said above, this sinlessness, this holiness of Jesus, is the moral presupposition of the atonement.

7

From the Cross to the Return of Christ

THE CROSS

Martin Kähler (1964) said that the Gospels are long introductions to the passion narratives. In a sense this is a very accurate statement. To believe in the death of Christ for one's salvation one must have some sort of an idea of the One who died on the cross. What did he teach? What did he do? What did he claim? How did he treat people? What was his life like? Did he love and hate? What sort of ethics did he teach and practice? The Gospels are filled with materials of this sort. They give us an image, a picture, a personality sketch of the One who died on the cross. Knowledge of the life of the person who died on the cross helps create a credence for believing in such a sacrifical death.

The New Testament never presents Jesus Christ as dying the death of a hero. It is the dramatic situation which creates the hero—the soldier who falls on the hand grenade to save his fellow soldiers. Nor is Jesus presented as a martyr, although there is a touch of that in 1 Timothy 6:13 (Jesus before Pilate). Jesus is presented as dying as a Savior, a Redeemer, and a Victim.

John's gospel has a very distinctive doctrine of the cross. The cross is seen as a date kept by the Son with the Father. (See Thusing: 1970.) This special meeting of the Father and the Son at the cross is brought out by the use of the word "hour" (*hōra*, 1:39, 2:4,11:9, 16:4, etc.), the word "season" (*kairos*, 7:6-8), and by the word "commandment" (*entolē*, 10:18).

87

Death by crucifixion was bloody and cruel.* Yet John's gospel turns the world of thought upside down and calls it an event of glorification. Under what possible considerations could a hateful cross be turned into an event of glorification? Apparently if John sees the cross as the event of world salvation (e.g., John 3:16), then it is transformed from an event of shame to an event of glory. Even Paul writes that he glories in the cross of Christ and apparently for the same reason (Gal. 6:14).

In the light of Hengel's research the very notion that the cross is an event of glory and even more so, that one can glory in the cross, stuns the mind. It adds immeasurably to our understanding of the love of God, the humiliation of the Son of God, and the cost of our redemption.

It was O. Cullmann (1962) who set out the death of Christ in a proper manner when he contrasted it so starkly with the death of Socrates. He contrasts the agony of Jesus in Gethsemane with the calm manner in which Socrates took the poison hemlock and died conversing philosophically with his friends. Of course Jesus knew as every person in the Roman Empire knew of the terrors of death by crucifixion. But Cullmann thinks that there is more than that. Jesus knew death as part of human alienation from God, and therefore it was a fearful event no matter how one died. No one could see death coming to them as Jesus saw it, for he saw it as the death of the Lamb of God (John 1:29).

As much as the writers of the New Testament tell us of the agony of the cross, they are careful to tell us that he did not die in some trivial village nor was he killed by a crowd of unruly ruffians. This would certainly trivialize the death of Christ. Rather they make it emphatic that he died under the authority of a high Roman official; he died in a capitol city; and he died as a verdict of a trial. Paul summed it all up rather tersely when he told Agrippa that the events around the death of Christ were not done in a corner, an idiom for some small, obscure town. Hengel lists the opinions of the Romans about the death of

---

* The practice of crucifixion in the ancient world is presented to us in great detail in M. Hengel's *Crucifixion* (Fortress, 1977). The great number of references to the cross in the New Testament have been listed in L. Morris, *The Cross in the New Testament* (Eerdmans, 1965). Until recently our knowledge of crucifixion has been limited to literary reports. However the skeleton of a crucified male has been found one and a half miles north of the Second Wall of Jerusalem and dated around AD 6. Details and sketches will be found in the article on crucifixion in *The Interpreter's Dictionary of the Bible: Supplementary Volume* (Abingdon, 1976), 199-200.

Jesus, showing that it had become common knowledge in the Roman Empire (ibid., 2ff.).

A number of books have been written about the trial of Jesus. They are efforts to recapture the Jewish and Roman legal procedures of that time and see how they might explain the trial of Jesus. Whatever the details of the trial might prove to be, the outline of events seems clear. The execution of Jesus by Pontius Pilate is an event known in the history of the world, and all the major steps in a crucifixion are mentioned in the account of Jesus' crucifixion.

Yet the New Testament nowhere dwells on the physical sufferings of Christ on the cross. The record is not silent about some obvious facts of suffering. It is known from accounts of crucifixion from that period that the two chief elements of suffering were an intense thirst and a headache that would seem strong enough to split the head open. The thirst is mentioned at the crucifixion of Jesus but not the headache. But the sentimentality found in Christian piety, Christian art, and Christian preaching is not found in the New Testament. The reason is that the weight of the crucifixion is upon its saving or redeeming worth. Its merit lay in its sacrificial aspect, not in the sheer amount of physical and mental suffering.

Medical discussions about the premature death of Christ are inconclusive. In most instances death followed crucifixion in about forty-eight hours. The cause was the combination of shock, exposure, and dehydration. The customary explanation is that Christ died prematurely from his intense spiritual suffering. In that it was routine to scourge the victims, Hengel's opinion is that Jesus received an extra strong lashing in which case the blood flowed freely. As a result he was too weak to even carry the cross-piece to the place of execution. And for the same reason he died in about six hours.

Such a premature death was unusual. It was a practice for the soldiers to tweek the ribs of the victims to see if they were still alive. In Jesus' case the tweek was a bold thrust of the spear into the viscera itself to be sure the victim was dead. Pounding the victims legs with hammers was a method of inducing death if the soldiers did not wish to wait out the two days of suffering.

There are several biblical passages which comment on how Christ faced the prospect of his death:

(1) There is the picture of Jesus in Gethsemane caught in the conflict of the terrors of crucifixion and the necessity to do the will of God (Matt. 26:30-46, Mark 14:26-31, Luke 22:33-34). The conflict was so

intense that his sweat were as drops of blood, which may mean either the sweat poured forth like a cut blood vessel or the capillaries in the sweat glands ruptured and colored the sweat red. In view of the agonized crucifixion to come, no wonder the conflict. It was a practice in many instances to leave the body on the cross to be eaten by birds and animals.

(2) In Hebrews 5:7-9 we are told that Jesus as the Son of God learned obedience through the things he suffered. This text reminds us of our Lord in Gethsemane, and intense spiritual striving to obey the will of God, as well as the great Christological text of Philippians 2:5-11. The plan of salvation was no empty drama nor fictional charade but was played out in the brutal realities of life and demanded the fullness of obedience to do the Father's will. The Philippian text is also a very unusual text, for the apostle mentions nothing about suffering, salvation, or atonement. The text presents the event of the crucifixion from the standpoint of the person of Christ. It reveals the maximum of humiliation to die on a cross and the fullest measure of obedience to the will of God until death, even the death of the cross.

(3) In Hebrews 12:1-3 we are told that Jesus was able to endure the cross through the joy that he anticipated after the cross. This is a most unusual text. How could any person have at the same time a sense of joy and a foreboding of death by crucifixion? There is certainly no joy revealed in the text of the Gospels about the crucifixion. This can be nothing less than a revelation to the author of Hebrews about the interior state of mind that Jesus had as he underwent crucifixion. There is hardly a greater contrast in human experience than that of the combination of joy and crucifixion.

One more point needs to be made about the cross. Hebrews 9:14 states that Christ offered himself up to God on the cross by an eternal spirit. Does "spirit" mean the Holy Spirit or the divine nature of Christ? Either way the point is the same. It was the dignity of the person who was crucified that gives the cross its merit and universal relevance. That is why the death of Christ on the cross is lifted above all the other thousands of that ancient world who also died on crosses.

THE RESURRECTION

In the resurrection Jesus Christ makes a transition from a state of humiliation to a state of glory. He becomes God's Lord and Christ. He is worthy of exaltation to the right hand of God. He stands forth as victor and as vindicated.

The New Testament witnesses that, after the third day of the crucifixion, Jesus Christ rose from the dead in a body that bore the marks of his crucifixion. Yet it was not the same body of humiliation but an "eschatological" body—a body for eternity.

The differences among New Testament scholars about the resurrection are many and they are severe. There is some concensus on the following points:

(1) There is a fullness of references to the resurrection in the New Testament, making it one of its most important themes.

(2) There is no easy harmony of the accounts of the resurrection. G. Ladd (1975, 80-82) has charted the accounts under twenty-five different headings so that the agreements and differences can be seen at a glance (cf. also Wenham: 1984).

(3) There are reasons to believe that 1 Corinthians 15:3-7 is the most primitive account of the resurrection in the New Testament.

(4) The methods used to discredit the resurrection accounts employed in the nineteenth century are considered dated and replaced by more sophisticated methods of gospel criticism. The older methods included the swoon theory of Schleiermacher, the mythical theory of Strauss and Bultmann, and the political theory of Reimarus.

(5) The cross is more than a revelation of the fullness of obedience of Christ. Its meaning is not exhausted in its triumph over death. As part of the gospel it is also a great theological event. In the first Christian sermon spoken by Peter and recorded in Acts 2, Peter draws out the theological meaning of the resurrection for the Jews. God has made Christ both Lord and Christ. In more recent research into the titles of Christ, these are among the most profound and significant.

VIEWS OF THE RESURRECTION

Again, it is granted that faith in a risen Christ permeates the New Testament. But not all New Testament scholars and theologians assess the materials the same way. Naturally the resurrection is a very controversial subject because it touches on so many other primary issues of theology and Holy Scripture. The following represents most of the major stances taken towards the New Testament witness to the resurrection of Christ:

(1) Those who hold to historic Christology believe that Jesus Christ

rose bodily from the dead on the third day. Although it was a body marked by the wounds of crucifixion to assure the believers that the crucified Jesus is the risen Jesus, his body was one of glory (Phil. 3:21). There is great variance in the resurrection accounts, but such variations are characteristic of the reporting of all great events. Those who believe in historic Christology are also very wary of attempts to spiritualize the resurrection and thus rob it of its status as the victory over death.

(2) Other New Testament scholars believe that God did truly exalt Jesus Christ as Lord and Savior after his death. But this was an exaltation of his person which did not involve Jesus' body. But to assure the disciples that God did exalt Jesus as Savior and Lord, God gave realistic visions of Jesus to the disciples. In fact they were so realistic that the disciples mistook them for a literal body and hence spoke of a bodily resurrection.

(3) Bultmann has a very individualistic view of the resurrection. A vicarious death for the sins of the world is a mythological concept and so is the resurrection from the dead. Bultmann prefers to take his stance in Romans 6. Hence the cross means the end of our old inauthentic way of existence. In the forgiveness and justification of God to the believer he has opened a new life, a new range of possibilities for the believer. He has granted the believer authentic existence. It is this new life that is the real meaning of the resurrection. Jesus was buried and there his body corrupted.

(4) Other New Testament scholars influenced by Bultmann approach the resurrection differently, although all agree (Käsemann, Marxsen) that the resurrection accounts are historically botched witnesses. It is claimed that the accounts themselves, properly sifted, reveal how the resurrection narratives came into existence. First there is the reported seeing (*Sehen*—an inward psychological interpretation and not the objective seeing as in the perception of an object) of Jesus among the disciples. From the *Sehen* of Jesus is deduced the conviction that Jesus lives. From the belief that he lives it is further concluded that he lives bodily. From his bodily existence the resurrection narratives are constructed in order to account for a bodily resurrection.

However from this interpretation a negative conclusion is not necessarily drawn. The resurrection has existential force. The kingdom Jesus announces continues. The concerns that Jesus had are still valid concerns. Whatever was authoritative in Jesus yet continues in his community as authority. Marxsen calls it the *Sache Jesu*—the cause of

Jesus. Käsemann calls it the faith of the post-Easter community, and he even speaks of Jesus as Lord. In the sense that this purposes to be a sophisticated advance in critical methodology and theological interpretation, it differs from the older liberalism which these men freely criticize.

For those scholars who deny the bodily resurrection but still believe that there is a message which stems from Jesus, the pattern of interpretation has hardly changed in more than a hundred years. First it is conceded on scientific, historical, and critical grounds that the bodily resurrection of Jesus cannot be accepted as historical fact. Then something is located in Jesus' teaching and ministry that has enduring worth or divine significance and that constitutes the message of the Christian church. Usually (but not in every case) it is some version of the kingdom of God. When the great acts of divine redemption in the cross and resurrection of Jesus Christ are rejected as the center and heart of his ministry, these are replaced by some version of the kingdom of God. Hence the concept of the kingdom of God becomes a theological litmus paper to test a person's theology.

(5) W. Pannenberg stands out uniquely in his belief in the resurrection of Christ. He is not in the conservative or evangelical camp, but he does believe in the bodily resurrection. He believes that Paul's list of witnesses of the risen Lord as recorded in 1 Corinthians 15:1-7 is valid historic material. And when one adds to that observation the witness of the empty tomb as recorded in the Gospels, Pannenberg believes we have interlocking (though independent in their origins) evidence of the historicity of the resurrection. If a historian would say that the resurrection cannot be believed because there is no other event like it in history (*Gleichartigkeit*), Pannenberg replies that all historical events are unique. If it is said that science does not allow such an event, then Pannenberg replies that not all the laws of nature are known as of now.

Pannenberg is with the few in taking the empty tomb as a serious witness to the resurrection. There is more substance to the empty tomb tradition than most New Testament critics will allow (see Stein: 1979, 8-12 and Wilckens: 1970). Their contribution is a refutation of the notion that the disciples pulled themselves out of their gloom after the crucifixion of Jesus. Only by the personal appearances of Jesus to the disciples could they really come to a belief that he was risen from the dead.

(6) A distinction between the Easter Event and the Easter Faith cuts across many different versions of the resurrection accounts. The Easter

Event is the bodily resurrection of Jesus which gave rise to the Easter Faith. This has been the stance of historic Christology. However liberal theologians already in the nineteenth century spoke only of the Easter Faith by which they meant the continuation in the hearts and minds of the disciples of the things Jesus taught.

An alternate version of this (with an attempt to give it more substance) has been argued by J. Knox (1967) and Pittenger (1970). There is a measure of obscurity to their thought. The resurrection is denied and affirmed at the same time. It is denied that the body of Jesus was raised from the dead by the glory of the Father (Rom. 6:4), while at the same time it is affirmed that an actual historical event took place which may be called the resurrection. The event is the coming of the Holy Spirit who simultaneously forms the Christian community and keeps fresh and powerful within it the memory of Jesus. And this memory of Jesus is not a matter of sheer recollection but has the power that unique personalities have to affect generations after them. Accordingly Knox and Pittenger make it a strong point to affirm their faith in the event of the resurrection, which in our view of historic Christology is but a strengthened version of the Easter Faith that denies the Easter Event.

A Primitive Witness

1 Corinthians 15:3-7 is considered the most primitive witness to the resurrection in the New Testament. As can be expected Bultmann and the post-Bultmannians uniformly discount the text, for regardless of an objective interpretation, if the text stands the Bultmannian position falls. We now wish to come to serious interaction with the text. Those New Testament scholars who see this as a most primitive piece of authentic Christian witness isolate the following elements in this passage:

(1) Paul uses traditional language in this passage (see Cullmann: 1954 and Bruce: 1970). This means that Paul is affirming that that which the church passed on to him is the gospel. Paul was converted somewhere between AD 33 and 35. This means we have a sample of what the church considered to be the gospel within three years after the crucifixion.

(2) The omission of appearances to the women is odd. Thus this list may be an official list or a "court trial list." Only the most substantial kind of evidence could be given. In that a feminine witness was not considered valid at that time, the appearances to the women were omitted.

(3) The use of the word "appeared" is a remarkable one. In the Septuagint it means a revelation of God in which God takes the initiative. In this passage it means that the risen Lord takes the initiative to make himself known to the disciples. The disciples did not come into Easter Faith by some kind of process of self-recuperation.

(4) The startling text also implies that the early church accepted the appearance of Christ to Paul as a valid resurrection appearance and not a vision. To indicate how unusual this was Paul calls himself an *ektrōma* which means something born out of time sequence. The appearance of the risen Lord to Paul three years or more after the ascension is certainly out of time sequence. Those who take *ektrōma* to mean how unworthy Paul thought of himself (so von Harnack: 1901) miss the real point of such an out of sequence event being reckoned a valid resurrection appearance.

(5) The chapter puts the empty tomb in perspective. A tomb may be empty for many reasons. Jesus could be risen from the dead for only one reason—the power of God (Rom. 6:4). When the risen Lord and his appearances are coordinated with the empty tomb, then a most significant reason is suggested for the empty tomb. In fact W. Pannenberg thinks that the evidence of the risen Lord in 1 Corinthians 15:3-7 intersects with the Gospels' witness of an empty tomb to give strong historical certainty for the resurrection of Christ. We can only agree that historic Christology is committed to the bodily resurrection of Christ.

THE BODILY RESURRECTION

Those who believe in the bodily resurrection of Christ differ in their understanding of its historical nature. D. Migliore (1977, 7-14) created a fictional panel discussion of the resurrection among Bultmann, Barth, Moltmann, and Pannenberg. It is a very accurate recreation of the opinions of these theologians. A panel discussion actually took place among some neo-orthodox theologians, some evangelical theologians, and one Roman Catholic theologian (John Montgomery, *History and Christianity*, pp. 81-110). In these two panels we can gather why there are sharp differences among believers about the historical nature of the resurrection.

(1) Basically the evangelicals argue that the bodily resurrection is a solid historical event. The resurrection took place in space, time, and historical sequence like any other event of history. It can be reported again with the same objectivity as any other event in history. This defense is posited against the numerous efforts by theologians in the past

hundred years to affirm belief in the resurrection, yet managing to deny a bodily resurrection. A hard line on the factuality, the historicity, and the reportability of the resurrection blocks off the sophisticated interpretations of the resurrection.

(2) The other group focuses on the uniqueness of the resurrection. Because it is such a unique act of God it consequently escapes ordinary historical reporting, and therefore cannot be set out as if it were an event like any other event in history. It is an event in which this world order is intersected by the eternal world order. The eschatological has dipped into the ordinary course of history. Therefore the resurrection must stand some measure apart from the ordinary writing of history. It is an important consideration that only believing eyes saw the risen Lord. If a Roman soldier had seen the risen Lord he would have no idea what he was seeing.

Barth has been the most sustained defender of this view. To begin with there has been a caricature of Barth as if he believed that there was a special space and time in which theological miracles take place. Barth believes in no such theological arena divorced from our space and time. In a virtually unknown little pamphlet Barth (1945, 6) comments on the nature of the resurrection. He states that the resurrection is not in the realm of thought and idea but is a real event in space and time. Nor is it in the realm of myth. The resurrection is about an empty tomb and about the person of Jesus who was bodily (*leiblich*), visibly (*sichtbaren*), audibly (*hörbaren*), and tactily (*betastbaren*) manifested to his disciples.

Barth's point is that historians do their research and write their books working with certain historical principles called historiography. One of these principles contained in a scientific historiography is that nothing supernatural can be considered an historical event. God can never be a character in any book of history. Hence when historians read the resurrection accounts in the New Testament they systematically rule them out as non-historical. According to their historiography they must do so. Hence historians will never report the bodily resurrection.

What is the status of an event which Christians believe took place in our space and time, but took place as God's act, and is on that plane, not capable of being written as an event in world history? Barth calls such an event a saga. The resurrection is a saga in the sense that it actually, literally, and bodily took place; but because it took place by the initiative of God, historians cannot report it as an historical event.

It is obvious from reading the discussions of the panels that both sides shoot past each other. Those who want so earnestly to guard the objectivity of the resurrection underplay its unique character as a proposed historical event; and those who want to guard the uniqueness of the event might not be aware of their tendency to shade away the historical factuality of the resurrection. Historic Christology can go with either view, although we think Barth's case is the best of the options because he has most thoroughly understood the nature of the historical issue.

THE RESURRECTION AND CHRISTOLOGY

However historic Christology does not see the resurrection as only a matter of defending against its factual denial. To the contrary the main emphasis is on the role the resurrection plays in Christology:

(1) The resurrection is part of the gospel and therefore part of what must be believed in order to be saved (cf. Rom. 10:9-10, 1 Cor. 15:3-7). F. X. Durrwell (1960) has worked out in great detail the way in which the resurrection of Christ fits into a total New Testament theology. Although Christian preaching and teaching is weighted in the direction of the cross, this is not the case in the New Testament where the resurrection is presented parallel to the cross. Therefore to eliminate the bodily resurrection of Christ from the Christian message is to damage all of New Testament theology.

(2) Paul writes that the greatest enemy of humankind is death (1 Cor. 15:26). Death is the end of a life unfulfilled, for all lives end short of their promise and potential. Although we concentrate on the tragic character of the death of a young person, it is nevertheless true that the aged also die tragically in that their lives too are unfulfilled. Death also causes the permanent separation of our loves. It is therefore the strongest of psychological shocks to the psyche.

The rule of Christ shall end the rule of death. The victory of Christ overcomes the sting of death (1 Cor. 15:54-57). The hope of the believer is in the risen Lord. If the bodily resurrection of Jesus is denied then there is no victory over death. The last and final enemy of the human race is victorious, not defeated. For those like Tillich and Bultmann who construct theology without the bodily resurrection the Christian faith means only the quality of life lived now in our present existence.

(3) That Christ is not only the divine sufferer but also the trium-

phant victor has always been a theme in Christian theology. The risen Savior is also the Conqueror. There can be no *Christus Victor* if Jesus was not raised from the dead. We may gain a social ethic, or a new theory of spirituality, or some kind of concept of the kingdom of God from the teachings of one who did not rise from the dead. But only in the risen Christ is there Christ the Victor over sin, death, and hell, which are all the great fearsome enemies of humankind.

(4) The resurrection is also part of the exaltation of Christ. So much are resurrection and exaltation joined in the New Testament that it is not unusual to have a writer go from the cross to the exaltation and not mention the resurrection (cf. Phil. 2:5-11). If there is no resurrection then there is no exaltation of Christ, no assumption of the glory of Christ, and no eschatological dimension to the victory of Christ.

THE ASCENSION

Both the Apostles' Creed and the Nicene Creed affirm the ascension of Christ to the right hand of God the Father. Therefore the ascension of Christ has been a central part of historic Christology.

The direct affirmation of the ascension and the texts which imply the ascension are very many. On this score J. G. Davies (1958, 45-46) writes:

> The witness of the New Testament writings to the Ascension of Christ is remarkable in its universality. We have observed references to it in all four Gospels, in the Acts of the Apostles, in the Pauline Epistles, in the Pastorals, in I Peter and in the book of Revelation. We may confidently assert therefore that the inclusion of the words "he ascended into heaven" in the Apostles' Creed is amply justified by the evidence.

Yet curiously the accounts of the ascension of Christ defy a set chronology. John Reumann (1968, 132) has made charts of the different versions of the ascension. In 1 Corinthians 15:3-7 Jesus seems to come from heaven for each appearance although the passage does not mention the ascension. John 20:17 suggests that the day of resurrection was also the day of ascension. Luke places the ascension after forty days of appearances, and the church calendar has followed Luke's version of the ascension (see Toon: 1984).

A new element has been added to the discussion of the ascension with the advent of modern astronomy. We know that not many miles above the earth the temperature drops far below freezing and that outside the protection of the atmosphere there is strong cosmic radiation. In addition modern relativity theory and astronomy have made such concepts as up and down meaningless. How does this knowledge influence our understanding of the ascension?

Jesus ascended into a cloud; he is not pictured as ascending endlessly upward. In Scripture clouds are one of the symbols of the apocalyptic and the eschatological (cf. TNDT, 4: 902ff.). The cloud then means that Jesus made a transition from this world of space, time, and materiality into the sphere of heaven. Elert (1960, 321) expresses this idea as follows:

> Heaven is the "place" of God, which limits the time-space of the earthly world, hence is the "otherside" of time and space. [Heaven] cannot be another kind of space in which one can rise into having left another kind of space. The single passages in the New Testament show clearly that there is a difference between the popularly spoken blue globe above us and heaven as the place of God, to which Christ was exalted.

However the most sophisticated writing on space is to be found in T. F. Torrance's (1969), *Space, Time, and Incarnation*. This is a discussion of the concept of space in Greek philosophy, among the church Fathers, at the time of the Reformation, and our current Einsteinian period of the understanding of space. He does much to correlate the action of God in the world and how it impinges on our understanding of space. He believes that the relational theory of space as found in Einstein's theory harmonizes well with the Reformed view of space as expressed in the incarnation (and by implication the ascension). The ascension thus fits into (i) the biblical understanding of how the actions of God are correlated with space and (ii) the relational view of space which Torrance finds in Scripture and modern astronomy.

Barth is perhaps right in affirming that the resurrection of Christ, the session of Christ, and the return of Christ are one doctrine. They express the exaltation and glorification of Christ as well as his universal rule.

THE SESSION OF CHRIST

After Jesus' ascension into heaven, the New Testament affirms that he was seated at the right hand of the Father. This is called the session of Christ. It is a far richer concept than most theologies represent, for it becomes involved in both the framing and understanding of some important theological topics.

THE INTERCESSION

The first and most obvious deduction about the session of Christ is that he enters into his intercessory ministry. It is puzzling that Paul makes only the minimum references about the session and intercession of Christ, for in his own time the Temple sacrificial rituals were being daily carried on. Only two verses (Rom. 8:34, 1 Tim. 2:5) refer to the intercessory ministry of Christ. It is the book of Hebrews which has the richest materials on this theme.

The book of Hebrews sets out the intercessory ministry of Christ within the imagery of the tabernacle, priest, and sacrifices. One finds these materials in Exodus and Leviticus. (i) The Son of God became incarnate so that he could experientially know what it was like to be a pilgrim in this world (Heb. 2:14-16). (ii) He is first of all a Savior because he offered up himself for the salvation of his people (Heb. 9:11-28). (iii) The place of his intercessory work is heaven itself, the true tabernacle (Heb. 6:19-20, 8:1-2). (iv) The basis of his intercession is his experience of temptation and suffering (Heb. 2:19, 4:14-16, 5:7-10). And the power of his priesthood is that he ever lives to make intercession (Heb. 9:11-28).

CHRISTUS PRAESENS

Christus praesens is a Latin phrase which speaks to the point of the presence of Jesus Christ on earth for individual Christians and for the church. It is a major theological topic and it has almost dropped out of theological literature. In the theology of the Eastern Orthodox Church and the Roman Catholic Church, Christ is supremely, uniquely, and literally present in the Eucharist, as mediated through the bishops and the priests. This is what gives them their authority and their sacramental power to make *Christus praesens*. However in the mystical and devotional literature of both churches there is also the personal doctrine of *Christus praesens*.

The Reformers had their doctrine of *Christus praesens* too. In all branches of the Reformation churches it was believed that Christ is present with each believer and in the church. Their basis for this were the texts of Scripture which affirmed the deity of Christ. But they added to that the power of the Holy Spirit to make the presence of Christ felt among his followers. In recent times Dietrich Bonhoeffer has expressed it as Christ present in the preached Word; Christ present in the sacraments; and Christ present in the fellowship of the Christian community.

The unmentioned tragedy of those theologians who deny historic Christology is that they have undermined the doctrine of *Christus praesens*. The version that Christ is remembered merely in the preaching in the church is a frail doctrine compared to the sturdy doctrine of *Christus praesens* among the Reformers.

COSMIC CHRISTOLOGY

In his session at the right hand of the Father, Christ begins his reign (1 Cor. 15:20-28, Phil. 2:9-11, Rom. 8:18-25, Rev. 11:15; 19-20).

In a very important and unexpected book Galloway added a whole new dimension to the understanding of the reign of Christ. The vision he had was that of Christ reigning until all enemies are defeated. This interpretation and the final victory of Christ he called cosmic Christology. Among other things the concept of the cosmic Christ is that it rescues Christianity from being a cultic affair located in Palestine. To the contrary the reign of Christ is cosmic in proportion, for Christ is Lord of Israel, the Lord of the church, the Lord over all demonic forces, and the Lord of the cosmos itself. If a theologian limits his vision and sees Christ as ruling only over believers and the church, there is then too much territory omitted from the reign of Christ. The gospel is personal, for only by faith do we become Christians. But from that original point of conversion, Galloway sees circle after circle as the reign of Christ is extended more and more until it becomes cosmic.

Galloway was a pioneer in developing the notion of cosmic Christology. George A. Maloney (1968) traces the thin line of cosmic Christology from Paul to the present, and mentions such moderns as Rahner, Schillebeeckx, and Teilhard de Chardin.*

---

* Teilhard is the greatest "Cosmic Christologist" of recent times. He solves the problem of the tension between the Christian doctrine of creation and the theory of evolution by "christifying" the whole cosmic and evolutionary process. Besides his own writings one may find summaries of his thought in Henri de Lubac, *Teilhard de Chardin: The Man and His Meaning,* and Christofer F. Mooney, *Teilhard de Chardin and the Mystery of Christ.*

THE SESSION AND ESCHATOLOGY

Historically speaking it is almost unanimous in Christian theology that Christ will reign until all his enemies are defeated, including death, the race's deadliest enemy. But this doctrine has provoked tensions about the nature of the reign and what forms it may take. There is a tension of how spiritual or how literal the reign will be, giving rise to the well-worn terms of postmillennialism, premillennialism, and amillennialism. Galloway has warned us that if we make the reign too spiritual, then part of the cosmos does not come under the cosmic reign of Christ. Standing with him on this point is the Swiss theologian Bietenhard, who is also apprehensive that such a spiritualizing of the reign of Christ will limit its cosmic dimensions.

From the other side comes the protest that if the reign of Christ is taken too literally and to crassly, the reign of Christ has been too materialized. As much as one may try, it has been impossible to find a mediating and reconciling solution to these tensions. But we can at least join in one chorus of harmony by proclaiming that Christ will in his good time be Lord of Lords and King of Kings, and so completely fulfill what is meant by cosmic Christology.

There are certain affirmations which all who believe in historic Christology have in common:

(1) According to Philippians 2:9-11 Christ shall one day receive universal adoration as Lord. The entire universe of created beings shall make that confession. The time or occasion of that event is not specified in the text, but all Christians believe that it shall come.

(2) Christ shall reign until all the enemies of God are conquered, including death (1 Cor. 15:20-28, Rom. 8:9-11). This means that the reign of Christ is more than spiritual or moral. That he shall conquer death is a reminder that the reign of Christ cannot be solely a spiritual one. All powers, authorities or whatever other term applies here shall be subdued by Christ. Further the kingdoms of this world will become the kingdoms of our Lord Christ, and he shall reign forever and ever (Rev. 11:15).

(3) The reign of Christ is universal and cosmic in that the cosmic order is recreated (Revelation 19-20). Although Christians may differ over the details of eschatology, they all unite in affirming that the human story is not over until there is a new heaven, a new earth, and a new Jerusalem. The reason for this is that human history begins in a cosmic way with creation. Adam and Eve were related to their cosmos

102

in the first creation. We are therefore related to the cosmos in our eternal state.

THE INTERCESSOR

In the heavenly session of Christ, Christ begins his ministry as high priest and intercessor for the Christians. The great model of the intercessory work of Christ is the great prayer of Christ recorded in John 17. Seen from the standpoint only of the literary character of its composition it is a masterpiece. In this prayer Christ devotes himself to praying for the total well-being and success of his disciples.

Paul presents us with a puzzling problem. As a young Jewish scholar studying under Gamaliel (Acts 22:3), and as one in Jerusalem when the Temple services were still being enacted, he says very little of the priesthood, the sacrifices, and the temple worship. He says nothing of tabernacle or Temple. In only two places he speaks of the intercessory ministry of Christ reflecting something of the Levitical priesthood (Acts 8:34, 1 Tim. 2:5).

The book of Hebrews is the richest with materials about the intercession of Christ. His intercessory work is set within the imagery of the tabernacle, priesthood, and offerings of the book of Exodus: (i) The Son of God became incarnate in the flesh so that he could experientially know what it was like to be a pilgrim in this world (Heb. 2:14-16). (ii) He is first of all a Savior in that he offered up himself for the salvation of his people (Heb. 9:11-28). (iii) The place of intercession is heaven itself, the true tabernacle (Heb. 6:19-20, 8:1-2). (iv) The basis of his intercession is his experience of temptation and suffering (Heb. 2:19, 4:14-16, 5:7-10). (v) He has a powerful priesthood for he ever lives to make intercession (Heb. 9:11-28).

THE RETURN OF CHRIST

Both the Apostles' Creed and the Nicene Creed affirm the return of Christ. The latter reads: "and will come again with glory to judge the living and the dead. His kingdom shall have no end."

In historic Christology future things are believed for two reasons: (i) it is a matter of divine revelation which informs us now in the course of history what shall be at the end of history; and (ii) the end of history so revealed is the logical development of what the Christian faith has said of events in the past and of the current experience of believers and the church. The eschatological and the apocalyptic materials about the future is the "unpacking" of what God has done, is doing, and will do.

Unfortunately the true nature of the return of Christ is confused by the speculations about the second coming, which turn it into some kind of political event like any other political event in human history, only bigger and more dramatic. On the contrary the second coming of Christ is unimaginable to us in that it is the event which ends time and begins eternity, and therefore it is an event beyond all human analogy.

The central verse which serves as a guide to framing the Christian understanding of the return of Christ is Hebrews 9:28: "So Christ, having been offered once to bear the sins of many will appear a second time, not to deal with sin but to save those who are eagerly awaiting for him."

A similar motif is found in 1 Peter 1:10-12, which speaks of the prophets of the Old Testament unable to juxtapose properly the sufferings of Christ and the glory that shall follow. Thus there is the pattern of humiliation and suffering death for world redemption in the first appearing of Christ, and the power and glory to conclude the purposes of God in human history in the second appearing.

The return of Christ is part of the total range of redemption and salvation. It is an event to be seen in that context lest it be grossly misrepresented. It can readily degenerate into an escapist doctrine, in which it is seen as the solution and end of present personal or world miseries.

The following elements are of significance with regard to the return of Christ and Christology:

(1) It is the breaking out of the reign of Christ into the open, which began at his session and is therefore part of the vindication of Christ. This is clearly the meaning of Revelation 1:7, "Behold, he is coming with the clouds, and every eye will see him, every one who pierced him; and all tribes of the earth will wail on account of him. Even so. Amen." It is currently obscure that this world crucified the Lord of glory. But at the return of Christ all this shall be clarified. This is the real and true *parousia* or presence of the Son of God (cf. Oepke in TDNT, 5: 858-71).

(2) As affirmed in the creed of Nicea the second coming or return of Christ (*parousia*) establishes the kingdom of God, finally, openly, and for all eternity. The doctrine is therefore part of the doctrine of the kingdom of God and the church.

(3) The salvation began in the believer by faith in Christ (justifica-

tion) and continued in this life (sanctification) reaches its perfection (glorification) at the return of Christ. (See Ramm: 1963.)

(4) According to the affirmations of the ecumenical creeds, the return of Christ is also the time of eternal salvation and eternal judgment. Some of the parables indicate the confusion of the kingdom of God at the present time. Wheat and tares are hopelessly mixed; the great net of the kingdom catches a bewildering variety of fish. Clarification comes at the end of the age with the return of the Son of Man.

(5) It is the day of the universal recognition of the Lordship of Christ as announced in Philippians 2:9-11.

It has been properly said that the kingdom of God has come, is coming, and will come. Christology has a similar pattern. There is the Christ of the historical Gospels. Christ has come. In the doctrine of *Christus praesens* Christ is ever coming to believers and the church. In the future victory of Christ, Christ will come. Also there is some truth in the claim that Christ was prophet in his earthly ministry as the teacher or the rabbi; that in his atoning death and its benefit Christ is a priest, and in the future reign and victory of Christ, Christ is king. A Christology that omits the fullness of this ministry of Christ is thereby a short-circuited Christology. In the thought of Martin Luther we must always have the total Christ. We must have the Christ of Now and the Christ of Then in order to have the total Christ.

8

Title Christology

TITLE CHRISTOLOGY AND RECENT RESEARCH

One of the means of enriching the Christology of the New Testament has been the study of the names or titles of Jesus in the New Testament. A tract in the historic tradition by B. B. Warfield (n.d., 307ff.) lists more than one hundred names for Jesus in the New Testament. W. Bousset (1865-1920) started a new phase in the study of the names of Jesus, which has come strongly to the fore in the past two decades (*Kyrios Christos*, 1913). Bousset asked what the name lord (*kyrios*) meant to the Christians of the early Christians of the early Christian communities. His method was to research all the literature which allegedly bore on the subject in the first Christian century. His method was far more important than his conclusion. His conclusion was that the first use of the term *kyrios* stemmed from the hellenistic Gentile church, and it was there that Paul learned it. In his method he founded the history-of-religion school (*religionsgeschichtliche Schule*). Bousset broke down the distinction between canonical writings and early church writings, as well as the distinction of the apostolic church and the later churches (cf. W. Kümmel: 1973, 270ff.). The full impact of breaking down these distinctions came in the New Testament studies after World War II and certainly in the thought of Bultmann.

Researchers in title Christology have some topics in common. Did Jesus ever claim one or more titles for himself? Did the disciples ever call Jesus by one of these titles? What are the roots of these titles—Old Testament, Jewish, Hellenistic? What did these titles mean in the early Christian churches? Do the titles reflect Hellenistic religious thought? Are there any mythological dimensions to them? What effect did the resurrection have upon the understanding of the titles?

Although the research in title Christology is diverse, scholars tend to fall into one of two camps: (i) The roots of title Christology are to be found in Jesus himself. Whatever developments or enlargements came in a later period are an outgrowth of what commenced with Jesus himself. Or (ii) the titles were created by the early Christian communities and were thus projected backwards into the mouth of Jesus or his disciples.

One corrective word must be said about title Christology. It is a temptation of New Testament scholars to limit Christology to title Christology or very narrowly to problems of the Gospels. But Christology is a much larger topic in the New Testament than the study of Christological titles.

EXAMPLES OF CHRISTOLOGY

B. B. Warfield finds more than one hundred titles for Christ in the New Testament. Only a handful of these have been intensively researched, but the material on those researched is very large.*

Our goals in discussing title Christology must accordingly be very modest. We wish to give some examples of title Christology and evaluate the materials for an understanding of historic Christology. The task is complicated by the very sharp divisions among the technical scholars on this subject.

A common assumption in current New Testament studies is that the Christian church spread out into three different cultural-geographic circles. Thus we may speak of three different clusters of churches. Further, the development of Christology can be traced as it moves from circle to circle. It is Fuller's book that sets this out in a clear, analytic manner. The three circles are: (i) Palestinian Judaism; (ii) hellenistic Judaism; and (iii) hellenistic Gentiles. However this is not accepted by all New Testament scholars, for the opponents of this three-circle theory believe that no such neat Christological circles existed (cf. Marshall: 1976).

---

* Cf. Carsten Colpe, "Son of Man," TDNT, 8: 400-77. Reginald Fuller's *The Foundations of New Testament Christology* (Charles Scribner, 1965) is an accepted text for the introduction into this phase of Christology.

LOGOS

On the Greek side of the origin of this term there is a long history of *logos* from the pre-Socratics to Philo of Alexandria. It could have its Semitic derivation from the wisdom concept of Proverbs 8 or the Aramaic word *memra* (in the expression, "the word of the Lord"). Bultmann (1951), Brown (1966), and Cullmann (1959, 249ff.) review the possible Hellenistic and Semitic origins, with Bultmann deciding for the former but Brown and Cullmann for the latter. Cullmann argues that John 1:1-3 is a deliberate echo of Genesis 1:1, and therefore Logos must have a Semitic origin. Further, Logos is a word for divine revelation which would make it fit the Semitic tradition better than the hellenistic tradition.

There is no exact equivalent of Logos in English. Logos has the sense of a word endowed with reason in contrast to a word as a part of speech. John uses it for the pre-incarnate name of the Son of God in order to bring out the notion of the incarnation.

As far as the early church was concerned the name Logos was used as a bridge from the Christian faith to the Graeco-Roman world. In the second century a Logos Christology was developed to bring together the tradition of God's revelation in Israel and in Christ with the Logos of the Greek philosophical tradition.

SON OF MAN

A phrase that for centuries appeared to scholars in the New Testament as an innocent title has now become the most complex title in current New Testament studies. All recent discussions of the title start out the same way; namely, with a complaint of the glut of literature on the subject.

First it would be well to note the data of the title in the New Testament: (i) it occurs eighty times, all of which are in the Gospels except Acts 7:36 and possibly Hebrews 2:6; (ii) the expression occurs in all the fundamental source documents of the Gospels, so it is not the preference of one writer; (iii) it is a title Jesus may have applied to himself; (iv) the title appears in no creed; (v) John's gospel has a special Son of Man theology; and (vi) the title defies any systematic representation.

Moule (1977) thinks that much current New Testament study is misdirected. He says that many New Testament scholars believe in an evolutionary approach to Christology. This is the assumption that Jesus had a simple view of himself and his mission, but in the procession of history in the early church the original simple Jesus of history is step-by-step transmuted into the theological Christ of the Synoptic Gospels, as they were finally composed. This means that the simple Jesus at the root of the Gospel tradition is a different person from the Christ of the finished Synoptic Gospels.

Moule calls his position "developmental." That which is a later so-called "higher Christology" is latent in the earlier "simple Christology." This means that there is a continuity and hence identity between the Jesus of the original tradition and the Jesus set forth in the Synoptic Gospels.

This discussion is relevant to the title of the Son of Man. Those New Testament scholars who follow Moule's developmental approach will view the debate over the Son of Man differently from those who follow the evolutionary view (e.g., Perrin: 1974).

Just to mention such names as Hahn, Todt, and Borsch (all authors of massive and learned works on title Christology) scares away the uninitiated. But venturing onward we can at least give I. Marshall's (1976, 79ff.) summary of the discussion. It should also be noted that Moule (Ibid., p. 11) is in general agreement with Marshall. Even though a minority report, Moule says that no scholar has given evidence to budge him from his position.

Marshall begins his remarks by stating that there is no interpretation of the title Son of Man without problems. (i) The title has its origin in Daniel 7:4 and other materials growing out of the Old Testament, such as 4 Ezra 13 and 1 Enoch 37-71. (ii) The Gospels shed new light on the content of the title by speaking of the suffering, dying, and rising of the dead and of the Son of Man as the foundation of the kingdom of God. They also speak of the Son of Man coming in glory. (iii) It has the most support among the titles as the title Jesus might have used for himself. (iv) It is an expression which raises Jesus above the rank of rabbi or prophet. And (v) it is apparently a transition title, as it is not found in the Epistles and the church creeds. Apparently all it intends to convey can also be conveyed by the title of Christ.

MESSIAH, CHRIST

The title *Christos* occurs 529 times in the New Testament, with 379 of them in Paul's writings (TDNT, 9: 528). So many occurrences suggest a richness of meanings. The title raises a number if issues: (i)

110

What was the current rabbinic understanding of a Messiah?* (ii) Did Jesus apply the title to himself or one of his disciples, or is it a title the early church gave him? (iii) Why did the title change from that of a name for a coming person to that of a proper name? (iv) Is there any claim by Jesus to the title from the accusation he bore with his cross? And (v) what effect did the resurrection have on this title?

From the discussions of this title we can summarize our own conclusions as follows:

(1) The root of the title is the Old Testament and more specifically the messianic materials. Jesus is the Christ, for he comes to us in the pages of the New Testament as the one who both announces and begins the kingdom of God. It is to be conceded that the Old Testament materials do not yield to an easy summary of its meanings. Hence there is both continuity and discontinuity in the picture of Jesus as the Messiah with Old Testament materials about the Messiah.

(2) We believe that Moule (1977) and Marshall (1976) reason correctly that the term of Messiah would not have been given to Jesus unless there were a basis for it in Jesus' own lifetime. There appears to be a core of historical reality to Peter's famous confession (Matt. 16:13-20, Mark 8:27-30, Luke 9:18-21).

(3) There is a good measure of truth in Pannenberg's assertion that the resurrection of Christ both clarifies and certifies the titles of Jesus. It is in the context of the resurrection that Peter says that God has made Jesus both Lord and Christ (Acts 2:36). It is also of some importance that when Paul spells out the gospel in detail in 1 Corinthians 15:3-7 he uses Christ to designate Jesus. Therefore the resurrection of Christ seems to have firmed up the title of Christ.

(4) The meaning of the word Christ as an office or an expected individual becomes a proper name for Jesus in the New Testament (cf. Kramer: 1966, ch. 1). With Paul Christ is a personal name alone and in many combinations (such as Jesus Christ, Christ Jesus, the Lord Jesus Christ). This use of Christ as a personal name would most likely grow out of the conviction that Jesus was the fulfillment of the Old Testament anticipation of the coming Messiah.

---

* Cf. E. Rivkin, "Messiah, Jewish," *The Interpreter's Dictionary of the Bible: Supplementary* vol., pp. 588-91.

LORD

Like all the other important titles of Jesus intensive research has been done on the word *kurios* or lord. (The pioneering work was done by W. Bousset: 1970 edition.) The following are some of the central conclusions of this research:

(1) The Greek word for lord, *kurios*, has a great number of meanings similar to the English word lord (cf. TDNT, 3: 1039-97). The meanings range from that of a human being to that of God himself.

(2) In 1 Corinthians 16:22 the Aramaic word for lord is used (*mari*) in connection with Christ. Kramer (1966, 23c.) believes that this is a name used of Christ prior to Paul. This means that Jesus was called Lord very early in the history of the church.

(3) In common with other titles there could have been a pre-resurrection meaning of the term and a post-resurrection one. In the pre-resurrection period it would amount to calling Jesus master, teacher, or leader. In the post-resurrection meaning it could be a term on the way to ascribing deity to Christ. It is a title which God gave to Jesus after the resurrection (cf. Acts 2:36, Phil. 2:9-11). It is the name that people confess for salvation (Rom. 10:9-10, 1 Cor. 8:6, 12:3). it is also pre-eminently the name used in Christian worship (Kramer: 1966, 63ff.).

(4) From confession and worship as Lord the name then borders on a confession of deity, or actually becomes such a confession. Because *kurios* is such a common name for God in the Septuagint (Greek translation of the Old Testament) Cullmann (1959, 307) thinks that the confession of Jesus as Lord is an incipient confession of his deity. This contention is re-enforced in trinitarian statements in which Jesus is identified as Lord (Eph. 4:4-6).

The Greek word for Lord (*kurios*) is as flexible as the English word. The term may be used to indicate respect for a person, to indicate nobility, or for God himself. Some of that flexibility is obvious in applying the word Lord to Jesus. In view of the resurrection and use of Lord to indicate how Jesus fit into God's program, the meaning became more and more sharply defined. Jesus Christ was called Lord in solemn confession, and Christian worship began to crystalize around the word Lord as applied to Jesus. And the climax of the development was the attribution of Lord to Jesus in the sense of affirming his deity.

SON OF GOD

Both the word *son* used in a religious sense and the expression of *Son of God* have a long and complex history (cf. Martitz: TDNT, 8: 334-

99). New Testament scholars have taken different stances in their interpretation of the title Son of God. Marshall (1976, 111ff.) has presented the options. (i) Jesus used the title himself and claimed that he was the Son of God sent into this world for human salvation. (ii) It is a title imported from hellenistic thought and signifies the myth of the divine man. (iii) Behind the title Son of God was a more primitive title, which in turn was changed to the Son of God; or else it was a term which expressed Jesus' special relationship to God. (iv) In the process of the development of the early church's Christology, the title Son of God emerges as one of the titles that was thought fit for Jesus.

From the standpoint of historic Christology the following observations may be made about the title Son of God:

(1) The title is so honorific and important that it is debatable if any church scribe would have given this title to Jesus without any claim to the title stemming from Jesus (so Moule: 1799, 23).

(2) The title is a messianic title similar to Son of Man. It has its historical roots in the baptism of Jesus. Moule argues that the entire theology of baptism in the New Testament hinges on Jesus' baptism, and this is strong evidence that the title of Son of God has its origin in Jesus' baptism (Moule: 1977, 29ff.; Hengel: 1976).

(3) Although previous writers interpreted the title to mean Jesus' special sense of sonship or filial piety, that interpretation is too mild. It is clear that when the expression Son is used the title means a special Son of the Father.

(4) Just as the resurrection heightens the meaning of most titles it heightens this one (cf. Rom 1:4, especially with the verb *horidzō*). If Christ's special sonship was obscure before the resurrecton, it is clarified by the resurrection.

(5) The title comes into its fullest meaning in John's gospel where in so many instances the expression the Son is used rather than the Son of God. In this light it may be seen that the Son of God is a transition title on the way to the affirmation of the deity of Christ, for much incipient material about the Trinity is to be found in John's gospel.

(6) According to Kasper (1976, 163) the confession of Jesus as the Son of God is the hallmark confession of the Christian church:

> The confession of Jesus Christ as the Son of God is therefore a brief formula which gives expression to what is essential and specific to Christian faith as a whole. Christian faith stands or falls with the confession of Jesus as Son of God.

CHRISTOLOGICAL HYMNS

It has been suspected for some time that some of the passages in the New Testament about Christ were originally hymns in the early church. As far back as 1928 Lohmeyer made an impressive case that Philippians 2:5-11 is such a hymn. More recently J. T. Sanders (1971) has written a work specializing on the Christological hymns of the New Testament. However there are two limitations to his work. First he is not interested in the theology of the hymns, in the sense that their study enriches one's Christology, but in the religious and social context of that first century which may have produced such hymns. Second he focuses his attention on the mythological configurations which would be the source of such mythologically saturated hymns (cf. Boers: 1972, 314ff.).

G. Delling is not happy with the current research in Christological hymns (TDNT, 3: 489-503). He says that there are no complete hymns but fragments suggesting that they were part of a hymn. Neither is there enough material to recreate the original hymn nor can it be known how the New Testament writer adapted the hymn to his purposes. Further the differences among New Testament scholars about the hymns show that the data about Christological hymns are not firm. A more sympathetic treatment is given by R. P. Martin (in Marshall: 1977, 239 ff.).

The "official" list of hymns treated by Sanders is: Philippians 2:6-11, Colossians 1:15-20, Ephesians 2:14-16, 1 Timothy 3:16, 1 Peter 3:18-22, Hebrews 1:13, and the Prologue of John. It is beyond the scope of this book to give an interpretation of each, but certain things stand out in reviewing these hymns: (i) In that hymns are confessional and liturgical they reveal the kind of Christological affirmations made by the early church. (ii) Because the hymns are earlier than their citation in the New Testament they are then more primitive than the New Testament. Therefore they bring us closer to the earliest days of the church. (iii) The hymns cannot be arranged in any order of theological progression. It has been said instead that they represent "Christological explosions" in the early church. (iv) The rich Christological content of the hymns suggest that very early in the history of the church, the church in praise, worship, and liturgy had a very high Christology.

In a word the hymns lend support to historic Christology. It shows that very early the church was affirming in worship that which would later be expressed more formally in the Nicene Creed. Or as B. B. Warfield (1929, ch. 6) put it, two nature Christology is not the invention of Chalcedon because it is not too far from the surface of every page of the New Testament.

CHRISTOLOGICAL CONFESSIONS

In addition to Christological hymns in the New Testament there are traces of Christological confessions. The beginning of creedal confession and Christological confession can be found in the pages of the New Testament itself. John Leith (1973, 14ff.) gives a list of the more important ones in *Creeds of the Church*: Mark 8:29, Romans 10:9, Acts 2:36, Romans 1:3-4, 1 Timothy 3:16, Philippians 2:5-11, 1 Corinthians 15:3-7, 1 Corinthians 8:6, Matthew 28:19, 2 Corinthians 13:14.*

Some confessions are the essence of brevity being directed towards a very specific goal such as "Jesus is Lord" (to the Romans where Caesar was Lord) or "Jesus is the Christ" (to the Jews). Other confessions speak of the redemptive activity of Christ, that is, the importance of the cross and the resurrection (e.g., 1 Cor. 15:1-7). Others are binarian, showing the direct relationship of Jesus as the Son of God to the Father; and others are Trinitarian (e.g., Matt. 28:19, 2 Cor. 13:14).

(1) From its very beginning the church was a confessional community. Kelly (1972, 7) speaks severely against those who think that the church was a fellowship of the Spirit which only later in its development added confessional statements. In his elaborate historic review of the concept of confession, O. Michel (TDNT 5: 199-200) has shown that the concept of confession is longstanding in both the Greek and Hebrew tradition. The Christian church (originally made up only of Jews) would naturally in the Hebrew tradition be a confessing community. And out of the simple confessional states of these early communities, the more articulate confessions of the New Testament emerged.

(2) The Trinitarian confessions of the later church are already both directly and indirectly in the New Testament. The same could be said

---

* Oscar Cullman has written on the subject in his work, *The Earliest Christian Confessions* (Lutterworth, 1949). J.N.D. Kelly's treatment is brief but very perceptive in his work *Early Christian Creeds* (Longman, 1972), ch. 1. Vernon H. Neufeld has screened the whole New Testament for its confessional materials in *The Earliest Christian Confession* (Eerdmans, 1963). Much of that which was said of the hymns could be said of the confessions. Of course Kelly is right when he says that the whole New Testament is one confession.

of the later Christological confessions. This means that as far back as scholars can go the church has a high Christology.

(3) These confessions reveal that to be a Christian meant (among other things) one must confess his faith. Confessions grow out of the baptistry even though later on they become more church confession than baptismal confession.

In the study of the titles of Christ and confessional statements about Christ we can see the beginnings of a later more elaborate Christology. Such studies help us to fill in the gaps between the early Christian communities and the later church in their mutual understandings of Christology. As such they are valuable contributions. Their limitation is obvious because titles of Christ and primitive confessional statements do not exhaust Christology. We have insisted a number of times that the early church also confessed what I have called the career of Jesus. This means that a Christology which ignores the career materials in the creeds will be an incomplete Christology.

9

Christology and Criticism

THE CRISIS OF CHRISTOLOGY AND CRITICISM

Historic Christology is based on the historical reliability of the Gospels. The critical writings of Reimarus (1694-1768) commenced a critical tradition in New Testament scholarship which has whittled away at the historical integrity of the Gospels (cf. Kümmel: 1973 and Neill: 1964).

If the criticism of the Gospels shreds them into a pile of historically inauthentic materials, then the case for historic Christology is lost. Any Christology which can be constructed from the few authentic scraps which remain is not worth the name. There is no question that redaction criticism of the Gospels has produced a crisis in historic Christology.

This is an embarrassment to the theologian. Form criticism, redaction criticism, etc., have become so technical that only the experts can use them. It is therefore very difficult for the person who specializes in theology to make judgments in a territory which calls for expert training of a very different kind. Can historic Christology be defended by theologians in the current situation?

A Theological Assessment

The thesis affirmed in the first chapter was that the final assessment in Christology is a theological one. This does not mean that it is the assessment of a theologian *per se*, for any given theologian may be incompetent to make the judgment. We do challenge the notion that New Testament studies have become so technical that only New Testament specialists may now have the only voice in Christology. It is our thesis that the final assessment in Christology is a totality assessment and this is what we mean when we say the last word in Christology must be a theological one. The reasons for this follow.

(1) We are all philosophers. Philosophical opinions and world view opinions are part of the critical process. The influence of Hegelian philosophy on Old and New Testament studies is a matter of record. The influence of Heidegger's philosophy on Bultmann and other New Testament scholars is also a matter of record in this century. We have already mentioned that if Bultmann had not bolstered his views with existentialism he would appear as a pure sceptic of the Gospels. When W. Marxsen becomes reflective about his world view, his philosophy surfaces. Käsemann's essay, "Is the Gospel Objective?" (1964, 48-62) is clearly existential in orientation, for the very question of objectivity and non-objectivity, as he discusses it, presumes something akin to Heidegger's existentialism and certainly to Bultmann's understanding of Heidegger. Opinions in New Testament studies are never purely critical, and therefore, in a phrase of T. S. Eliot's, lions still need keepers.

(2) All historical writing involves a philosophy of history. We know that the writing of history is not a painstaking, careful transcript of the past. The writing of history has been likened to plastic surgery. The critic of the New Testament is also a historian and as such has a philosophy of history. In spite of efforts of idealist philosophers like Croce and Collingwood a strong positivistic theory of the writing of history prevails in biblical studies. Bultmann's theory of myth permeating the ancient world and therefore deeply influencing the writers of the New Testament is a historical judgment. If New Testament scholars need keepers because they are philosophers, they also need keepers because they are historians.

(3) Specialization can have an inhibitory function on the decisions of the scholars. One of the merits of Pannenberg's (1976) *Theology and the Philosophy of Science* is to show that the broader and more comprehensive stance we take in making judgments the more likely that they will be correct. A given "fact" is always in a circle of closely related facts, which in turn are in circles of other facts. This means that Gospel criticism is also involved in a circle upon a circle of facts. The critic who isolates out one mode of investigation and grants it a status of independence is not clarifying the case but obscuring it.

An obvious instance of this is Bowman's book *Which Jesus?* (1970). As a summary of different pictures of Jesus held by scholars, it is a good book. But a hostile attitude towards philosophy runs through the book. That circle is eliminated! However, hostility towards philosophy is a species of philosophy. The old Greek proverb still holds: "No philosophy is a philosophy."

This leads us to the following statement, which is an oversimplification, but it focuses on the point we want to make: The mentality of the believer in historic Christology is a *confessional mentality*; the mentality of the gospel critic is a *problem-centered mentality*. It is an oversimplification because many believers in historic Christology are professional New Testament scholars engaged in critical studies; and most critics of the historical authenticity of the Gospels belong to some Christian communion.

The *confessional mentality* means that the Gospels are viewed primarily as witnesses of God's love; of the concrete expression of that love in the incarnation of God in Christ, the figure in the Gospels; of man's participation in salvation by faith in the Son of God. As important as critical studies may be they are secondary to this fundamental passion; namely, the gospel as the saving grace of God in Jesus Christ. No doubt there is a wide range of opinion about critical matters among those who hold a *confessional mentality*, but in the ultimate decision they stand on the same side of the dividing line.

The *problem-centered mentality* is one which sees the Gospels as historical documents which must be assessed by proper historical and literary methods. It is not so much interested in the theological content of the Gospels as it is in a sociological study of the first century to see how such Gospels could be produced. It studies Christological hymns in the New Testament not to round out a Christology but to trace out their mythological origins.

It boils down to this: The Gospels are the witness of God to the redemption of the world through his incarnate Son or they are a collection of documents posing fascinating problems for historical and literary research. And that is why the final decisions in Christology must be theological and not narrowly critical.

We have made the issues starkly either/or, and we think at the dividing line they are. But it is not a case of criticism or no criticism. New Testament scholars who hold to historic Christology engage in critical studies. Nor is it a case of belief or unbelief. Most of the scholars that we label as critical have some minimum Christology and do belong to some Christian church.

One cannot appeal to the divine inspiration of the New Testament in order to resolve some of the problems. In his book, *I Believe in the Historical Jesus*, I. H. Marshall shows that the doctrine of revelation is not a panacea. There are problems common to all students of the Gospels and the New Testament. All who comment on the Gospels must face such things as the lack of a common chronology and presumably the different forms of the same parable. And certainly James D. G. Dunn's *Unity and Diversity in the New Testament* raises yet other valid questions for students of the New Testament, regardless of their theological persuasion. Nor is it a simple classification of scholars into believers and non-believers in order to escape the problems. For example Peter Stuhlmacher and Martin Hengel are competent New Testament scholars but in strong reaction to the kind of New Testament scholarship which characterized Bultmann and his followers. Neither men see a disparity between their critical methods and their more positive theological stance.

Our procedure in the following pages will be one of discussing fundamental strategy. That is where the issues are. In many instances the New Testament scholars do not state their assumptions, so these must be brought to the surface. But only in polemics are the issues truly faced, and in this sense all good theology is polemic.

APOSTOLIC CONTROL IN THE EARLY CHURCH

Historic Christology is based on the assumption that there is a substantial historical connection between Jesus and his disciples, between the disciples and the early church, and between the early church and the New Testament.

To the contrary, the modern critical assessment of the New Testament denies this. Modern critical New Testament scholars open up an enormous gap between the historical Jesus and the New Testament documents. This will be much discussed in the following pages but we will cite two New Testament scholars to illustrate the point. E. Käsemann (1964, 34) writes:

> For our Gospels believed, in all good faith, that they possessed a tradition about the earthly Lord, which was reliable over wide stretches of its content. Historical criticism has shattered this good faith as we ourselves are concerned. We can no longer assume the general reliability of the Synoptic tradition about Jesus.

Speaking of the historic faith of the church as expressed in such documents as the Nicean Creed, Bornkamm (1962, 59) writes: "It is essential for us to admit that this tradition of faith and of doctrine has been irrevocably shattered by the emergence of recent science and especially the science of history."

A chart of the emergence in historical time of the various books of the New Testament commences with the death of Jesus at AD 30 and ends around AD 90, in which sixty-year period all the books of the New Testament were written (see Reumann: 1968, 35). Whatever the evolution of the mission and message of Jesus, it had to take place in that time period of sixty years. The question to be asked is whether the disciples of our Lord had anything to say about the events of this period, especially when most critical theory makes such a great difference between who Jesus was and what he taught and that which we find on the pages of the Gospels. It has been said that if the radical scholars are right then the disciples were raptured to heaven on the day of Pentecost. Generalizations obscure the differences between critics, but if we center in Bultmann and his school we are faced with a most unusual solution to this problem. The world view (*Weltanschauung*) and the world perspective (*Weltansicht*) in the first century were such that religious thought could not be expressed except in mythological concepts. It then follows that the disciples too must have been so influenced, and they therefore expressed themselves in myths, legends, stories fabricated under the best of intentions, and the like. This then forces the next conclusion that the disciples did not correct the great elaborations of the early Christian communities because they shared in the process. And if they shared in the process how do we exempt Jesus?

If it is true that Jesus, his disciples, and the early churches were all caught up inevitably in expressing themselves mythologically, then that is an end to Christianity and the church. Why bind the modern person with ancient mythology? But it seems that those who follow the mythological thesis and yet remain Christian do think that there is something in Jesus that is not mythological, such as his understanding of the coming of the kingdom of God, or the manner in which he acts in love and acceptance towards the wayward of this world, or in the authoritative manner in which he corrected the Jewish tradition and offered his own program. But if Jesus could escape the mythological net, why not his disciples? And if his disciples, why could not the early church scribes? Briefly the claim that Jesus' message and mission were non-mythological, yet the framing of the same in the early churches is thoroughly mythological, is an undigested thesis.

Most critical scholarship reckons that the disciples were such children of the first century and its culture that they participated in the transformation of the original message and mission of Jesus into the high Christological documents which the Gospels are. Is this also true of Paul who was active in the churches from AD 35 to AD 64? Paul's conversion is dated somewhere between 33 and 35, which places him within five years after the death of Jesus. Further it is almost universally conceded that Romans, 1 and 2 Corinthians, and Galatians are authentic Pauline letters. There is much agreement that 1 Corinthians 15:1-7 and 16:22 are pieces of very old church tradition. Paul mentions his knowledge of the pillars in the church at Jerusalem: James, Peter, John (Gal. 2:9, *pillar* being a strong word for leadership; TDNT, 7: 734ff.). This means that Paul was in the center of the life of the early church around the year 50.

Is Paul's Christological thinking totally mythological? It could hardly be maintained that the Gospels reflect a Christology in mythological terms whereas Paul had a non-mythological Christology. Hence Paul too must be understood as having a Christology expressed in mythological concepts (cf. Jones: 1956, part II). But this thesis has its problems with such a man as Paul, for he does not appear to be a person totally determined by mythological ways of thinking, as seen in his ministry in the book of Acts.

In Paul's speeches and conversations in the book of Acts Paul speaks of the saving death of Christ and the bodily resurrection as factual assertions, that is, not as myths. As he is understood by his listeners in the same mode of speaking. When he speaks of the resurrection of Jesus he frames it as a historical event. There is a difference between a myth and a mistaken notion or factual understanding. The resurrection is a factual claim to be settled by the historical evidence and therefore cannot be written off a priori as an impossible historical question (see O'Neil in Sykes: 1972, ch.12). Paul may have been wrong about factuality of the resurrection; he was not wrong in understanding it as a claim to be a factual event in history.

It is true that most critical scholars do not think we have reliable history in the book of Acts and so no appeal may be made to it. It is currently said that in Martin Hengel we are watching a rerun of the experience of Sir William Ramsay (1851-1939). For reasons of health Ramsay went to Asia Minor. He began to read the inscriptions on the various remains of antiquity and began to find references which paralleled the book of Acts. Making New Testament archaeology a lifetime occupation he moved more and more in a conservative direction. In his book, *Acts and the History of Earliest Christianity* Hengel said that he presumed the history of the book of Acts to be reliable until proven otherwise.

However the mythological thesis has to keep true to itself and maintain that Paul exerted no control over the transformation of the mission and message of Jesus. Yet at the same time Paul stands out as one of the universal geniuses of the human race; a Roman citizen, a world traveler, and one who gained the respect of all the higher authorities he had to deal with. The mythological theory cloys at this point.

Another problem about the mythological transformation of the mission and message of Jesus is the matter of possible written accounts and the sheer powers of memory possessed by people at that time. Written documents and excellent memories would be a check on the mythological elaboration of the mission and message of Jesus. B. Gerhardson's (1961) work, *Manuscript and Memory*, has been challenged for the validity of his materials and conclusions, but M. Wilson (1976, 350-63) calls attention to the nature of Jewish education at this time. Jewish education stressed perfect memorization of large pieces of material, so that remembering things decades after they happened would not be the problem it is for us today. Wilson points out that the writers of the Gospels, who were so educated, would be reliable reporters of the life of Jesus, whereas people with a modern bookish style of learning would find this very difficult.

Another thesis has been argued by R. Gundry (1967). He points out that Matthew's job as a tax collector could require a person concerned with note-taking. He makes the same point as Wilson does about note-taking, the development of shorthand, and the education of people at that time. Even more, Matthew was posted on the important Great West Road, which would force him to be competent in Greek as well as whatever languages he had to know. Hence the detailed notes of Matthew could well be common background for all the writers of the Gospels.

Therefore with a well-remembered tradition, and with a copy of a notebook possibly from Matthew, it would be difficult for the critical theory to maintain itself. To put it in theological terms, there was an apostolic control over writing the Gospels, even though it may be difficult to chart.

The radical thesis is breathtaking. When the radical critics list the number of things that we really think we know about Jesus, it is a very small list. The thesis then asserts that in the sixty year period some very elementary or basic things taught by Jesus, done by Jesus, and proclaimed by Jesus were elaborated into the four Gospels as we have them in the New Testament. Is sixty years enough time for such an elaboration? According to Grillmeier's (1951-54, 33ff.) summaries of the Christologies of the Apostolic Fathers (commencing shortly after AD 90) their Christologies are in the tradition of historic Christology so they form a firm cut-off date.

However, even the sixty-year period can be shortened. If Mark's gospel and other significant materials were written before the destruction of Jerusalem in AD 70, the period is limited to forty years (Käsemann: 1964). If Paul started writing about authentic Christology in the church about the year AD 50, the period is cut to twenty years (Hengel: 1976, 58). If 1 Corinthians 15:1-7 is taken very literally—*au pied de la lettre*—we have the Christology of the church but a few years after the death of Jesus. It must be further noted that things moved much slower in that day in terms of transportation, communication lines, means of publishing, and distribution of materials.

Every year the period of elaboration is reduced makes the critical theory that much more fragile. It is our conviction that the time period is too short for such a great elaboration to have taken place. And it is the opinion of the Cambridge historian, H. Butterfield (1979, 105), that the essential form of the Gospel materials was settled by twenty years after the crucifixion. Further, on the very issue of the role of the disciples in the early church, Butterfield (103-04) states that secular historians are apt to be more emphatic on the role of the disciples than New Testament scholars.

> All [secular students] would agree, I imagine, that some of the things in the Gospels—the Crucifixion and the Resurrection for example— must have been in the preaching from the very start. This was the reason for everything else that happened, *and the evidence must have come from the disciples. Indeed, I think there can be no doubt that the belief of the disciples in these events was of an overpowering nature* (italics are ours).

Breaking step with much of recent New Testament critical theory are the works of Martin Hengel. On the theme we are currently discussing he has expressed himself rather forcefully in *Between Jesus and Paul* (1983). He argues for an unbroken sequence of the teachings, ministry, and claims of Jesus to the writings of Paul. If his case stands it means that many thousands of pages written on the Christological develop-

ments in the early church are dated pieces of New Testament scholarship.

INFLUENCE OF HELLENISM ON THE NEW TESTAMENT

The development of an advanced culture in ancient Greece is one of
the great occurences in the history of the world. The Greeks called
themselves the Hellenes; hence their culture is called Hellenism. Hellenism as a cultural movement was the spread of Greek culture out of
Macedonia and Greece into the surrounding countries. Before the time
of Alexander the Great the Greek culture had already begun to spread.
Alexander gave it an enormous impetus. He was taught by the great
philosopher, Aristotle, and so he had a bent towards acculturation,
which was rare for a military conqueror. To spread Greek culture
wherever he conquered was a major thrust in his life.

Like all huge historical concepts Hellenism too has its fuzzy edges. In
the narrow sense Hellenism is limited from the time of Alexander to
the emergence of Christianity. In a larger sense it is the filtering of
Greek culture through many centuries and into such distant places as
England and India.

It is not contested that there were hellenistic influences in Palestine
(cf. Kasper: 1976, 194, fn. 27). The question is how pervasive it was.
Was it so strong that nothing could be written without being power-
fully influenced by hellenistic and mythological concepts? That is the
stance of the more radical critics. But it raises certain problems.

If there was this powerful hellenistic influence in Palestine and/or
among the earliest Christian churches, it makes it very difficult to as-
certain the events in the life of Jesus and what he taught. For one thing
if the entire culture had such hellenistic influences this must apply to
Jesus too. It is then a meaningless task to find something about the
teaching of Christ or the person, for there would be no non-hellenistic
or non-mythological materials either in his person or teachings.

This borders on a kind of sociological determinism by which we
mean that the person of Christ and his teachings, as well as the writings of the apostles, could not break out of the cultural shell in which
they lived and wrote. It means a lid is put upon the conceptual materials of the New Testament. That this is not an exaggeration is seen in
the essays of some of the contributors to *The Myth of God Incarnate*
(Hick: 1977). Further, Roberts has shown how firmly the writers of the

125

New Testament were caught in this sociological web, according to the mind of Bultmann.

Sociology is not a strict science so there is no way we can measure the impact of concepts on a culture. And human personalities have so many variables we cannot predict the inner composition of their minds. Hence studies of hellenistic influences or Palestinian influences on given writers will always be imprecise. Our concern is that no arbitrary lid be set upon Jesus and the writers of the New Testament which would limit the range of their concepts.

The matter of Hellenism is interesting when turned back to Greece itself. One of the reasons that Greece reached such preeminence in the age of Pericles is that it produced so much metacultural material! There is a strong multicultural character to the whole history of Greek philosophy from Thales to the hellenistic period. Some of Aristotle's works are still the point of departure for modern studies as *Poetics*, *Rhetoric*, and *Organon*. Plato's *Republic* is still one of the finest introductions to the theory of the state. If such men could escape their cultures, why not the writers of the New Testament?

Frances Young's article (Hick: 1977, ch. 5) in *The Myth of God Incarnate* ("Two Roots or a Tangled Mass,") is a historical survey arguing that an incarnational belief was in the air around New Testament times. Many of the concepts used by Jesus were common in that period. She modestly claims that she has not demonstrated that the belief in the incarnation rose out of such a set of concepts but that it would not be surprising if it did. However another essay needs to be written. That is to show how some people of that period transcended their environment; who wrote beyond their culture. This would not demonstrate that the writers of the New Testament escaped their cultural grid, but it should not surprise us if they did.

Their is no need in historic Christology to presume that the writers of the New Testament miraculously in every way escaped their culture. One has to be part of a culture to meaningfully speak to it. But the point is that if other writers of that period can transcend culture, why not the writers of the New Testament?

In this matter of the world view in the first century, and its impact upon the writers of the New Testament, the contest between Barth and Bultmann is worthy of brief review. In that Barth accepts the New Testament as is, in its totality, he has to accept its whole world view. According to Bultmann, a person of the twentieth century cannot do this. Barth in return thinks that Bultmann has a definite theological-philosophical grid and Bultmann will believe only what filters through the grid.

Barth pictures a whale (the largest sea creature) and an elephant (the largest land creature) meeting in some lagoon. One blows water through his trunk and the other air through its air hole. But communication is impossible. So if Bultmann grants such royal rights to critical scholarship he cannot help but see Barth as holding an impossible archaic view about the nature of the New Testament. And Barth thinks that Bultmann, having accepted this critical grid, can never hear what the New Testament is saying. In other words, Barth reads the New Testament as a document with its own integrity and the right to speak for itself. Bultmann reads it as a document that is profoundly determined by an ancient world view, and it can only be heard through a thorough critical investigation.

THE EARLY CHURCH AND CHRISTOLOGY

Historic Christology is based on the belief that Jesus Christ came teaching, preaching, healing, and making strong claims about his person; for example, as Son of Man or Messiah. It is further accepted that the Gospels, for all their variations and problems, preserve a record of historic integrity of Jesus Christ. It is yet further believed that the advanced Christology of the Epistles of the New Testament is the logical outcome from the earlier, simpler Christology.

The early church did not compose its own Christology; it received it. Unfortunately, some believe that somehow the early church made a serious blunder, that Christology rests on a mistake (see M. F. Wiles in Sykes: 1972, ch. 1). The early church said things of Jesus that should not be said of any man. Or as Knox (1967) expressed it, the church made the error of presuming that God worked a divine work in Jesus which meant that Jesus was somehow God. According to Wiles, Knox, Bultmann, and others the early church wrote its own Christology.

However all who hold such a belief do not believe that the early church scribes are guilty of intentional fraud. They did not wilfully fabricate matters. Their mistakes were innocent and sprang from good intentions. To the contrary much of current Gospel criticism shows how such elaboration was an innocent working out of processes within the early Christian communities. The various situations in these communities (*Sitzen-im-Leben*) produced needs which summoned into existence miracle stories, messianic claims, or resurrection accounts.

If there is advancement in redaction criticism it is its attempt to show how from simple, innocent beliefs, ideas, or experiences the larger Christology belief grows. A good example of this is Willi Marxsen's (1965a) *Die Auferstehung Jesu als historisches und als theologisches Problem*. From a report of a vision of the risen Jesus derives a conviction of having a vision of Jesus; from the vision of Jesus comes the notion of a bodily vision; from the bodily vision comes the notion of a bodily resurrection; from the bodily resurrection develops the resurrection stories to account for the bodily visions. In all of this there is no historical fact; it is all elaborated from reports. The conclusion is that the bodily resurrection of Jesus was not invented, fabricated, or devised; it, rather, developed naturally out of the time and needs of the early churches.

It once was a common apologetic assertion that either Jesus is God incarnate or he is a mad man and the world's greatest deceiver. Current Gospel criticism would say that this attitude is a sad error. Jesus never made all these claims! These claims were made by the early church and reflected backwards to Jesus. And as indicated, these Christological developments came innocently (i.e., by natural sociological processes) and were not instances of deception or fraud (see Perrin: 1974, 54 and 1977).

This may be an improvement over some of the opinions in the nineteenth century, and we should grant that recent criticism preserves the innocence of Jesus and the early church scribes. Nonetheless the conclusion is the same: the church wrote its own Christology. This reconstruction of the high Christology of the completed Gospels has many advantages for the contemporary critic of the Gospels. He is under no obligation to believe the Christology of the Gospels because now he claims to be able to trace its evolution. Miracles in the Gospels form no problem as they are again elaborations within the early church and not events in the life of Jesus. Nor need it be denied that there are historically reliable materials in the Gospels, for they are outgrowths of a historical process which started with John the Baptist and Jesus. But even so, the verdict cannot be avoided that the church wrote its own Christology.

It follows that the church created its own image of the Savior. The Christology of the completed new Testament is a Christology in which Jesus is Lord and Savior. There was not only elaboration in the early church about the titles of Jesus but also about the work of Christ (see Boers: 1972, 319ff.). The images of salvation in the New Testament must also be ascribed to church creation. The early church rewrites its Christology and its soteriology.

Before this issue is left a point of clarification is in order. It is not an issue between (i) Gospels that are the products of great elaborations in the early Christian communities or (ii) pure and simple reporting of the words and deeds of Jesus. Evangelical New Testament scholars know that the composing of the Gospels was a complex matter. Previous generations were too naive on this score. But it is the belief of those who hold to historic Christology that the Christology of the New Testament has its origin on Jesus Christ himself and the early church did not write its own Christology. According to Moule (1977) and Marshall (1976), the Christology of the New Testament develops consistently out of the Christology of Jesus Christ himself, and is not an evolutionary process resulting in a Christology in the Gospels far different from whom the historical Jesus was and claimed. With reference to the historical Jesus, J. Schneider (1958, 18) notes that the common point of departure is the sudden origin and powerful spread of the early church.

> There is only one explanation [for this phenomenon], that at the beginning of the great religious and spiritual movement we call primitive Christianity [*Urchristentum*] stands a powerful, all-towering figure [*Gestalt*]: Jesus of Nazareth who was conscious that he was the Messiah and, who out of this certainty [*Selbstgewissheit*] and out of the authority granted him, did wonders and signs.

DEGREES OF PROBABILITY

Although an amateur in New Testament criticism C. S. Lewis (1967, 162ff.), himself a literary scholar, made an important observation about literary theories. All literary theories are probability statements; and as one theory is based on another the probability of such a theory decreases.

One meaning of the term *logic* in modern philosophy is a critical self-analysis of a given subject matter, especially in terms of the nature of its knowledge, the kinds of procedures it follows, the degree of precision within which it works, and the nature of verification. The only theologian in recent times who has investigated the field of theory-construct and theory-verification, applying it to his own work, has been W. Pannenberg (1976). What may be learned from the study of the philosophy of science can be applied to New Testament scholarship in the following ways.

(1) An overall assessment can be made of any science or human discipline, with reference to such items as the degree of precision with which it works, the kind of control it has over its subject matter, and the specific clarity of its results. Pride of place usually goes to physics. It works with the greatest measure of precision, the most refined of measurements, excellent control over subject matter, and with vigorous processes of verification. At the opposite end of the spectrum are the social sciences, which work with (in contrast to physics) sloppy parameters, large fluctuations in measurements, poor control of materials, and dubious verification.

New Testament study is in the general territory of the social sciences and not physics. Therefore its theories partake of the same character as social studies. In that all studies today are mixed and overlap, it is possible to have a statement from physics or chemistry applied to something in New Testament studies (e.g., chemical composition of an object in an archaeological dig, the dating of the dig, and carbon-14 dating of materials). But we are here assessing the overall nature of New Testament studies and not particular items.

(2) All theories in science are probability statements. A probability statement is one that has evidence for its truthfulness but no final validation. Although in popular language we speak of proving a theory, in reality experimentation may heighten the evidence of a theory and so increase its probability. This means that New Testament studies work with probabilities. Theories of New Testament scholars are probability statements and not demonstrated theories.

(3) If a theory is proposed, some mode of its verification must also be proposed. There are sharp differences among philosophers of science over verification theory. Under what conditions can any theory be verified? Or is it that theories can be falsified but not verified? If the matter of verification is so difficult in the sciences it is even more so in literary criticism. It is obvious if one reads New Testament studies that theories in some cases can be readily falsified, but it is very difficult to see how they are verified with any degree of high probability.

(4) One of the most provocative books in philosophy of science has been Thomas S. Kuhn's *The Structure of Scientific Revolutions* (1970).

His thesis is that science does not progress (at the theoretical level) on the gradual increase of the boundaries of knowledge. Rather novel paradigms replace the older ones. Again the logic is obvious. If scientific theories can be upended by a revolutionary paradigm, how much more so can theories in literary criticism? It does not mean that scholarship should be less vigorous but only more humble.

Failure to recognize such limitations to any kind of literary critical theory manifests itself in a number of ways; for example, scholars citing articles in journals as if they had the same substance as experiments in physics; the omniscience of Bultmann in assigning sources in his *History of the Synoptic Tradition*; or the manner in which Marxsen (1965b) treats history as if it were as scientific as physics.

All work in biblical criticism from the most radical to the most conservative is subject to these limitations. It would be healthier all the way around if the limitations of critical work were recognized. In his essay "Epilogue" in *The Myth of God Incarnate* (Hick: 1977), D. Nineham comes close to facing the issue of verification in literary theories. He shows how embarrassing the gap is between Christological claims of some current New Testament scholars and the actual historical evidence with which they work. He could have pressed the case harder (see also Katz in Sykes: 1972). But in any case we do not have as yet a major work on the nature of scientific knowledge as it bears on critical studies and in turn how this bears on the current discussion in Christology.

There is a growing literature on the attitude of experts in literary criticism towards New Testament criticism. It is common knowledge that such British experts in literature who were also convinced Christians (T. S. Eliot, C. S. Lewis, and Dorothy Sayers) believed that radical New Testament critics had gone to seed on literary criticism. The thesis of these literary critics is that the application of the methods, as used by the radical New Testament scholars when applied to literature in general, proves to be useless if not harmful.

Typical of this inter-disciplinary criticism is R. M. Frye's (1979, 207-19) article, "Literary Criticism and Gospel Criticism." First he indicates that the same kind of methods used on the Gospels were used on Shakespeare and Hamlet, all done with great learning and immense attention to detail. Yet in both instances the effort collapsed. Secondly, he takes up particular points of analysis in the Gospels as carried on by current radical New Testament scholars. He shows in each instance that such methods and/or criteria when carried over to studies in "secular" literary criticism fail. Then he concludes by saying that there will be progress in New Testament studies only as the New Testament scholars get away from their idiosyncratic methods and back to mainstream methods of literary criticism.

This will not be easy. Walter Wink (1973) charges New Testament scholars with having a "Guild Mentality." Current methods have become so intrenched and have become so axiomatic in their logical status, that any question of their adequacy is vigorously contested. A young scholar is admitted to "The Guild" only if he will comply faithfully with the rules of the Guild.

A SPIRITUAL DIMENSION IN THE GOSPELS

One of the major theological encounters of this century was between Adolph von Harnack and Karl Barth in the pages of the German journal, *The Christian World* (cf. Robinson: 1968, I: 165-90). Harnack was a defender of the religious liberalism of Ritschl. His (1901) book, *What is Christianity?* is considered a classic expression of this liberalism even though popularly written. At the time of the exchange of correspondence (1923) Barth was just emerging as a theologian. Harnack had heard an address of Barth at an earlier period, and the more he thought about it the more he became upset. Accordingly he initiated a correspondence with Barth in *The Christian World*.

In essence the issue is as follows: how far is the theologian to be guided by scientific methods of biblical criticism in the interpretation of Scripture? According to Harnack there was no limit to the application of scientific interpretation to Scripture. To insist otherwise was to retreat to the pre-scientific era in biblical studies. Barth had no quarrel with the method as such. But as a theologian studies Scripture, at some point there will be a confrontation with the Word of God in Scripture. At that point a significant change will be mandatory, for now it will no longer be a matter of the scientific understanding of the text but a matter of obedience or disobedience.

The debate stalemated. Harnack could not imagine any situation in which the interpreter had a right to abandon the methods of scientific biblical criticism. Barth could not imagine any serious view of the Word of God in which the interpreter would ultimately remain critic of the Scripture. This debate has relevance to Christology because it relates to the study of the Gospels. But it is clear at this point that if there is a spiritual or theological dimension (as Word of God) to the Gospels, Harnack's method has no means of identifying it.

Barth also faced the same issue in debate with Rudolph Bultmann. Bultmann insisted that Scripture be interpreted as any other book from classical antiquity. Barth agreed. But he added that as one went the ordinary way through Scripture one encountered the extra-ordinary Word of God, and at that point theological interpretation was mandatory. Granted, Bultmann had in addition to his critical methodology an existential interpretation of the New Testament, but the latter may never challenge the results of the scientific interpretation of the text (e.g., one could never say on existential grounds that Jesus rose bodily from the dead).

Barth wrote in the tradition of Luther and Calvin that Jesus Christ comes to us in the garments of the Gospels. If this is the case then there is another dimension to the intepretation of the Gospels other than the historical-critical one.

According to Kierkegaard (1962, ch. 4) every person is contemporary with their own generation and with Jesus Christ. Those who saw Christ on earth have no advantage over those of later generations. In other words, no person is a disciple by second hand as if we know Jesus only by the report of others. Each person confronts the present, contemporary living Christ and so is a disciple by first hand. But how does one do this? One becomes the contemporary of Christ by the mediation of Christ in the Gospels. This means that there is more to the interpretation of the Gospels than the historical-critical method.

Helmut Thielicke (1947, Vol. 1.) also discusses this issue as a loyal disciple of Luther. Luther taught that the Old Testament was the written Word of God but the gospel was the proclaimed Word of God. To maintain the purity of the gospel it too had to be written, but its nature as proclamation must never be overlooked. Sinners meet Christ in proclamation! If students are introduced to the Gospels first of all as the subject of critical studies, the possibility of meeting Christ in them is very slim.

Thielicke also attacks biblical criticism on theological grounds. He insists that the primary encounter with the Gospels in critical studies stultifies students theologically and spiritually and ruins their preaching. The Gospels and the gospel must first be encountered in proclamation.

Thielicke then relates the study of theology to his thesis of proclamation. If a student begins his study of Scripture for the first time as so many critical problems of biblical introduction, he might never hear the Word of God in Scripture. When such a student is confronted with Scripture he will turn the confrontation into a methodological discussion and not into a confrontation with God. "Here the counter-question yields to never ending reflection, and the perversion is complete" (Ibid., 202). The preaching of students who have come to the Scriptures primarily *via* biblical introduction and not *via* hearing the Word of God in proclamation is so entangled in matters of biblical criticism that it cannot interact with the substance of Scripture. The result is uncertain preaching.

HISTORICAL INTEGRITY OF THE GOSPELS

Historic Christology is built upon the belief that the Gospels are historically substantial. Serious critical and historical reflection on the Gospels as historical documents began with Reimarus (1694-1768). Up until this time it was generally acknowledged in the church that the Gospels presented a picture of Jesus that had historical substance.

Gospel criticism since Reimarus has challenged the main tradition in the church. First of all, historical information about Jesus outside the New Testament is scant. The kind of corroborating materials historians require for substantial history are too fragmentary. Further the chronology of the life of Christ among the Gospels is so different that no sketch of his life can be made in the serial order of events. Hence no biography of Jesus is possible in a technical sense of the word. However it must be said that a lack of sequence in the Gospels does not mean that there is no historical substance to the individual events. In the light of the historical and literary-critical studies of the Gospels, how much historical integrity of the Gospels is necessary for historic Christology to remain a valid option?

(1) The fact of so many variations among the Gospels is not new. It was never considered a serious problem. Already in the second century Tatian attempted to create one story out of the Gospels, which is itself a confession of their diversity (*Diatessaron, ca.* AD 150-175). For this reason the differences among the Gospels has been underplayed in the history of the church. Calvin has been criticized for lumping together the Gospels in a harmony in his commentary on Holy Scripture. However the study of the Synoptic Problem is not something new in the sense that the newer studies embarrasses historic Christology.

(2) It is true that the composers of the Gospels were Christians and wrote from a Christian perspective. It is also true that historians are suspicious of history written from a partisan viewpoint. Therefore the historical integrity of the Gospels is suspect.

Butterfield (1979, 133-50) wrote a graceful essay on this very theme. He makes the odd suggestion that the best historian of Christianity would be a believer, who could thus understand the inner side of the Christian faith, but who had given up his faith and could thus write as an objective historian. Of course the matter of the proper historian is more complicated than this. Christians suffer the severe temptation of reading the record in their favor; and unbelievers may not have the perception to understand the powerful inner dynamic of the Christian faith. But Butterfield does say that, in the long wash of the centuries, the Christian faith has been part of the making of a great modern historical science. And it is true that in some instances only the believer can write the valid history.

The first thing to be said in reply is that all historical writing is partisan. The scientific ideal of an impartial writing of history is recognized as impossible. Modern historians have criteria for the writing of substantial history and they are not to be contested. In that history can be written only as there is a selection of events, the partisan element enters. The real issue is whether the partisan commitment thoroughly distorts the writing of history, as is believed to be the case in a Marxist rewriting of history.

There is yet another side to the issue. In some instances only the committed partisan can write a good history. We would not expect a physicist to write a history of art, nor an engineer the history of philosophy. It is the learned partisan who can in some instances do the best job of writing a history. Therefore the Gospels cannot be discounted as reliable history solely because their authors were Christians.

It is the Christian contention that only a believer in the person of Christ could do justice to the life of Christ. A neutral observer could well botch the record. It is folly to think that a Marxist who believes that religion is the opiate of and for the common people would do justice to the life of Jesus. In this instance a Christian would be the best possible chronicler.

This becomes clearer with reference to the resurrection. All witnesses of the resurrection as recorded in the New Testament are Christians (more specifically, witnesses of the risen Lord). This is so because of the phenomenological category of the *Holy*. Only people in the circle of the *Holy* may witness a holy event. Unholy eyes do not know what they see. If a Roman soldier had looked upon the risen Lord he would have seen a total enigma. There would be nothing in him to enable him to understand what he saw. Therefore only those people standing in the circle of the *Holy* had the inward qualification to know what they perceived when they looked upon the risen Lord.

The modern critics of the Gospels do not admit the category of the *Holy* and its implication for the historical knowledge of Christ. If nothing else, the concept of the *Holy* applied to historical knowledge violates the concept of the intersubjectivity of scientific knowledge (i.e., a proposed thesis must be open for investigation to all qualified researchers). All of this is in sharp contrast to believers in historic Christology, for to them only persons standing in the circle of the *Holy* can bear historical witness to the risen Lord. The kind of partisan writing of history, of which historians are the most uncertain, may in this case be the only kind of authentic history that can be written.

Peter Carnely (in Sykes: 1972, ch. 10) has challenged the historical scepticism which is behind so much gospel criticism, taking his cue from the philosopher N. Malcom. It is logically false to presume that, if one or even many historical judgments are false and hence reversible, then all historical judgments are capable of revision. Gospel critics have as an operating rule that all historical judgments are reversible and apply this to the Gospels. Carnely accuses them of being naive of the latest critical writings on the nature of historical knowledge.

Different interpretations of a historical event may contradict each other. But it may also be the case that the event is described from two different perspectives. In that case both explanations are valid. That a balloon is red does not clash with the assertion that it is also round. Critics of the Gospels presume all alternative descriptions of the same event mean at least one of them is false or botched. But the logic of alternative interpretations does not permit that easy sort of judgment.

(3) No doubt in the history of historic Christology the impression has been given that the four Gospels were based on solid historical materials in such a way that we have four versions of the life of Christ each with a ring of solid, hard, historical factuality. Some of this stems from an interpretation of Luke 1:1-4, which reads an entire scientific historiography into the writing of the Gospels. And certainly this kind of hard, solid, historical claims for the factuality of the Gospels has been created by theories of inspiration which demanded at all points in Scripture such a hard, compelling factuality. Further, such so-called high views of inspiration felt uneasy with the plurality of the gospel

witness and with all the variations among the different reports. There is nothing like an extreme fundamentalist view of Scripture to generate its opposite extreme critical view of Scripture. Thus the critical assessment of the Synoptic problem has turned the Gospels into one of the most complicated and fascinating crossword puzzles in history, and has provoked many an elaborate scholarly effort to decode the puzzle. (Cf. William Farmer's life-long concern with source-criticism of the Synoptics.)

In our opinion both the very literally-minded, fundamentalist understanding of the Gospels and the critical understanding are inadequate. Berkouwer's (1975) views are far closer to the facts of the case. The Christian church started with the mission and message of Jesus Christ, including his saving death and victorious resurrection. His life is a gospel (Mark 1:1). It is the good news of the love of God, of the coming of the kingdom, and of reconciliation in Jesus Christ. Jesus himself employed the custom of public proclamation of this message. He was both evangelical and evangelistic in his public ministry . His disciples-apostles were those whom he called, trained, and commissioned to be his representatives after his ascension. As such they formed the nucleus of the church and inaugurated the church at the day of Pentecost. That day was in keeping with the ministry of Jesus Christ: it was an evangelical and evangelistic day. The gospel is to be preached to all nations. The large area around the gospel (the *penumbra*)* is composed of all the sayings and doings of Jesus Christ which illuminate the person who died on the cross and rose from the dead. To rephrase Kähler's famous remark, the larger evangelical activity of Jesus in his three-year ministry is the basis for understanding his particular evangelical fate of the cross and the resurrection.

Therefore as the Christian church grew and spread, it grew with the pattern of preaching the gospel within the larger context of the so-called life of Jesus, for the gospel only means something as seen in the context of the life and deeds of Jesus prior to his death on the cross and the resurrection. Hence the "gospel" is always in the context of the "Gospels." As the church spread different traditions of Jesus, his teachings and his deeds followed along the different routes. The notion of a "school of Matthew" and a "school of Mark" and a "school of Luke"

---

* A *penumbra* is the band of half-light in an eclipse between the dark center of the eclipse and the bright light farther out.

and a "school of John" is a sound one. It specifies how the different traditions of Jesus radiating out from Jerusalem took on particularized forms.

Seen in this perspective the function of the Gospels (and the traditions before them) was not to give an exact, precise, notarial, historically perfect account of every word and deed of Jesus. The function of the traditions and then the Gospels was to create the necessary *penumbra* around the gospel of Jesus Christ in order that the person who died and the person who rose from the dead be given a measure of credibility. This is what Luke expresses in his prologue to his gospel (1:1-4).

The Gospels are primarily witnesses with authentic rootage in history. They are authentic impressionistic scenes; they are authentic graphic pictures. Such scenes and such pictures illuminate the person who dies for the sins of the world and rises from the dead for the justification and reconciliation of the world.

That is why the early church put its entire Scripture (the New Testament) in the Greek language. As far as we can judge Jesus spoke Aramaic and maybe Hebrew too. A rigid theory of inspiration would demand that the *ipsissima verba* of Jesus be in Aramaic; but if the Gospels are primarily witnesses they must be in the *lingua franca* ("the universal language of ambassadors") of the times—the Greek. That is why there is no exact chronology in the Gospels but great freedom of arrangement. The message is in the pictures, images, and scenes of Jesus and not in the chronicling. That is why there is so much variation in details of events, parables, speeches, etc. among the Gospels. It is not notarial reporting of a life but witnessing of a life which in itself is a gospel. That is why fundamentalist views of inspiration always stumble at the Synoptic Problem, and critical views make too much of the differences.

Seen from this perspective the Synoptic problem allows that:

(i) There is a richness in the witness of Christ as seen in the four Gospels. Positive, affirmative Christian faith has seen this diversity in the analogy of a banquet and not as a series of vexing critical questions.

(ii)There was a great adaptablity in the early church in its mode of witnessing as it spread out into the Roman Empire. The identical phenomenon can be found today among the churches in the different parts of the contemporary world.

(iii) The Synoptic problem is also a commentary on the route of the traditions about Jesus as the church spread into the Roman Empire.

(iv) The important concern of the Gospels is their witness to Christ given in images, scenes, dramatic events, speeches, and encounters with a diversity of people. To reduce the Gospels to a test case of notarial reporting is the demand of a rigid theory of inspiration that quails before ambiguities; to reduce the Gospels to elaborate critical crossword puzzles is to destroy their function as an authentic historical witness to the Person who is in his life and in himself The Gospel.

The Gospels are gospel. That is why there is no scientific biographical materials in the Gospels. They are witnessing, confessing, and theological documents. If they were not that there would be no gospel. As witnesses they come with a footing planted in history, for a witness is worthy only as he stands on fact. But at the same time they do not come to us heavy with the scholar's documentation; nor as official documents with metalic seals (bullas) stitched to them or clay seals stamped upon them. They do not make an obvious appeal to authenticity as one finds in the signatures in the preface of the *Book of Mormon*. Their *imprimatur* is the self-witness (*autopistia*) they bear of the saving grace of God in the person and work of the Lord Jesus Christ.

Therefore the Gospels have a strange historical impress, for at the same time they are history and sermon; event and message; biography but not scientifically biographical; never pure message and never pure event; a foot in history and a foot out of history; the natural and the supernatural in the same paragraph; datable events and eternal kerygma. But never is it a confusion of fact and fiction; superstition and reality; magic and sanity. These are the reasons why the Gospels are so difficult to get into focus. At the same time their phenomena perplexes tight-fisted theories of inspiration and mythological explanations.*

JESUS IS NECESSARY TO CHRISTOLOGY

What would a theologian or New Testament scholar do if biblical and historical scholarship demonstrated either that Jesus never lived or that the amount of material we have about him is trivial? This issue has a profound way of flushing out what is both basic and hidden in Christological belief.

A follower of historic Christology would reply that such a conclu-

---

* For views very similar to this cf. Peter Stuhlmacher, *Historical Criticism and Theological Interpretation of Scripture* (Fortress, 1977). Martin Hengel, *Acts and the History of Earliest Christianity* (Fortress, 1980). Brice D. Cjilto, "An Evangelical and Critical Approach to the Sayings of Jesus," *Themelios* 3 (1978), 73-85.

sion would be the end of historic Christology because it is based on the authenticity of the sayings and events of Jesus Christ as found in the Gospels. If that material is declared to be historically spurious, then the foundation of historic Christology is destroyed.

However theologians with other types of Christology claim that their theology would not be endangered by such an undermining of the Gospels. In our opinion all those theologies which would survive if it could be shown that Jesus never lived or that the details about him are trivial are versions of Hegelian Christology. The Hegelian theologians taught that there was a distinction to be made between the Christ idea and the Jesus of history. The Christ idea is a theological principle which affirms the unity of God and man, which if not pantheistic borders on it. If it can be shown to one who holds Hegelian Christology that Jesus never lived, nothing essential would be lost. Christ as the symbol of the continuity of God and humankind, of the infinite in the finite human spirit, continues as valid. Jesus is the historic manifestation of the unity of God and man, but he is not absolutely essential for the validity of the Christ principle. Those theologians whose Christology is not undermined by the loss of the historical Jesus are not necessarily Hegelians; we affirm only that their solution is Hegelian. It is Hegelian in this sense that whatever Jesus stands for or represents is not absolutely tied in with the historical Jesus and therefore survives if it can be show that Jesus never lived. This, as indicated, could never be tolerated in historic Christology, for Jesus Christ is himself his truth, his message, his gospel.

John Knox's views on the subject are not totally clear if one compares *Christianity and Criticism* (1952) with later works. In *Christianity and Criticism* he claims that the memory of the historical life and teaching of Jesus is in the church firmly, and that is what the church lives by. Historical criticism is necessary, but historical criticism can never undermine that picture. This would seem to add up to the Hegelian idea that the memory of Jesus in story and parable could be detached from history and still be valid. Yet in *The Humanity and Divinity of Christ* (1967) he insists that there is the historical Man as both the center and origin of these memories. One need not pick here and there with Knox's solution to the problem of how the vitality of faith can hinge upon contingent historical events, for the problem is deeper. It is the problem of carrying water on both shoulders. It is a very difficult, an exceedingly difficult position, to accept major critical and historical strictures against the Gospels and then attempt to erect upon whatever remains a credible Christology and substantial Christian message. One can hear the creaking of the timbers as Knox discusses this is the opening pages of *The Church and the Reality of Christ*.

Tillich argues two ways. First he thinks it is necessary that there appear in historical life one person who perfectly manifests New Being under the conditions of historical existence. Next he argues that if criticism shows that Jesus never lived all is not lost. There remains the hard datum of Jesus as New Being, which is pictured in the earliest Christian communities. Carnley (in Sykes: 1972, 185ff.) assesses this as double-talk.

Bultmann's views on whether Jesus is essential to the Christian gospel or not are a matter of debate (cf. Fischer: 1970 and Wolf: 1965). Bultmann (1934) says that if critical investigation eventually proves that we can know nothing of the historical Jesus, then nothing is changed. He makes the amazing statement that Jesus stands as the code word for the historical phenomenon (i.e., of the early church with its kerygma, ibid., p. 14). Although not totally sceptical of the Gospels he reckons there is not too much historically valid about Jesus in the Gospels. Thus in a Hegelian manner we can save the Christian kerygma even if we cannot establish the historical Jesus.

However, later in Bultmann's career he was faced with those who claimed that his system consistently led to a religious existentialism in which Jesus was unnecessary. Bultmann reacted against that by insisting that without the historical Jesus and the event of the cross there would be no kerygma. How severe a shrinkage of historical materials this is for the kerygma will be discussed in the next chapter. The historical connection has become so slim that nothing of the personality of Jesus can be found in the Gospels and indeed is not necessary to the kerygma. Further the Christian faith is interested only in that *thatness* (*Dass*) of Jesus and the cross and nothing more. Bultmann reduces the historical element of the kerygma to the absolute minimum, and certainly upon such a minimum there is no base for historic Christology.

It can be said that scholars like Knox, Tillich, and Bultmann pale at the historical risk. Historic Christology is pledged to the historical risk. John McIntyre correctly says: "To hold an historical faith is to have a faith which stands or falls with the records" (1966, 41). Dorothy Sayers comments that there are many stories of gods incarnate but only one with a historical date: Jesus suffered and died under Pontius Pilate. It is only with the risk of history that historic Christology sustains the gospel. If the Christian *message* is in the final analysis only a series of concepts—idealistic in Hegel, existential in Tillich and Bultmann—then it is the kingdom of God in word but not in power. Only in the incarnation of God in Christ is the kingdom of God in word and in power, for the power stems from the atoning cross and the victorious resurrection. Historic Christology boldly takes the risk of history, for only in our space, in our time, and in our historical sequence of events can an event occur which is the redemption of the world. We are not saved by concepts, truths, and schemas which can in principle be loosed from history.

This same kind of Hegelian logic is to be found in Norman Perrin's (1977) *The Resurrection According to Matthew, Mark and Luke*. Perrin's belief that the meaning or significance of the resurrection can be detached from the bodily resurrection of Jesus is analogical to Hegelian Christology. Although very much in the Bultmannian tradition he breaks with Bultmann over myth. He quotes Amos Wilder's eight different definitions of myth and accepts a positive view (1977: 12) of myth; namely, myth as primordial archetypes of the race and myth as giving "structure of identity and cohesion [to] particular human groups and ways of life."

Whether Jesus rose from the dead is a question to be solved by scientific historians according to Perrin. But the meaning of the resurrection is in the realm of myth and is therefore independent from the decision of the "hard-nosed" historians (as he calls them). The meaning of the myth of the resurrection as a primordial, archetype myth and a myth for meaning and structure in daily life is not then based on what happened to the body of Jesus. At this point the believer in historic Christology must join with the opinion of Pannenberg that modern theology, for all its devotion to scientific history, irrationally flees from history, where the only true knowledge of God can be found. With a resurrection without a body we are back to the familiar aphorisms about the smile of the cat without the cat, or the king who is naked.

JOHN'S GOSPEL

John's gospel is a paradox to any writer on Christology. On the one hand it has a beautiful Christology. It contains a Christology of the Son of Man and a Christology of the "I am" statements. Yet on the critical side it is a nest of problems (see Brown: 1966, 1970; Kysar: 1975; Barrett: 1978)

(i) It has a long discoursive passages and conversations all with much theological content that is not matched in the Synoptic Gospels.

(ii) It reveals meticulous knowledge of Palestinian matters, such as peoples' names, peoples' relationships, customs, geographical sites, numbers of things, precise movements of peoples, etc.

(iii) It makes rich use of abstract nouns such as world, darkness, sin, truth, life, death, resurrection.

(iv) Its conceptual language, which came as a distinct surprise to scholars, is closer to that found in the Dead Sea Scrolls than the other Gospels.

(v) It is very sharp in its attitude towards the Jews and is called by some an antisemitic gospel.

(vi) Its concept of miracle as sign is different from the Synoptic Gospels as well as its many referrences to glory.

(vii) It records the dramatic raising of Lazarus, and this poses the question of why the Synoptic Gospels fail to report such an astounding case. In other instances of raising people from the dead they had been dead a short time, suggesting possibly a deep coma; but Lazarus was decomposing and hence stinking.

(viii) It reflects some kind of encounter with a philosophical mind (logos?) or a hellenistic mentality far beyond anything found in the Synoptic Gospels.

The question of the authorship of John and the answer to the uniqueness of John are linked together. Conservative writers still hold to John, the disciple, as the author of the Gospel (cf. Guthrie: 1971, ch. 8; Barker, Lane and Michaels: 1969, ch. 25; and Morris: 1971).

How, then, do we account for such a strange gospel in contrast to the Synoptic Gospels? Is it a historically worthless gospel (Käsemann: 1964, 60)? Or is it the greatest of all the Gospels in its theological vision? Some of the theories about the nature of John's gospel follow.

(1) It has been claimed that the many speeches found in John's gospel given by Jesus are either a series of *asides* spoken to John or materials that the other gospel writers failed to include in their gospels, which John in turn adds to his gospel to fill out the record. This notion has the virtue of keeping all the words of the Gospels spoken by Jesus authentically from Jesus; but it utterly fails to come to terms with the seriousness of the problems of the gospel of John.

(2) It has been claimed that these are the words of the Risen Christ to John. This too is an attempt to perceive the words of Jesus in the gospel of John as authentically from Jesus, but as a solution to the problems of John it is pure escapism.

(3) Raymond Brown believes in the core of the gospel as the work of

John but postulates five rewrites of the gospel to account for its present state. This mediates between the historic belief of the church that John the disciple is the author of the gospel and modern critical opinion.

(4) Barrett still remains with the thesis of the first edition of his commentary that a "school of John" gathered in Ephesus and it was such disciples who in consort wrote the works attributed to John in the New Testament. Although there is some doubt about John's relationship to Ephesus, F. F. Bruce (1978, 339-61) has summarized the evidence in favor of a long stay by John in Ephesus.

(5) Clement of Alexandria said that John wrote a spiritual gospel: "Last of all John perceiving that the [external] facts had been set forth in the [other] Gospels, at the instance of his disciples and with the inspiration of the Spirit composed a spiritual Gospel" (Guthrie: 1971, 273). The implication of the remark seems to be that John drew out of the synoptic materials and his own personal knowledge the full theological meaning of some of the sayings of Jesus, and some of the claims about him.

Hence we would say that he wrote a "theological gospel." There is a rule in logic which says that in asserting a proposition one asserts everything which can be deduced from the proposition. If we say Mr. Green is a man, we have also asserted all the propositions that define manhood and humanity. If the Gospels call Jesus Lord, Son of Man, Messiah, or Son of God, then the Gospels have also asserted all that can be deduced from such names. Hence statements in John's gospel that Jesus is the Logos, Lamb of God, or Bread of Life are deductions from that which is affirmed of him in the Synoptic Gospels. It may put a strain on our sense of the historical, but formally or logically speaking John is within his rights.

It has been our occasional contention that the Gospels are primarily witnessing and proclaiming documents. They came into existence in the process of the various Christian churches as witnessing, evangelistic, and missionary centers. There is an element of truth in *Gemeinde Theologie* (i.e., the church as writing the life of Jesus) such that the Gospels are productions of the early church. This is mandatory from the nature of the Christian message. The church receives *the original gospel, kerygma,* or *kingdom proclamation* from its Savior and Lord through the apostles and their writings and *frames it for their locality.* Studies in the parables show that to some measure the parables were shaped so that they would be intelligible to a given audience. Therefore John's gospel represents a very special and highly technical framing of the Christian message for a very special locality.

This is being done all the time in missionary work around the world. A missionary who has spent thirty or forty years among Buddhists in Japan cannot but think in terms of a "Buddhist-shaped Christianity." That means in the encounter with Buddhist thought the missionary frames the Christian message to best encounter Buddhist mentality. This is not a distortion of the Christian message but an intelligent presentation of it. The same could be said of a missionary working among Muslims who creates a "Muslim-shaped Christianity." One could also speak of a "Hindu-shaped Christianity." We have the more extreme kind of reshaping of the Christian message in Christian novels, Christian drama, and Christian films. John's gospel is to be seen in the analogy of all shaping and reframing of the Christian message.

It is a sustained tradition that John lived out the latter part of his life in Ephesus. Alexandria was the greatest cultural center in the Roman Empire, even though Rome was the administrative center. Ephesus ranked second to Alexandria, especially in theological and philosophical reflection, and excavations in Ephesus reveal that it was a rival of Athens, Pompei, Rome, and Ostia.

What kind of gospel would John write if he lived in Ephesus about thirty years and carried on a Christian dialogue at a high level in its most sophisticated community? He would write a gospel (in the analogy of Clement and modern missionaries) that would reflect his effort to reframe the original Christian message to make it most effective to his audience in Ephesus. He would first of all be faithful to the origin of his message with Jesus in Palestine. Much has been made of the similarities of John's gospel to the Qumran materials, but Barrett does not believe there has been material help from the scrolls. At any rate it shows why the gospel of John attempts to be as faithful to the local color of Palestine as possible.

The focus of attention is certainly on the Jewish mind. John 20:31 reveals the obvious intention of the author: to convince Jews that Jesus is the Messiah, the Son of God. So many of the dialogues and the discourses are centered in Jewish traditions, Jewish history, and Jewish concepts. Yet there is this radical contrast from the style of the Synoptics.

John's gospel is then the attempt of John to make the gospel of Jesus

Christ meaningful and compelling to the Jews at Ephesus. Or it could be said that the gospel represents the final summation of his years of missionary witnessing in Ephesus. Such a view does not cause all the problems to vanish. Barrett is very testy with all theories of the gospel because the complications are so many that no one theory resolves them all. Nevertheless some sort of a venture must be undertaken (as Barrett himself does).

John's gospel is a paradigm (as we understand it) of creative missionary preaching and teaching. It took a theological genius to bind his faith to the historic Jesus of Palestine and at the same time to reframe that original message for the people of Ephesus.

This is not at the edge of matters but at their very center. A major concern of the twentieth century has been that of the translation of the gospel into the idiom of contemporary culture. This is the inspiration of Tillich's kerygmatic, apologetic, and systematic theology. This was the genius of Barth's *Römerbrief.* This is the heart of Bultmann's synthesis of critical studies and existentialism. And it was one of the major considerations in Thielicke's effort to write an *Evangelical Theology* (3 vols.).

It is Thielicke who clarifies issue the best. In the effort to translate the gospel into the modern idiom there is the danger of translating the gospel out of one's theology, which Thielicke thinks is the case with Schleiermacher, Tillich, and Bultmann. He objects to the conservative and/or orthodox theologians who do no translating and hence betray their generation in that they make no meaningful communication to it. A good biblical, Christian, and evangelical theology does make the translation from the historic Christian faith and its Holy Scripture to the modern person. And our point is that this is precisely what John's gospel did for his day.

Further, Pannenberg says that this process can be found in the New Testament. Certainly Matthew and Hebrews are books written to people with a Jewish background and mentality. But books like Ephesians, Philippians, and Colossians are the Christian faith retooled for a more Gentile or a more Greek mentality. Hence Pannenberg argues every culture must take the original Christian revelation in documents and translate them into its own idiom. We believe this is what John's gospel was all about in Ephesus.

Our thesis is fleshed out by Stephen Smalley (1984) who has written a small but very judicious book on the gospel of John and its diverse problems. He accounts for much of the shape of the gospel by affirming that there are two groups that John addressed who were in Ephesus. John had to make peace or reconciliation with these two groups. The first group was the Jewish Christians who were highly protective of their Jewish heritage and the second was the hellenistic group. John had to correct items in the beliefs of the Hellenists, which were pulling them back into their former gnostic concepts.

10

The New Quest for the Historical Jesus

FROM SCHWEITZER TO BULTMANN

It had been the common assumption in the Christian church, believed until the time of Reimarus (1694-1768), that the historical person of Jesus, the Lord Jesus Christ of the Epistles, and the Christ of the church creeds were one and the same. It was Reimarus who first set it out that the picture that is found of Jesus in the Gospels and the actual historical personage were very different. He began the differentiation of the Jesus of history from the Christ of apostolic preaching (Jeremias: 1960, 7).

From Reimarus to Wrede (1859-1906) a number of lives of Jesus were written which expanded one way or another the basic thesis of Reimarus. Albert Schweitzer (1910) achieved enduring theological fame by his famous summary of these lives in his book *The Quest of the Historical Jesus*. Schweitzer's verdict was that these lives were a failure. The writers of such lives were reconstructing Jesus in their own image. Schweitzer believed that the eschatological element in the Gospels was not some Jewish excess to be ignored but the very key to the historical Jesus. The eschatological coming of the kingdom of God was the central message of Jesus.

There were a number of assumptions in this historical quest such as: (i) the Gospels reflect a highly developed Christology; (ii) as historical and factual documents the Gospels are suspect; (iii) the miraculous events and many of the theological claims in the Gospels are contrary to what a modern person may accept; and therefore (iv) some sort of critical methodolgy is necessary to work through the Gospels and discover what is historically authentic.

Schweitzer's indictment of the lives of Christ under review did not stop the writing of such lives. A great number of them appeared on both sides of the Atlantic in the period from Schweitzer to Bultmann. However it is due to the thought of Bultmann that a new crisis arose over the historical Jesus, and the second or new quest began. However something of the Bultmannian program was already contained in Wilhelm Bousset's famous work, *Kyrios Christos*. In the fifth edition of this work (1970) Bultmann wrote a very sympathetic foreword.

To understand why Bultmann's thought sparked a new quest for the historical Jesus, a sketch of Bultmann's total range of thought must be rehearsed. Bultmann makes a severe division between (i) existential statements and (ii) objective or scientific (including the historical and critical) statements. Each territory is separate from the other, and each is autonomous. There is one point of overlap, and that is the event of crucifixion. It is a paradox because at the same time it is a genuine event of history and the event of world salvation. In New Testament studies it means that all matters of authorship, history, critical investigation, literary origins, and world views belong to the objective and scientific statements. According to Bultmann and his school, to go against these kinds of statements for reasons of faith is to crucify the intellect. That which appeals to faith and decision belongs to the existential. The criticism of the Gospels is a scientific matter; the kerygma within the Gospels is an existential matter.

Kerygmatic and existential matters of the New Testament do not conflict with critical-scientific studies because they are compartmentalized. Theology so understood is concerned with the existential meaning of the New Testament. Because there is this severe division of the existential from the critical and scientific, nothing of the critical, scientific or historical authenticates faith, nor even helps to authenticate faith.

Faith is defined as an existential decision. It cannot be verified by that which is non-existential. Neither history nor more critical investigation can validate faith or give us more assurance of faith. Only something existential which is of the same species as the kerygma can assure us that we have believed the truth.

This may give the impression that Bultmann does not believe that the Christ of the kergyma is related to the Jesus of history. Bultmann does believe that the Christ preached in the kerygma is connected with the Jesus of the Gospels. He does believe that there are some authentic materials of Jesus in the Gospels. But he does not believe that establishing historical facts about Jesus makes the kerygma any more believable. The scientific cannot shore up the existential.

This radical division between the scientific and the existential has a strong apologetic value. It means among other things that the scientific, critical, or historical can never embarrass the existential kerygma. Like jetliners flying east and west they fly at separated altitudes, eliminating any possibility of collision. When asked about his own paradox of a passionate belief in the kerygma and a cold scepticism in his critical work in the New Testament, Bultmann replied he never once felt a tension between the scientific and the existential. The obvious reason is that Bultmann has assigned specific tasks to each one so that a collision is impossible.

Bultmann limits the interest of the kerygma as far as history is concerned to the event of the cross. He speaks of the *Dass* or *thatness* of the cross. The events in the life of Jesus prior to the cross are not part of the cross and, as we previously remarked, can add nothing to the credibility of the cross. This six hours of the cross, this sheer *thatness* of the cross, began to appear to some of Bultmann's followers to be far too slender a territory upon which to build the Christian faith. In an effort to widen the base of the Christian faith one of Bultmann's most able students, Ernst Käsemann, delivered a lecture which in turn was printed (1954, 125-53). This essay opened up the new quest for the historical Jesus and generated a mountain of literature.

There are three things that the students of Bultmann wanted to do in correcting their mentor: (i) to think through their common assumptions; (ii) to clarify their problems; and (iii) to correct any onesidedness. One of the main goals was to correct the onesidedness of Bultmann's understanding of the historical element in the kerygma. It was felt that Bultmann had the narrowest of linkage between the life of Jesus and the kerygma. Accordingly they set out to correct this by expanding the historical element in the historical Jesus (Reinhardt: 1970, 271).

Käsemann was careful to assert that the new quest would not fall into the errors of the old quest (although V. A. Harvey and S. Ogden do not think the new quest is that new; in Braaten and Harrisville: 1970, ch. 1). Bultmann did not approve of the new quest by his former students. He reaffirmed his basic position that existential matters and historical matters are separate, and that it is impossible to shore up an existential kerygma with more data on the historical Jesus.

THE NEW QUEST AND HISTORIC CHRISTOLOGY

Historic Christology recognizes no distinction between the Jesus who actually lived, the Jesus as reported in the Gospels, the Lord Jesus Christ of the letters of the New Testament, and the Jesus Christ of the Christological creeds. If there was an error in historic Christology it was to overlook the historical development and uncritically fuse the different pictures of Jesus.

However to break up the various versions of Jesus into contradictory pictures is fatal to historic Christology. Historic Christology does not believe that it can harmonize all the pictures of Jesus in the New Testament. The New Testament witness to Christ is too rich for that. In this sense there is no one Christology but many Christologies in the New Testament. But it does insist that there are certain beliefs that underly all the diversity in the New Testament. Further, the amount of gospel criticism accepted among defenders of historic Christology varies. There is certainly a "conservative-liberal" spread here. But no large rift can be made among the versions of Jesus without damage to historic Christology.*

To a believer in historic Christology it is a very serious matter if the Jesus of historical research is radically different from the Jesus in the Gospels. It is also very damaging to historic Christology if the Jesus of history has no continuity with the Christ of Chalcedon. The believer in historic Christology has a vested interest in the new quest for the following reasons.

(1) The interest in the outcome of this quest is of maximum interest to the believer in historic Christology because the issue is much more than academic. The Nicean Creed stated that the purpose of the incarnation was *for our salvation*. If God did not become incarnate then there is no salvation as the church historically understands salvation. If there is no salvation, then the personal faith of the believer in historic Christology is undermined. The new quest, therefore, cannot be divorced from the most fundamental issues of life; it can never be a

---

* It could be said accurately that the most suppressed item in New Testament studies is the great diversity within its pages. James D. G. Dunn has devoted important time to this matter in *Unity and Diversity in the New Testament* (Westminster, 1978). The one position to beware in this kind of study is that it might convert diversity into contradiction. The diversity in the Christologies of the book of Ephesians and the book of Hebrews are very great but they need not be understood as contradictory.

purely academic matter. The stakes of historic Christology in the authenticity of the gospel records is maximum. If the new quest shows with great certainty that the Jesus who actually lived is radically different from the Lord Jesus Christ of historic Christology, then there is no more salvation. As Paul wrote, we are to be pitied above all men (1 Cor. 15:19).

(2) The believer in historic Christology is committed to an extra dimension in his understanding of history. Historic Christology cannot be defended within the structure of a positivistic writing of history. By a positivistic theory of history we mean the writing of history which confines itself completely to the immanent factors of human life, completely to ordinary cause-effect relations, and completely to the rejection of any overarching meaning of history. The positivistic view of history admits no metaphysical principle operating in history, no overall philosophical stance as the right perspective on history, and nothing supernatural to be taken as historical data. If the new quest is conducted from the stance of a positivistic view of history then there is no question that the new quest and historic Christology are on a collision course. A new quest carried on by positivistic assumptions will produce a Jesus far different from the Jesus of historic Christology.

Any theory about the historical Jesus is at the same time a revelation of the scholar's view of history (Marshall: 1977, ch. 1). In this connection a look at Bultmann's view of history is relevant (Ott: 1960, ch. 7). In his critical work in the New Testament Bultmann operates with a positivistic view of history, which is an impossible task. It is impossible to write history without philosophical assumptions and therefore the ideal neutral, objective, scientific, and non-partisan stance of the positivists cannot be achieved. Bultmann cannot really interpret the New Testament with such a view of history. Those who are positivist in their view of history believe that their view of the historical Jesus is objective and free from theological or metaphysical overlay; and that those who have specific Christological convictions cannot help but write about Jesus with distortion. On the contrary, the postivists have as much intrusion of theological and philosophical materials into their description of the historical Jesus as they presume in those of the other camp.

It is true that some of the "new questers" reject the positivistic view of history that has characterized much of gospel criticism. They do appeal to the British philosopher Collingwood, who has a more idealistic view of history. And some still trade on the distinction between *His-*

torie (history as written scientifically) and *Geschichte* (history as written from an ideological or theological perspective). But the kind of history written either under the influence of Collingwood or the distinction between *Historie* and *Geschichte* does not answer to the demands in history of historic Christology. One can accept all of this and still in principle reject the incarnation, the virgin birth, and the bodily resurrection of Christ.

Käsemann repudiates a purely positivistic view of history, for it represents the intrusion of scientific categories into historical knowledge. History is about both facts and meaning (*Bedeutung*, or significance). Therefore the gospel reports of Jesus may be part of the kerygma, for they are both fact and meaning. Bultmann had said this much in *Jesus and the Word* (1934) but later abandoned it (Reinhardt: 1970, 274). Even so it is not enough for the support of historic Christology.

Believers in historic Christology do not believe they are the best historians. Much solid history can be written regardless of faulty methodolgy. It is radical givenness of revelation, the belief in the participation of God in Israel's history and all history, and "that great exception" (Chesterton) of the incarnation, that gives the Christian a different perspective in his or her view of history. It is the gift of grace and the invasion of grace that also invades our idea of history. The incarnation not only challenges our pretensions to self-righteousness, but it also challenges our pretentions to know all the factors which make for history.

(3) Contrary to the positivistic mood that governs gospel criticism and the new quest, the believer in historic Christology cannot dispense with the category of the supernatural. In a very sturdy article B. B. Warfield (1952) makes the point that a non-supernatural Christianity is not Christianity. One of his major points is that the doctrines of God, creation, and redemption are supernatural. To identify the supernatural in Christianity solely with miracles or divine revelations is to misunderstand the category of the supernatural. The miracles are but one example of a more fundamental supernatural activity. Therefore to profess to be Christian and also to be naturalistic is to assert a contradiction.

With this understanding of the supernatural in mind it is apparent that historic Christology is thoroughly supernatural. From the event of self-humiliation and incarnation, to the exaltation, and to the right hand of God is all supernatural. All the incarnational passages are supernatural. This of course means that those who accept historic Christology cannot but clash with those New Testament scholars who understand history only in positivistic terms, which in principle exclude the supernatural. Again it does not mean that such Christians are better historians, nor that all the positivistic historians write chaff, nor that the New Testament scholars have nothing important to say. It means that at the fundamental vision of reality those who accept historic Christology believe that historic Christology commits them to the category of the supernatural.

(4) Historic Christology presupposes the biblical doctrine of sin. Then presuppositions of the creeds with their Christology presuppose the sinfulness and fallenness of the race. One cannot discuss Christology apart from the necessity of propitiation (*Versöhnungsnotwedigkeit;* Elert: 1960). Or Anselm has argued that whoever has pondered the weight of sin (*quanti ponderis sit peccatum*) must follow with a doctrine of Christ and the atonement.

Such doctrines as creation, the human race, sin, Christology, salvation, and faith mutually define each other. Christology cannot be discussed in isolation from the whole fabric of Christian theology. For example one of the cardinal weaknesses of so much of the discussion of title Christology is to separate the discussion from the much wider circle of other doctrines.

(5) Historic Christology always vigorously defended the complete humanity of Christ, yet that needs reaffirming in light of the historical quest. Historic Christology in its equal affirmation of the deity of Christ appears to some theologians as a reaffirmation of docetism; that is, underestimating the humanity of Christ. Because historic Christology believes so firmly in the humanity of Christ it has a profound concern with the Gospels. It is in the Gospels that the humanity of Christ is set forth in its earthly and social setting. John 1:14 says that the incarnate Logos *tented* (the verb is from *skēnē,* a tent) among us; that is, Jesus lived as a first-century Jew among other Jews and in the common routine of daily life.

Therefore to the degree that the new quest is a quest for our Lord in his full humanity it is a noble and valid quest. The debate involves the premise of scepticism about the historical integrity of the Gospels. But if the intention is to see Christ in his full humanity, then we need all the study of the Gospels available. Faith in the full humanity of our Lord demands this.

The intercessory work of Christ as a high priest, as set out in the letter to the Hebrews, is based upon the gospel record of our Lord in the days of his flesh. The argument from Hebrews is not based merely on the humanity of Christ but upon that humanity as revealed in the gospel incidents. Again this means believers in historic Christology must be much interested in gospel research.

As previously cited Martin Kähler said the Gospels were long introductions to the passion narrative. This means it is the public ministry of Christ that creates for us the image of the person who dies on the cross. This is another reason why those who espouse historic Christology believe that gospel research is so important. It impresses us that there is something seriously wrong with Bultmann's theology when he affirms that we should have no interest in the personality of Christ (or better perhaps, Christ as a person), and that he can reduce the cross to a bare *Dass* of six hours. To believe in such an eviscerated *Dass* is to us certainly a crucifixion of the intellect, for it asks us to believe in an event from which every shred of the personal must be abstracted. More thanks to the new quest if it enriches our understanding of the person who dies for the sins of the world.

From above remarks it should be clear why those who accept historic Christology have a great interest in the new quest. The basic issue is how much authentic materials are in the Gospels. Historic Christology is built upon the premise that the Gospels are authentic historical documents of the original historical Jesus.

THE METHODS OF THE NEW QUEST

The new quest grows out of the old quest. In the new quest for the historical Jesus certain assumptions are those of the former quest, such as the freedom of inquiry into sacred matters, and the assumed discrepancy between the picture of Jesus in the Gospels and what he actually was. But the new questers represent an advance over the old questers. This advance is principally in newer methods of gospel criticism. A brief summary of such methods is in order. These methods were often developed by German scholars, and the translation of some of the terms is either difficult or awkward.

(1) History of Religion (*religionsgeschichtliche Schule*). This is a

method of research pioneered in Bousset's *Kyrios Christos*.* The basic idea behind it is that religious concepts have a history. There is such a thing as "historical sociology," which recovers in the best as possible way the social milieu of a given period of history by an intensive study of its literature. Out of such a historical reconstruction of social milieux of the past the scholar can also learn the meaning of its religious concepts. Bousset's task was to see what the word lord (*kyrios*) meant in the first Christian century.

This is not exactly new, for older books on biblical interpretation discussed the *usus loquendi* of a word or term by investigating the manner in which a term was used at the time of the writing of the New Testament. The method of History of Religion criticism is more extensive and more thorough. It also carries with it the presupposition of the strong influence of Hellenism on the scribes who wrote the New Testament and the further presupposition that the New Testament is much more the revelation of the life of the early Christian communities than a historical account of the life of Jesus. It changes biblical interpretation from the theological exposition of the text to a sociological commentary on the origin of concepts.

(2) Form Criticism (*Formgeschichte*). Form criticism is based on the premise that a culture preserves its heritage by putting the various items of it in certain literary forms or genre (cf. Travis in Marshall: 1977, ch. 9). According to this theory the life of Jesus was preserved in the early church by putting the various elements of it in stylized forms. Further, as the church enlarged and elaborated on the life of Jesus it did so continuing the use of these literary forms. Martin Dibelius was famous for his pioneering work in form criticism and in turn he had a strong influence on Bultmann. Examples of these forms are as follows: *Paradigm*—A brief, epigrammatic saying of Jesus followed by the reaction of the onlookers (Mark 3:31-35); *Tales*—Stories of the miracles of Jesus; *Legends*—Stories of Jesus' birth and infancy; *Myths*—The transfiguration; *Exhortations*—The teaching materials in the Gospels.

This means that the Gospels are in no sense a biography of Jesus but

---

* For further reading on the faith and history issue, the following may be consulted and their bibliographical materials noted. Carl E. Braaten and Roy Harrisville, *The Historical Jesus and the Kerygmatic Christ* (Abingdon, 1964). Carl E. Braaten, *History and Hermeneutics: New Directions in Theology*, Vol. 2 (Westminster, 1966). Norman Hillyer has compiled a very excellent bibliography in I. Howard Marshall, editor, *New Testament Interpretation*, (Eerdmans, 1977), 367-88.

documents stitched together. Or a common illustration of form criticism is that it reduces the Gospels to necklaces. Each form is artifically linked to the next form. This led some scholars to describe the Gospels as sub-literary products (*Kleinliteratur*).

The task of the New Testament researcher is to identify the forms and attempt to reconstruct the situation in the early churches which would create the demand for such a form. Although the general drift of form criticism is against the authenticity of the Gospels there are New Testament scholars who use form criticism in a helpful way. The most prominent of such scholars has been O. Cullmann.

Travis lists the limitations of form criticism as follows: (i) There is no common agreement among scholars about the list of forms; (ii) the assumption that there was a period of oral tradition before anything was written is gratuitous; (iii) it cannot be established that there were such church scribes who were doing this kind of elaboration; and (iv) efforts to find parallels in non-biblical materials may be more harmful than helpful. Travis concludes that the method of form criticism is only as good as the scholar who uses it. If used to get closer to the original sayings of Jesus it is acceptable; if used to break the authenticity of the Gospels then it is not.

(3) *Source criticism* (*Quellenkritik*; Wenham in Marshall: 1977, ch. 8). Source criticism is the attempt to discover what written sources were used in the writing of the Gospels. The oldest source theory was that of Augustine, and with modifications is known today as the Griesbach Hyphothesis. Matthew wrote first and Mark used Matthew as his source; Luke wrote after Mark and used Matthew and Mark as his sources; and John wrote last using the three former Gospels as his sources. Griesbach puts Luke before Mark.

A more recent theory is that the two basic sources are Mark's gospel and the Q document. The Q document is composed of all those passages that Matthew and Luke have in common to the exclusion of Mark. Streeter has constructed a complex four-source theory for the composition of the Gospels. All summed up, eighteen different sources are often projected behind the Gospels (Soulen: 1976, 157).

(4) Tradition criticism (*Traditionsgeschichte*). It is presumed that before the Gospels were written there was a period of oral tradition (although some have postulated that the disciples themselves could have started taking notes during Jesus' ministry in analogy of students of rabbis). Tradition criticism is a study of the phenomenon of oral tradition and as it could apply to our understanding of the formation of the Gospels.

The most controversial feature of tradition criticism is the criteria of authenticity. Although it is held by Marxist propaganda writers that Jesus never lived and that the Gospels are pure creations of the imagination, this is not the view of even the most radical Gospel critics. There is a minimum of historical materials about Jesus in the Gospels. The myths and elaborations of the church scribes who wrote the Gospels did not completely block out historical materials about Jesus. The question is then, how can such materials be recognized? This has created "criteria of authenticity." However there is no accepted list of such criteria, for scholars vary somewhat (cf. Fuller: 1962 with Perrin: 1976), but the agreements are much more than the differences. D. G. A. Calvert (1971-72) lists five criteria of authenticity which at least illustrates the issue (*New Testament Studies*, 18: 211):

(i) If a saying is dissimilar from Jewish or Hellenistic traditions it could be authentic.

(ii) If a saying seems to be primitive, that is, something before the formation of the post-Easter church, it could be authentic.

(iii) If a saying agrees with material already judged authentic it can be assumed to be authentic.

(iv) If there is convergence of materials in the three Gospels it could be authentic.

(v) If the saying seems to be Aramaic or Palestinian it could be authentic.

In reviewing the literature on the criteria of authenticity certain presuppositons are obvious: (i) The basic premise is that the Gospels are untrustworthy as historical documents until proven otherwise. It is the reversal of the rule that the charged is innocent until proven guilty. The Gospels are assumed guilty of historical untrustworthiness until proven historical. This sceptical approach must not be overlooked nor underrated. Calvert also listed five criteria of inauthenticity, and that is the area where most sayings are concentrated. (ii) The other presuppostion is that the materials which historic Christology so values are all mythological. (iii) it is difficult to counter the assertion that something can be granted to be authentically from Jesus if it can be shown to be irrelevant or trivial.

However, every kind of quest for the very words and deeds of Jesus is worthy of serious attention and may be commended by those who follow historic Christology. In this context we can agree with D. R. Catchpole (in Marshall: 1977, 178) in his conclusion after reviewing the criteria of authenticity.

But [the research in Criteria of Authenticity] does at least have the merit of recognizing that the gospels do belong to Jesus and also to the churches. For Jesus this means that he is seen as not merely *historisch*, a figure of the past, but also one whom we can see within the developing tradition as truly *geschichtlich*, that is, a person whose relevance is explored and exploited ever and again in places far removed from Galilee and Jerusalem in times long after A. D. 30.

(5) Redaction criticism (*Redactionsgeschichte*). The English verb *redact* is not much used, but it means to edit something for publication, which is so necessary in the printing and publication industry. Redaction criticism is the most specialized and most controversial method for the study of the Gospels which has developed after World War II (cf. Smalley in Marshall: 1977). It is closely associated with *Composition Criticism (Kompositionsgeschichte)*. R. T. Fortuna (IDB Suppl., 733) defines Redaction Criticism as follows: "Redaction is the conscious reworking of older materials in such a way as to meet new needs. It is editing that does not simply compile or retouch but creatively transforms." Hence it is also related to tradition history, which also involves close attention to the theological convictions of the editor to see how that influences the manner in which he shapes his materials.

Redaction criticism presumes four stages from Jesus to the finished canonical Gospels: (i) the original sayings and deeds of Jesus; (ii) the elaborations in the period of oral tradition; (iii) the emergence of the documents assumed in source criticism; (iv) the final editing or redacting of these materials into the canonical Gospels. Like form criticism, redaction criticism reflects the scholars who use it. Some evangelicals use it for constructive purposes to get back closer to the original Jesus, and others such as Willi Marxsen use it to establish a great gulf between the original words and deeds of Jesus and the materials in the Gospels.

(6) Content criticism (*Sachkritik*). It has been an accepted division of labor to assign the role of criticism to matters of biblical introduction and the role of interpretation to the meaning of the text. Content criticism breaks up this division of labor. It contends that the critical investigation characteristic of biblical introduction must also apply to what a text teaches. The teaching of a text is as much a matter of scrutiny as are the matters of which are part of biblical introduction. In simple language this means that the critic is not under obligation to believe something because it is affirmed in Holy Scripture. The teaching's of Scripture (*Sache*) are as much subject to critical judgment as are mat-

ters of introduction. If the New Testament teaches the bodily resurrection of Christ, it does not mean that the New Testament scholar is under obligation to believe it. It can be said that *Sachkritik* is the presupposition of all the critical methods of modern scholarship, for they all presume the right to theologically criticize the text (or philosophically or scientifically criticize it).

The issues in content criticism broke out fiercely between Bultmann and Barth. Barth held strictly to the historic division of labor which separated the critical assessment of the text from its theological interpretation. Bultmann believed that the New Testament scholar must be as scientific, critical, and objective with the teaching of the New Testament as he was with matters of biblical introduction. For Barth this was a rerun of his famous debate with Harnack mentioned earlier.

Klaus Reinhardt (1970, 242ff.) clarifies why Bultmann believes in content criticism. Bultmann believes that there is a difference between what the text says (*Gesagte*) and what is meant (*Gemeinte*). Texts usually are mixtures of different kinds of materials, and content criticism is able to judge what is adequate and what is unusable. Reinhardt comments that what is really at work here is an existential approach to the text, and Bultmann saves the worth of an ancient text by restating its meaning in modern existential concepts. This means that unless we use content criticism we will believe things in the New Testament no modern person should. And to believe such things is the crucifixion of the intellect. According to Barth this procedure determines ahead of time (a priori) what the text may say.

In this debate historic Christology is on the side of Barth. If the interpreter may become the final authority over the Word of God, then the concept of the Word of God has become superficial. Certainly in Bultmann's content criticism the ship of historic Christology is sunk.

There is a point that Barth made which is systematically overlooked. In going behind the materials of the Gospels the researcher expects to find a more authentic picture of Jesus than appears in the Gospels as they are. Barth does not think this is impossible. If a person looks at a portrait he has no way of knowing how accurate or realistic it is unless he knows the person who has been painted. Hence Barth reasons that if a scholar rejects the picture of Jesus in the Gospels he has no idea what kind of Jesus to find in its place. Though gospel critics usually do produce their Jesus picture, they have no way of knowing if Jesus were ever like that. Barth's position boils down to accepting the kind of picture of Jesus we have in the Gospels or agnosticism about the historical Jesus. It is not a popular stance these days, but nevertheless it seems closer to the facts than the other options. Speaking of the current leaders in New Testament studies Barth (1966, 69) writes that "to my amazement [they] have armed themselves with swords and staves and once again undertaken the search for the 'historical Jesus'—a search in which I now as before prefer not to participate."

THE NEW QUEST AND MARTIN KÄHLER

Martin Kähler's famous book on Jesus Christ and criticism was published in 1896 (see the 1964 translation). The book anticipated many of the issues in the current new quest, and it has a number of seminal ideas from which different recent scholars have chosen selectively (cf. Braaten: 1964, ch. 6).

(1) Kähler wrote in his book that the most important thing about the Gospels is the powerful picture they paint of Jesus; and that faith was independent of the results of historical research (and by implication, biblical criticism). Tillich (in Kähler: 1964) latches on to both of these ideas. The important thing in the Gospels is the picture of Jesus Christ as the historical incidence of New Being. Even if Jesus never lived the picture is still valid. As we have seen, Tillich desires a person in history, in genuine human conditions, to be a model or archetype of New Being, so he accepts the historical Jesus. But if hard pressed he can retreat to the picture of New Being.

Further, he wants faith divorced from outcome of critical scholarship so that the kerygma is not dependent for its validity either on the historian or the New Testament critic.

(2) Bultmann finds other things to his liking in Kähler. First he likes Kähler's emphasis on preaching and the Christ in the center of preaching. Bultmann's theology centers on the Christian kerygma. It is in the kerygma, in the preaching, that Christ is presented as crucified and risen. Of course Bultmann does not believe in a historical atonement or a bodily resurrection from the dead but in their existential counterparts in preaching (the cross being the end of inauthentic, worldly, fleshly, etc., existence, and the resurrection being new life, authentic life, the life of obedience, the life of openness to the future). Preaching in Bultmann's theology almost reaches the point of becoming charismatic and sacramental.

Further, Bultmann likes the distinction Kähler makes between scientific history (*Historie*) and theologically interpreted history (*Geschichte*). In ordinary German prose the terms are synonyms. But if one adopts Kähler's distinction a New Testament scholar can claim to be as scientific in matters of history as the historian (*Historie*), but as a Christian the scholar can see depths of meaning in a text which carry us into the area of theology (*Geschichte*). Those theologians who do not make this distinction cannot but run into the heavy firepower of modern scientific historians.

(3) Some evangelicals have been appreciative of Kähler. First, he frees the gospel from the lordship of critical scholars. The church cannot live under the perpetual threat that someday the critics will undermine the Gospels and with that the gospel. Second Kähler refuses to divide Jesus up into the historical Jesus, the preached Jesus, and the Jesus of the history of Christology. It is the one and the same Jesus in all instances.

(4) W. G. Kümmel (1973, 225) sounds a necessary note of warning. Kähler makes the message of Jesus free from the threat of any historical judgment. There cannot be serious faith in the importance of Jesus Christ if he does not have some contact with history, and if there is contact with history the judgments of the historians cannot be excluded. Historic Christology has always insisted that the incarnation pledges its believers to the risk of history. Otherwise the gospel becomes moral exhortation (as it really is in Harnack), or existential New Being (Tillich), or a lesson in existential authenticity (Bultmann). Kähler did see the issues sharply and for evangelicals took high ground; but it must never be without the historical risk, for there is no real redemption in religious concepts. The kingdom of God becomes a kingdom only in word but not in power or action.

(5) The most sympathetic treatment of Kähler is by C. E. Braaten. His doctoral work on Kähler included a translation of Kähler's book into English. In an introductory essay to the translation, his thesis is that Kähler shows the impossibility of any meaningful quest for the historical Jesus either by the old questers of the nineteenth century or the new questers of the latter part of the twentieth century. That is for two reasons: (i) the Gospels do not contain the kind of data from which any sort of a biography can be written; and (ii) the Gospels are absolutely unique because there is no historical in an incarnation. The two theses interlock.

Further, while Kähler attempted to give history and criticism its proper due (and so broke with conservatism in biblical criticism), he also wanted to preserve the theological integrity of the witness of the Gospels to Jesus Christ (and so broke with the critics of the time). It was not critical research which discovered Jesus for the believer but the Holy Spirit in its witness to Christ. Hence it is only in faith that the Christian finds Christ in the Gospels and not new Testament critical scholarship. Further the weight of Scripture is not to be found in some theory of inspiration but in that the Scripture is Christ-bearing or Christ-witnessing. Braaten does not believe Kähler puts down history and biblical criticism, rather he shows that only in the great doctrine of justification by faith does the believer encounter the living Christ.

SUMMARY

(1) Historic Christology is based on the historical integrity of the Gospels. The Gospels are confessional materials but they must have rootage in history.

(2) Historic Christology does not call for an end of critical studies. Critical studies cannot be stonewalled. Under the theory of descriptions it can allow critical studies without necessary conflict. Nor does historic Christology regard the divine inspiration of the Gospels as a source of refuge from critical theories.

(3) Historic Christology does not rule out the notion that the church helped produce the Gospels. The church is both the recipient of the gospel and the evangelist of the gospel. It is therefore normal that it share in both the reception of the gospel and its transmission.

(4) Historic Christology believes in the continuity of the historical person of Jesus and the New Testament documents. There is not enough time (thirty years) for the historical teachings of Jesus to be so transmuted into a theological Christ, as is the claim in much criticism.

(5) Historic Christology believed that the disciples lived on in the church for many years, and therefore critics cannot develop theories which would be possible only if the apostles were absent from the church.

(6) Historic Christology affirms that Paul is an important person for Christological studies. His conversion dates within about three years from the death and resurrection of Christ, and that he was not only conversant with the other apostles but accepted into their ranks as a peer. 2 Corinthians 5:17 does not mean that Paul was ignorant of the

historical details about Jesus Christ, but that there is a difference between a pure human understanding of Christ as over against a knowledge of Christ in divine revelation.

(7) Historic Christology concedes that the Gospels are not biographies in the modern technical sense, but the Gospel materials do reflect authentic history.

(8) Historic Christology believes the Gospel not only convey to us teachings of Jesus and words of Jesus. They also reveal to us the kind of person he was.

(9) Historic Christology believes that it is an odd thesis to affirm that the Gospels tell us more about early church history than they tell us about Jesus Christ and his public ministry.

(10) Historic Christology does not believe it is based on a mistake; a mistake that claims the early church was over-impressed by Jesus and converted him into Lord and Savior, and in the creeds as God the Son. To the contrary the New Testament witness is the true reflection of who Jesus Christ was.

(11) Historic Christology does not believe that the New Testament is highly tainted with myths, nor that its high Christological claims can be undermined by calling them mythical materials.

When Bultmann declared that the whole cultural context in which the church arose was governed by all kinds of myths, mythological terms, and mythological constructs he created a serious problem. It turned out that everything that is held valuable and central in historic Christology is myth. It is not that part survives and part is discarded; the whole Christology must go. However Bultmann's concept of myth is so elastic that all Bultmann does not like in the New Testament could be myth, and at that point it becomes a definite subjective prejudice.

However some efforts have been made to save myth from being so totally objectionable as it is in Bultmann.

Myth can be saved from being the sort of thing impossible for a modern person to believe by two suggestions: (i) A myth gives genuine insight into the nature of reality. It is *ontological*, which means that although a myth has a shaky logical character it nevertheless is a means of expressing something that is true in human experience. It can be a literary means which gives us a window on a reality that may be difficult to set out in analytic sentences (Perrin: 1977). If a myth has no ontological element it is worthless. (ii) Myths can have historical roots. They need not be timeless truths. Hence the myth of the incarnation has its roots in the historical Jesus (Wiles in Hick: 1977, ch. 8).

165

C. S. Lewis is very severe with Bultmann, for he believes Bultmann does not understand what a myth is. It could be presumed that he could agree with much that Wiles and perhaps even Perrin might say of the function of myths in general. Lewis too admits that there are good myths and worthless myths. But there is this severe difference: *in the incarnation myth has become actual history.* As the Nicean and Chalcedonian creeds teach, God the Son literally took flesh (*assumptio carnis*) and appeared in history as the person of Jesus Christ. Therefore all mythological interpretations of the incarnation (in the attempt to do it justice) as a symbol, an insight, a paradigm, or a model of the relationship of God and man (e.g., Wiles) are betrayals of the incarnation. The reason why most followers of historic Christology are so allergic to the concept of myth is that, whether used in Bultmann's sense of that which is unbelievable or in a more constructive sense (Wiles, Perrin), it still amounts to a denial that the Logos of God truly, at a moment in time, stepped into human history in the person of Jesus Christ (John 1:14). Without that there is no salvation for the human race, and again, as Paul says in a somewhat different context (if it did not happen), "we are of all men to be pitied" (1 Cor 15:19—or as the word can also mean, "to be sympathized with").

One of the more enlightened discussion of myth and Christology is by H. Thielicke (1974-82, 1: 66-115). He grants that there are mythical elements in all our thinking and writing, even in science. But the Christian message is never myth as such. It is super myth or disarmed myth. The heart of his protest against Bultmann and his theory of myth is that the New Testament is plainly recording history. It is therefore very odd to convert history into myths. When the New Testament speaks out about the cross and resurrection as the historical basis of our redemption it has no intention whatsoever to be speaking mythically.

11

Historic Christology
in the Twentieth Century

RECENT CHRISTOLOGICAL THOUGHT

As stated in the prologue it would take an encyclopedia of Christology to do justice to the full range of Christology reflection. The range in one tradition alone can be both very rich and very complex. *An Expository Times* series of reviews of great books in the British tradition revealed how complex that tradition was (starting with Vol. 64, October, 1952). K. Reinhardt (1970) has written a very compendious and very serviceable survey of Christological thought. It has two limitations: it is limited to writings in the German language, and it does not closely link New Testament critical studies and their impact on Christology. The following is a survey (admittedly limited) of some of the Christological options in the twentieth century, as a preparation to the defense of historic Christology in the twentieth century.

LIBERAL CHRISTIANITY

Although we are commenting on Christologies of the twentieth century something must be said of Schleiermacher (1768-1834). He is recognized as the father of liberal theology and its Christology. Liberal theology as it came to be known in America in particular is closer to Ritschl than to Schleiermacher, but the fundamental scheme of the new Christology is set out in Schleiermacher. A few follow the precise lines of Schleiermacher's thought, yet Schleiermacher's Christology is a shadow cast over all of them.

Schleiermacher does not build upon an interpretation of biblical

Christological passages but commences with a philosophical scheme. He talks about being (*Sein*) which comprises the being of God and all the other beings (roughly, "objects") of the world. Man is dependent for his existence on the objects in his world (food, air, etc.), but he is absolutely dependent upon God for his spiritual or religious existence (*Existenzverhältnis*). When man has this sense of absolute dependence upon God then he has a God-consciousness. But this sense of God-consciousness Schleiermacher calls a feeling (*Gefühl*). Hence the feeling of absolute dependence and God-consciousness are the same. Sin is the disturbance of this God-consciousness in that we depend upon this world and not on God (i. e., sin is sensuousness or a misguided consciousness).

Christ is interpreted within this pattern. Christ had an undisturbed God-consciousness. This gave him a personality with great spiritual power. As such he is the divine type (*Urbild*) of a perfect God-consciousness, and thus he has in his personality a power to arouse a similar God-consciousness in us through the event of preaching. Because Christ's personality has the power in preaching about him to effect a change in us so that we too can come to God-consciousness, he is boldly called our Redeemer by Schleiermacher. Christ's sinlessness is a comment on his ability to maintain his God-consciousness undisturbed. His sufferings and his death reveal that firmness of his God-consciousness, for he maintained it unchanged until death.

Schleiermacher excluded from his Christology everything in the New Testament and historic Christology which did not fit this pattern. Some of the items that were so excluded were: the deity of Christ, the pre-existence of Christ, the virgin birth, the atoning death, a bodily resurrection, the ascension, and the return of Christ. Also excluded were the Christologies of the Creed of Nicea and the Definition of Chalcedon. As Reinhardt comments, this is Christology built totally on Schleiermacher's understanding of Melanchthon's famous words, which Reinhardt translates into the German as follows: "Christus erkennen, heisse nicht seine Naturen erkennen, sondern, seine Wirksamkeit" (to know Christ does not mean to know his natures but his efficacy [ibid., 65]).

Schleiermacher criticized both the New Testament and historic Christology. Sometimes he simply asserted that events such as miracles could not happen. Or he would reinterpret the older doctrine. For example, the pre-existence of Christ he reinterpreted to mean that Christ occurs in history by the providence of God.

Other things are matters of hagiography, such as the birth narratives or hyperbole as the language of our Lord's prayer in John 17. He could not advance his own Christology without such an attack upon the older Christology. It is not surprising either that so much of that which passes as current criticism of historic Christology is reprocessed Schleiermacher. In a sentence, Schleiermacher stands at the head of both modern or liberal Christology and the attack made upon historic Christology.

John Macquarrie thinks that Schleiermacher's opinions prevailed over historic Christology (1976, 36-39). He notes three items in which Schleiermacher's opinions were accepted: (i) that Christ as a truly human person replaces the Christ of a divine incarnation; (ii) that Greek vocabulary be dropped from Christological discussions; and (iii) that our faith in Christ be based on experience and not on the historical credibility of the Gospels which, as a matter of fact, historical criticism was eroding away. To repeat, much twentieth century and even recent Christology is reprocessed Schleiermacher.

A recent representative of the older views of Jesus in the liberal tradition is difficult to find. However in H. P. Van Dusen's (1963) *Vindication of Liberal Theology: A Tract for the Times* we have a bold, forceful defense of Jesus as understood in the classic, liberal American tradition. The book is composed from a series of lectures and therefore has a rhetorical character to it, with much overstatement.

Van Dusen lifts selectively from the gospel accounts a picture or version of Jesus which becomes the authoritative lens through which the Christian understands God and his purposes. Further, by looking through this lens we understand ourselves and the nature of the moral and spiritual life we should pursue. It is the faith of Jesus, the religious life of Jesus, the moral and ethical perception of Jesus which is the bedrock of the Christian faith. Shorn of Van Dusen's rhetoric, that which is defended is Christian faith based upon the religion that Jesus himself practiced and not a religion based on Jesus.

That Jesus Christ is the lens through which Christians look upon God, the world, history, and themselves (to see things as they really are) is not difficult for a follower of historic Christology to affirm. It follows from the doctrine of the incarnation. However Van Dusen has neither philosophical, theological, nor historical foundations for exalting one man to such a crucial relationship. It is an astounding decision to designate one man, one historical man, as the guide for all people of all ages. One must have profound theological and philosophical bases

169

for making such a claim. If Jesus Christ is not God-incarnate then Van Dusen's claims border on idolatry. Liberal theology has no theory of inspiration or revelation which can support such an enormous claim. Certainly in the light of current logical theory, philosophy of science, and stringent rules about writing history, this exaltation of Jesus must appear as arbitrary.

An odd question in Christology is, Was Jesus a Christian? For liberal theology, Jesus Christ was the first Christian. He was the ideal (*Urbild*), the model, the type, the paradigm of what humankind is supposed to be before God. We are Christians to the degree that we incorporate in our lives the kind of spirituality one finds in Jesus. In liberal theology Jesus was a Christian (and so in all paradigmatic Christology we shall discuss later).

Historic Christology affirms that Jesus was not a Christian. He is the Savior, the Lord. He stands apart from sinners as their Redeemer ("holy, blameless, unstained, separate from sinners," Heb. 9:26). Because he has not become totally one of us he can be the Savior. The first Christian is the first believer.

EXISTENTIAL CHRISTOLOGY

Kierkegaard is regarded as the founder of existential Christology. Both Bultmann and Tillich are deeply indebted to Kierkegaard's existential thinking about Christ. It is clear that Bultmann sees Jesus in existential categories, although it is also clear that his theological system is grounded in existentialism, especially with additions from Heidegger. An existential Christology is most apparent in Tillich.

Heidegger had used the terms authentic and inauthentic to describe human beings in the relationship of their responsibility to the call of Being. These terms can be roughly retranslated into faith and sin. Tillich retranslates them into New Being and Non Being. By New Being he says that he means the same thing as Paul does in 2 Corinthians 5:17, where he writes of being a new creation in Christ. Non Being describes the destructive forces of sin in a person. Salvation is to move from Non Being to New Being. But Tillich believes there must be one example in history where a person was able to live out New Being without falling into Non Being. That person is Jesus. Jesus as the Christ (Tillich's favorite expression) is Jesus as the one person who lived the authentic Christian life (or New Being) in the changes of history. Therefore he is the center of the Christian gospel. When Christ is preached there is the possibility that the listener can make his transition from his Non Being to New Being.

Admittedly such a short presentation of a system which runs to three volumes (*Systematic Theology*) is scarcely adequate. But an existentialist Christology arouses various apprehensions in a follower of historic Christology. The first apprehension is the same that we have with process Christology, namely, a philosophy intrudes itself too deeply in Christian thelogy. Tillich's system is a combination of Kierkegaard, Heidegger, and Schelling. And it is precisely this system which distorts the message of the New Testament.

There is no genuine interpretation of the Christological texts in Tillich. Tillich has his kind of interpretation. He takes a New Testament concept, gives it an existential reinterpretation, and says this is what the New Testament means. But jumping from New Testament texts to modern existential concepts is not an adequate interpretation of the New Testament. His Christology must be assessed as a philosophical and not a biblical Christology.

Finally, there is no Savior. Tillich has rightly been accused of being a gnostic, that is, regarding a Christian as one who sees and accepts this philosophical-theological system. In Tillich's system the offense of the cross has vanished, the miracle of the forgiveness of sins is gone, and justification by faith has been reduced to the modern psychological concept of self-acceptance.

We do not comment at this point on Bultmann's existential Christology since it has been considered throughout the body (of this work). However Reinhardt provides a compact summary of his system and Christology (1970, 240-270). Fritz Buri (of Basel) fits generally into the existential framework in Christology but takes his departure from the philosopher Jaspers (who finished his teaching career at Basel). He departs from Bultmann in seeing the Symbol as the bearer of the transcendental message of the Gospel and not the myth. In our analysis he comes close to a Hegelian type of Christology. Jesus Christ is not the unique Symbol of divine transcendence through whom we come to our own self-understanding, but by historical accident he is the Symbol for us who have grown up in the West. In other words, the historical Jesus is dispensable; that which is forever is our discovery of our own self-understanding through the encounter with some Symbol of transcendence. Reinhardt rightly criticizes this as virtually pure theologizing (or better, philosophizing) with the absolute minimum attention to scriptural texts (1970, 308-16).

171

There is also a measure of the existential in Gogarten's Christology although he prefers to use personalistic terms. His Christology need not be reviewed, but his radical distinction between personalistic concepts and objective concepts leads to the same split world that Bultmann has and upon which no adequate Christology can be built (cf. Reinhardt: 1970, 306-07).

The most massive effort of a Christology using an existential framework, yet at the same time seeking to be true to historic Christology, is that of Karl Rahner (1978, ch. 6). The entire volume is Rahner's summation of his theology with no footnotes and the absolute minimum of references to other scholars and works. One could contrast him to another existentialist, Kierkegaard. If Kierkegaard's goal was to set out the incarnation as an absolute shock to the human mind, arousing it to maximum passion, Rahner's goal is to show the continuity of fundamental theology with the special theology of salvation. He does this by setting up an understanding of God, the world, and humankind in which an incarnation does not necessarily happen, but if it did happen it would appear as part of the scheme of things. He everywhere gives the impression that we cannot simply confront a modern reflective person with the incarnation and ask him to believe it. Rahner works between two foci: (i) the natural order of created things with the mutual relationships of God, creation, and anthropology and (ii) the special saving actions of God. He wishes to avoid a purely rational theology from which one could even deduce the incarnation. And he does not want a special kind of theology which we must accept uncritically. So consciously working with insights from Heidegger's existentialism he builds up fundamental theology which leads to but does not demand salvation or soteric theology. Here the incarnation comes not as an oddity but something implicit in the scheme. From the absolute savior of fundamental theology comes the specific Savior, Jesus Christ, in salvation theology.

Such a rich exposition of an effort to make the incarnation (and historic Christology) believable to our generation deserves its own reading from each serious student. There is an interlocking of concepts, from the nature of God, to the nature of creation (the unity of matter and spirit), to the nature of human beings, so that the incarnation for all its historical speciality fits into the scheme of things. This is an impressive achievement in Christology.

Within the limits of this survey we can but express some apprehensions. (i) Rahner says himself that in such a sophisticated version of

Christology there is the danger of reducing Christology to a philosophy. Therefore he insists that he wants to preserve at all times the unique saving and personal character of the incarnation so that it does not become part of some Christian metaphysics. For all that self-conscious awareness of the danger, and all the efforts made to counter it, we may doubt if he has succeeded. (ii) Has Rahner felt the full weight of Kierkegaard's understanding of the incarnation, namely, that the incarnation requires such a mixing of categories that it shocks the reason as nothing else can? Granted there is overstatement in Kierkegaard, but can we ever really modulate the shock that an incarnation must give the human mind? (iii) We may not ignore the priority of the texts of Scripture. Whether Barth does a good job with the texts or not is beside the point; he does get to the texts of Scripture. One is bound to feel uneasy when such a great theme as Christology with all its impressive subthemes is discussed apart from the texts of Scripture. This must be the point of departure even though it may ultimately lead to such a graciously well-conceived system as Rahner's.

PROCESS CHRISTOLOGY

The process philosophy of Whitehead has created two waves of process theology in American theology. Out of the second wave of process theologians has come a process Christology written by D. R. Griffin (1973). He mentions three sources of his ideas: the New Quest (in which he sides against Bultmann), the neo-orthodox idea of revelation, and process philosophy.

Griffin's goal is to put Jesus in the center of the Christian faith, Christian preaching, and Christian worship by use of the philosophy of Whitehead, and not by the traditional procedures of historic Christology. He wants to show that Jesus is God's decisive revelation for the world and especially for the church but how can one elevate a person to that high status without going contrary to natural causation? Griffin claims that Whitehead's philosophy, while denying all supernatural events, nevertheless admits of special events, even a supreme event. And on those Whiteheadian premises he attempts to show that Jesus is God's supreme event, as it were, or God's decisive revelation. The other side of this coin is that Jesus' vision of reality is normative for Christians. In other words, Jesus does not teach a dogmatic system such as could be destroyed by critics and relativized by the panorama of history. But his vision of the kingdom of God and what God is doing in the world is the substance of Christian faith through the centuries.

Obviously we cannot do justice to any person's Christology in such short space nor tediously record all our apprehensions. But from the standpoint of historic Christology several points should be made.

First of all, it is clear where Griffin will not stand. He rejects the bodily resurrection of Christ, any strong doctrine of divine revelation, any doctrine of divine inspiration, and anything (historically understood) supernatural. He accepts much of the current sceptical conclusion of gospel criticism. This means that historic Christology is excluded.

Second, Whitehead receives nothing short of adulation:

> It is the formal thesis of the present essay that Whitehead's metaphysics provides us with a conceptuality never before equaled in its combination of appropriateness to the Christian faith and intrinsic excellence as measured by the normal rational and empirical criteria (1973, 165).

There is no question that a person can have his favorite philosopher. But by reinterpreting the whole Christian schema from the stance of Whitehead's philosophy Griffin runs the risk of making Whitehead look better than Jesus. The common sense of the church must eventually prevail that no one philosopher and no one philosophy is to be the canonical support of the Christian faith.

The principle logical flaw in his exposition is that from only natural resources Griffin attempts to make Jesus in some sense absolute. From relativities one cannot derive absolutes. It is not at all possible by natural methods to denote that Jesus' vision of reality *"was the supreme expression of God's eternal character and purpose"* (1973, 218; italics are his). Later he writes: "the Christian believes that *Jesus was God's supreme act of self-expression, and is therefore appropriately apprehended as God's decisive revelation"* (1973, 227; italics are his). There is nothing in the canons of logic nor of empirical science that permits statements about "supreme expressions" and "supreme acts." Whatever flaws maybe found in historical Christology it cannot be challenged about the grounds it has for affirming the highest lordship of Christ.

Finally, those who accept historic Christology must reject the distasteful pretension that in reality what the church has lived by through its many centuries has not been historic Christology but Jesus's vision of reality. The same claim is found in R. B. Mellert's account of process Christology (1975, ch. 7). But it is even more distasteful when

Mellert gives the impression that the only believers in historic Christology today are young, uneducated, misguided neo-fundamentalists and charismatics (1975, 76).

John Cobb's (1975) Christology in *Christ in a Pluralistic Age*, is also in the tradition of process theology with much emphasis on the writings of Whitehead. Although he has much in common with Griffin, Cobb approaches the Christological issues differently. In broadest compass his book attempts to answer two questions: (i) how can we speak uniquely of Jesus in an age of religious pluralism? (ii) how can we speak uniquely of Jesus in an age of full Enlightenment with its critical mentality in all departments of human study?

Before considering the basic theses of Cobb's Christology we should note that his Christology is a radical departure from historic Christology, although Cobb is at pains to indicate that he wishes to stand in the Christian tradition and so not appear as a radical innovator. In the historic meaning of the terms there is no deity of Christ, incarnation, sinlessness, virgin birth, atoning death, bodily resurrection, *Christus praesens*, nor return of Christ. Cobb freely states from time to time that historic Christology is an impossible position for him, even though at other times he tries to keep the tradition.

The book presents some astounding efforts to set up logical dilemmas (and in each case he claims a resolution on the side of the angels). How can we affirm the reality of pluralism in religion and yet not drown in a sea of relativities? How can we make Jesus totally human and yet maintain his uniqueness? How can we grant the conclusions of current New Testament criticism and still find within the Gospels normative materials about Jesus? In view of process philosophy souls must be declared impermanent, but how can we then affirm that they are important? How can we yet be Christian in an age that is so scientifically critical and philosophically agnostic?

Cobb's Christology is based on the concept that God is at work in each of us as a lure to coax us on to being better persons. But Cobb does not use the expression "better persons," preferring a more philosophical concept of "creative transformation." This activity of God in human persons Cobb labels as the Logos or the Christ. However this Logos or Christ activity going on in all persons came to a unique manifestation in Jesus. Cobb can then affirm the incarnation in the sense that in a historical person and in his historical life the Logos came to its fullest manifestation in Jesus (the parallel here with Tillich and Jesus as the historical example of New Being is very close). Hence the words of

175

Jesus and the pictures of Jesus in the Gospels (Cobb is not a sceptic about some knowledge of the historical Jesus) still have a working power to effect changes in us and thus creative transformation is possible. The similarities here with Schleiermacher's notion of the continuing power of Jesus' personality to affect people should not be overlooked. The Logos as the principle of creative transformation came to a unique manifestation in Jesus. Hence the pictures of Jesus in the Gospels and his words still have a working power to effect a change in us so that creative transformation takes place.

In the assessment of such a Christology the following may be briefly said:

(i) There is the same problem in Cobb as with Griffin. Whitehead threatens to come out looking better than Jesus, for apparently Cobb can believe in Jesus only if Jesus is placed in the rationale of Whitehead's philosophy. (ii) He attempts the usual rescue mission with its resulting Christology of the paradigm. He grants the radical conclusions of current New Testament critics and then attempts to salvage something for Christology from the authentic scraps which remain. At this point the shadow of Schleiermacher falls across Cobb's Christology. Soon another Albert Schweitzer will write a summary of the New Quest for the Historical Jesus showing that the New Questers were guilty of the same errors as the Old Questers. (iii) His solution to the Christological issue is essentially Hegelian. Namely Jesus is the incarnation of the Christ-idea. In principle this means that if Jesus never lived the Christ-idea (or Logos-idea) would yet remain valid. This means that the historical Jesus may be important to Cobb but his existence is negotiable. (iv) In a number of instances Cobb states that he cannot believe something in historic Christology because it is based on substance philosophy and not process philosophy, so it has to be given up or restated. But he never asks the question: what do New Testament texts state? Historic Christology claims its roots are in the New Testament and not substance philosophy. (v) Cobb is to be commended for setting out his logical knots. His Christology is only as good as his solution of these logical problems. In view of contemporary science, logic and scientific history, Cobb takes the position of the small minority and attempts to turn the logic in his favor. This is a very precarious situation for a Christology. (vi) He makes the kingdom central to Jesus' teaching and mission. That is always (or usually) the case when historic Christology is given up. It means that the cross and the resurrection along with the church as the redeemed people of God are not the center of Christian faith or theology. (vii) He has a severe problem by assenting to pluralism as a fact of our times and yet making Jesus unique. At one point his logic really fails. He asks the question whether other persons could have had the same fullness of the Logos in themselves as Jesus and admits that it is an outside possibility but lightly dismisses the problem on the grounds that we have no such records. But it is an enormously important point, records or not. If there are conceivably ten other persons who had the same fullness (or even more in theory!) of the Logos as Jesus, then Christology as a theme in Christian theology suffers a severe reversal. (viii) Cobb also gets into severe problems of a logical nature when he speaks of how full the Logos was in Jesus. There is no conceivable basis (apart from divine, special revelation) that Cobb can know that "Jesus existed in full unity with God's present purposes for his life" (1975, 141) or that "Jesus was fully open to the Logos" (1975, 146). How much Jesus was open to God or the Logos or the Christ is a spiritual-psychological fact that perished when Jesus died. There is no way of recovering that kind of datum about Jesus in the twentieth century. (ix) Again as in Griffin there is the patronizing attitude that what the church really believed (or—which is apparently the same—ought to have believed) was not the impossibilities of historic Christology but some version of process Christology. For example what the consubstantiality of the creeds really affirmed was not that Jesus is very God of very God but the Logos within him was truly God working as the lure to creative transformation. (x) We come back again to Brunner's observation that those who give up historic Christology ought to give up its vocabulary. When the incarnation of God in Christ is denied all such terms lose their meaning. Relevant here is H. Nicholson's (1971) thesis that if Jesus is really dead in a Palestinian grave we ought to admit the implications flat out. This means, Nicholson argues, that we cannot give numinous religious afterglows to Jesus as if in some mysterious way his influence spreads through history. Cobb's Logos-idea incarnate in Jesus is such a numinous afterglow attributed to Jesus.

Paradigm Christology

We have already mentioned how so many New Testament scholars have, for a variety of reasons, given up historic Christology. But such scholars have not given up the Christian faith (at least their own understanding of it). They have reworked their Christology. Reinhardt has asked the central question in Christology: "How can the once-for-all historical event (*Geschehen*) in Jesus of Nazareth possess final validity for the salvation for all persons? That is the heart question (*Kernfrage*) of Christology" (1970, 251).

These Christian scholars who have rejected historic Christology have worked out their own answer to Reinhardt's question. We call such attempts paradigm Christology. A paradigm means a model, a pattern, or an example. A paradigmatic Christology is one in which something about Jesus is declared to be unique in Jesus and therefore paradigmatic for all men. It involves an important methodological shift, which if not understood leaves the Christology blurred. The shift is from (i) Jesus as the one exhibiting something unique or paradigmatic in his life to (ii) Jesus as the theme of Christian preaching and object of Christian belief in virtue of this paradigmatic something. Or to express one such interpretation as a kind of motto: Jesus as the man of authentic faith becomes the Jesus as preached in the church and hence the object of our faith.

Jesus may be made paradigmatic in one of the following ways:

(i)   He exhibits that which God expects of humankind.

(ii)   He exhibits faith in its truest meaning.

(iii)   He aligned himself with the poor, the socially outcast, and the oppressed.

(iv)   He exhibited a special filial piety.

(v)   He exhibited a special nearness to God.

(vi)   He dared to speak with the authority of God.

(vii)   He was uniquely the Man for other men.

(viii) He was God's agent for introducing the kingdom of God.

(ix)   He is the model case of the life of God in the life of all people.

(x)   He was totally transparent to God or totally dedicated to the will of God.

(xi)   He was a completely authentic existential person.

(xii)   The will of Jesus was identical with the will of God.

(xiii) It is the cause-of-Jesus that carries over from Jesus to us.

(xiv)   Jesus loved as no other person loved.

(xv)   Jesus believed what he believed unto the death of the cross.

(xvi)   Jesus had an unprecedented intimacy with God.

(xvii) Jesus was the most Spirit-filled of all people.

(xviii) Jesus was God's representation and representative.

(xix)   Jesus is the paradigm of openness to God and willingness to be transformed.

178

Granted none of these are appealing when reduced to one sentence, but we are attempting to set out as clearly as possible both what is meant by paradigmatic Christology and the wide range of the current options. However, there is one logical flaw in all paradigmatic Christologies: in logical terms each one is built on a foundation of sand. Yet from this foundation of sand an absolute claim is made for Christ (except by those who, like Buri and Braun, do not make this absolute claim).

C. S. Evans (1979, 139-57) has written a remarkable essay in connection with such paradigm Christology. Evans distinguishes three kinds of people: Unbelievers have rejected the concept of God incarnate; Believers have maintained the tradition of the church and affirm the incarnation; and Adaptors have rejected the incarnation but add something else in its place to make Jesus central to faith. Evans remarks that having rejected the incarnation the Adaptors are quick to absolutize their own version of Jesus.

His main point is that terms should be used with consistency if there is to be meaningful communication. He gives an example from philosophy in which a materialist eventually comes to idealist convictions. At that point philosophers would demand that he give up the title of materialist. He refers to Kierkegaard's contention that because the Danish Hegelian Christians were not talking about the Christianity of the New Testament they therefore did not deserve the title of Christian. Evans thinks that Kierkegaard was right.

His conclusion is that only people who hold to the traditional view of the incarnation have the right to the name of Christian. The retoolers or reworders of the message of the New Testament do not deserve the name of Christian.

Paradigm Christology raises certain serious issues which apply also to process Christology and the Christology of religious liberalism.

(1) How can Jesus Christ in any sense be a person with universal saving significance if historic Christology is denied? Granted some modern writers (Hick, Buri) no longer hold to such a universal character for Jesus Christ—yet it seems that the defenders of paradigm Christology still do. But in view of all the denials about the nature of the New Testament, of the supernatural, and of historic Christology, defenders of paradigm Christology have surely undermined any possible universal significance for Jesus Christ.

It is a logically difficult matter to claim one historic person has universal significance for all persons. The doctrine of the incarnation

179

solves the issue at the logical level for historic Christology. If God becomes incarnate, then the incarnation has universal relevance. But what gives Jesus Christ universal relevance if the incarnation is denied? There is to our way of thinking no answer to this in paradigm Christology.

(2) How can one avoid the dilemma that, by declaring one human being who is only a man as having universal significance for the salvation of all people, one is in danger of lapsing into idolatry? The prophets of the Old Testament proclaimed the Word of God and never became saviors or mediators. If Jesus Christ is a man and only a man, he is a creature. It is by definition idolatry if the creature, any creature, is made to function in the place of God. How can Jesus Christ, regarded as only a man, as only a creature, be definitive and decisive in my relationship to God?

(3) H. Nicholson's (1971, 60) book, *Jesus is Dead,* is neither learned nor profound, but there is a rugged honesty about it. He attacks men like Tillich (and in our mind all defenders of paradigm Christology) who deny the resurrection and must therefore affirm that Jesus is dead yet seek to give Jesus a quasi-resurrection status. If Jesus is dead, reasons Nicholson, he is dead with all his claims. To pretend that Jesus lives on in some sense, in any sense, Nicholson calls *the primitive hangover.*

> [Jesus] does not motivate the people who wear the Christian label, nor does he activate the services that are rendered in the name of the institution. It is impossible for Jesus to do that because he is dead, and has been dead for nearly two thousand years. It is not Jesus who lives. It is rather a primitive hangover which insists on this assumption that persists. It is out of such primitive persistence..., that grave religious frustration grows.

We seem to be caught here between total scepticism about the Gospels or accepting the affirmations of historic Christology. But, as we have seen, many recent writers (Griffin, Cobb, Pittenger, Knox, Käsemann) shy away from a total scepticism about Jesus. Käsemann (1954, 61-62) pleads:

> There are no grounds for lapsing into a defeatist scepticism; there are at least some things about which we can have maximum certainty and which free us from the necessity of judging the faith of the community [of the early Christian church] to be arbitrary and meaningless.

Yet how can Käsemann speak of Jesus as the Lord of the church, or

Cobb describe him as the Logos, or Marxsen appeal to the Cause of Jesus (*Sache Jesu*) if Jesus is dead? Nicholson is right as far as he goes. If Jesus is dead we ought to be rid of all notions of a "primitive hang-over," an afterglow, or a continuing powerful personality and the like. Admittedly, historic Christology may be wrong, but its logic is right in its understanding of the continuing power of Jesus Christ in the church and in the world: *Christus Victor!*

(4) In an effort to update recent studies in Christology and yet present the various views in a manageable way we have employed the concept of paradigm. The concept of a model or paradigm comes from scientists (in the nineteenth century) who imagined pictures of their theories. In fact one famous scientist said he could *only* imagine theories if he could imagine pictures of them. Of course, modern atomic science is so complex that the day of picture-models is over with, but the notion of a model has been carried on and has been brought into theology. The procedure followed here is to describe a given Christological model, list the advantages and disadvantages of the model, and conclude with a very important list of criteria that any valid Christological model must contain. To the extent that is done here, paradigm Christology has its proper focus.

LIBERATION CHRISTOLOGY

Liberation theology is a very broad term, but we are limiting it here to Latin American Christianity. Even so, it covers both Catholic and Protestant writers, as well as evangelical and non-evangelical. However these share some common themes.

The context of liberation theology and its Christology is the terrible conditions found in Central and South America. The following all exist in an acute degree: hunger and starvation, numerous diseases (many of which can be traced to malnutrition), high rate of unemployment, fluctuating labor markets, exploitation by foreign capital, oppression by military governments and/or dictatorships, radical division between the rich, powerful class and the poor class, which exists in terrible slums. This situation is structural because there is nothing in their national constitutions which permit a meaningful change of course. All these miseries could be summed up in one word: oppression. And if there is one word which sums up the Christian response, it would be liberation. Some of the common traits of liberation Christology are represented in Jon Sobrino's *Christology at the Crossroads*.

(1) The development of Christology in the Patristic period, the Reformation period, and the post-Reformation period is seen as too philosophically oriented, too cerebral, too abstract, and too divorced from the sufferings of life.

When a Christology is so written and so defended it cannot help but support the current oppressive political and economic order. So today those who vigorously defend Chalcedon are also unwittingly defending the economic and political *status quo*.

(2) Jesus Christ is seen primarily as the Liberator. One can contrast this with Augustine's quest for the Christ as Purifier, with Justin Martyr's Christ as the Logos, or with Luther in quest of the merciful and gracious Savior.

(3) Jesus Christ is seen as a political rebel. Rather than being put to death as a blasphemer (traditional view) he was executed as a political rebel.

(4) The picture of Jesus "meek and mild" can be painted only by neglecting the full picture of Jesus in the Gospels. There are the incidents in which Jesus is morally indignant. There is the blistering attack of Jesus upon the religious leaders of the times (e.g., Matthew 23). There is the Jesus who speaks a sharp word against Herod. And there is the Jesus who does not cower before Pilate but puts him on the defensive.

(5) The cross and the resurrection are not to be seen in a narrowly individualistic manner as the means by which we are each saved. Rather they are to be seen in the context of liberation from oppression (cf. Moltmann: 1974).

(6) It is a *von unten* Christology. Christology must commence with the historical life of Jesus since all other points of beginning are too abstract or too theologically shaped already. It is in the historical Jesus that one can see Jesus' concern for the poor, the socially outcast, and the politically powerless, that is, Jesus' own praxis.

(7) The kingdom of God and Christology mutually interpret each other. The kingdom of God is interpreted as the gradual (or sudden!) transformation of this wicked world order into the order of God's justice and love.

When one reads of the wretched conditions of these Latin American countries in Bonino's *Doing Theology in a Revolutionary Age*, criticism of such a Christology seems impious. But we have seen that if we reject criticism under any circumstances we simply invite the possibility of even greater evil. We therefore list a few of our doubts concerning a Christology of liberation.

(1) It represents an excessive reaction to the regional situation, whether in Latin America or Africa. Certainly Christians of all ages and places have seen Christ through the grid of their own culture and their own problems. Christians in oppressive countries have every right to see Christ from their perspective. Our concern is that the total rewriting of Christology from such concerns must in the long run produce a limited, parochial Christology. If Christology loses its universality it loses itself.

(2) The second concern is with the centrality of *praxis*. The concept of praxis means that only those in a situation know the dynamics of the situation and therefore are the only ones qualified to make decisions. Even a theologian as sympathetic to liberation theology as Moltmann was denied the right to offer advice to the churches of South America on the grounds that he lived in Europe.

Praxis thinking seems simply that those who so think are exempt from the logical and ethical scrutiny of their opinions. This was the *reductio ab adsurdum* of existential and situational ethics, for if we know the right decision in the context of the decision then all others not in that context are incompetent to judge the decision. There is an element of truth in the assertion that only those in a situation know its factors and dynamics. But it has always been unhealthy to exempt any movement from the moral, factual, historical, and ethical scrutiny of its opinions.

One other item that makes us restless with the concept of praxis is that it derives from Marx. According to Marx it was not the intellectuals nor the economically intrenched persons who understand the social situation. Only workers and those identified with the workers can know what the plan of action must be. This then cuts off any criticism of praxis, and labels the thinking of the intellectuals as specious. But in our opinion to cut off in principle any criticism of a movement by whatever maneuver is dangerous. In fact sometimes it is the outsider who has the clearest vision of things. An anthropologist living with a tribe to learn its structure knows more about the tribe than the tribal members. And in linguistics it has been said that those who were raised outside a given language group can be a more accurate student of that language than its speakers.

(3) Chalcedon cannot be so readily discarded as being too abstract or too philosophical. As we have already pointed out more than once, the issues of Chalcedon are in the New Testament itself. If a theologian is going to deal responsibly with the text of Scripture, one must wrestle

with the problems of Chalcedon. If Chalcedon were all that formal, all that theological and philosophical, all that divorced from the gospel texts itself, it never would have gained such a hold in the church. And we have also noted that those who reject Chalcedon cannot propose an alternate theory commanding general assent.

Finally, a theoretical concern may be a valid concern. The great defect of the pragmatic mind has been its failure to realize that a theoretical question can have as much relevance and passion for some thinkers as concrete problems have for others. In fact if some men did not have this passion for the theoretical we should not have science. So even if Chalcedon be written off as speculative this does not mean that it did not express a valid passionate concern of the fathers in the early church.

POST-AUSCHWITZ CHRISTOLOGY

M. B. McGarry (1977) has summed up the reaction among Christian theologians to three recent developments: (i) Hitler's effort to exterminate the Jews and the issue of antisemitism; (ii) the emergence of the state of Israel; and (iii) recent rabbinic studies which show how Jewish Jesus' background was. Among the key issues discussed are: (i) did historic Christology have anything to do with the persistence of antisemitism, which was a large factor in Hitler's thought; and (ii) how does the Christian concept of the finality of Jesus Christ relate to our understanding of the Old Testament and of the Jewish people? Some of the important matters emerging from McGarry's survey follow.

(1) The relationship of the Christian church to the Jewish people, the synagogue, and the Old Testament is complex because the Christian faith is rooted simultaneously in the Old Testament and first-century Judaism; but it also claims to go beyond the Old Testament with the New Testament and beyond the synagogue with the church. Jesus Christ is at the hinge of this transition, hence the issue is Christological.

(2) The church has commonly taken a *supersessionist* view, which means that the church replaces Israel as the people of God, and hence there is no future for Israel except in the church. But this approach has unwittingly aided antisemitism. Hence the New Testament itself has been called an antisemitic book.

(3) Opposite the supersessionist theory are various dialogical theories: Jews and Christians have such common roots that they ought to be in conversation. This is not a question of mere fraternizing but gen-

uine dialogue aimed at mutual correction and enrichment. All supersessionist language is to be avoided.

(4) The two-covenant theory is that God has really two people (Israel and the church), under two covenants, each to go its own way with mutual respect through history.

(5) The Jewishness of Jesus is to be clearly set out in our Christology to show how seriously the church understands its roots in the Old Testament, in Judaism, and in the synagogue.

(6) All church documents, hymnology, etc. are to be purged of anti-semitic statements.

(7) The most difficult problem of all for Christians is how to understand the finality of Jesus Christ. Some see it leading inevitably to supersessionist views and so look for the conversion of Jews to the Christian faith; others understand it as leading to some kind of two-covenant theory, whereby God has never repudiated his covenant with Israel but has added on another covenant in Jesus Christ; and members of both covenants are to keep peace with each other.

In current theological studies the manner in which the two Testaments are to be related is a very controversial one. This raises the issue of supernaturalism. There could be an intimate relationship between the two Testaments only if God guided the course of human history to such an end and supernaturally revealed his purposes to the prophets. If a theologian denies such supernaturalism one cannot accept the traditional Christian view of the relationship of the Testaments. Others believe that there is a valid connection between the two Testaments but reject the church's historic view as too artificial. It also tended to undermine the integrity of the Old Testament. Hence the relationship of the two Testaments must be restated in more acceptable terms.

However it seems unavoidable that as articulate Christians we must face the scandal of affirming that the Old Testament comes to its central intention in the person and work of Jesus Christ. However this need not be affirmed crudely or offensively. Regin Prenter (1960, 298) has stated the relationship in an excellent way. He affirms that whatever we say of Christ and the Old Testament can be said only in a backward, reflexive way. Only in Jesus Christ can we decode the intent of the promise character of the Old Testament. Hence there can be no charge against Israel as if her scholars were mentally dull, prejudiced, or unable to see the Christological character of the promises of the Old Testament. The promising must be understood by the nature of the fulfilling and not the reverse.

Brevard Childs (1979, ch. 44) has responded to such scholars as Gese and Ludberg who wish to make a radical difference between the Christian Old Testament as a book and the Jewish Bible as a book. Childs will not allow a division either in the matter of the text of the Old Testament or its canon so as to create a distinct Jewish Old Testament and a distinct Christian Old Testament. He seeks to preserve the unity of text, canon, and message, and with this we concur.

A very unusual and important book, *The Jewish Reclamation of Jesus,* by D. A. Hagner, preceives that Jewish scholars have now come to a fuller realization that Jesus is a Jew, and therefore there must be some authentic Jewish materials about Jesus in the New Testament. Jewish scholars in modern Israel have produced recently more material on Jesus than in the whole history of the subject matter up to that point. There are also some beginnings of the study of Paul strictly as a Jewish person to see what measure of authentic Judaism one might find in Paul. This interest from the Jewish perspective may lead to a new appreciation for the unity of the testaments.

CRITICALLY RECONSTRUCTED CHRISTOLOGY

By a critically reconstructed Christology we mean a Christology that accepts in general the current methods of New Testament studies and some of its conclusions but seeks to maintain some continuity with historic Christology. Even so the variations among practioners of critically reconstructed Christology are large.

Catholic theologians such as Schillebeeckx (*Jesus: An Experiment in Christology*) and Küng (*On Being a Christian*) have much in common. Both list detailed modern bibliographies, especially of critical New Testament studies, showing extensive reading in the Christological literature. Both are Enlightenment men, believing that we must come to terms with the Enlightenment before we have the privilege to speak as Christians. Further, both believe that a theologian must come to terms with modern critical studies of the New Testament as a condition of voicing opinions in Christology. Both men believe that they are trying to save the gospel for this age. Both are influenced by European and Third World versions of liberation theology. Finally, both believe that the *von unten* approach is the only option for modern theologians (even Roman Catholic ones).

The case of Schillebeeckx is a bit more complicated. He exerts an enormous influence on Roman Catholic thought in Holland and ministers to a student body of more than six hundred. One gets a very personal insight from an interview with Teofilo Cabestrero, who wrote a book based on interviews with fifteen theologians. The more specific theological details are reviewed in Peter Hebblethwaite's book, *The New Inquisition? The Case of Edward Schillebeeckx and Hans Küng.* Schillebeeckx was requested to come to Rome for a dialogue and conversation about his famous book, *Jesus: An Experiment in Christology.* The theological guardians of the true Catholic faith posted at the Vatican came to the conclusion that Schillebeeckx had compromised the historic Catholic creedal Christology (Nicea, Chalcedon, Athanasian), and that his statements about the virgin birth, the miracles of Jesus, and the resurrection appeared ambiguous. Both Hebblethwaite and Cabestrero picture Schillebeeckx as the purely scholarly type, very much divorced from settling matters by a courtroom procedure. But he did make his reply. He said that he was denying nothing of Roman Catholic faith. His book on *Jesus* was an effort to see what could be saved of the Gospels if one subjected them to the sharpest critical analyses of the time. Further, he had planned a trilogy of Christology, in which he would affirm his positive Christological beliefs; his questioners should wait for these publications. He argued that one could not simply unload the Christology of the Patristic period on modern students or congregations, for this way of thinking would have no real meaning to them. If one writes on Christology or preaches on it one has to do it within the life and in the conceptual circle of the modern person. So Schillebeeckx argued that he is not denying historic Christology but trying to put it in such language and in such a way it could have meaning to modern people. And so one must decide whether Schillebeeckx is saying the old dogma in a new way, or is denying the old dogma by the use of modern learning and its concepts.

It is perhaps unfair to lump together two thinkers and their massive books under a few words of criticism, but we have no other option short of a book on the subject. However both Küng and Schillebeeckx display certain common features. Both are Roman Catholic scholars. Both suffer from a serious ambiguity. Both claim that they are doing their best to restate Roman Catholic theology for the times. But do they really do this? Is the Schillebeeckx account of the resurrection really what the Roman Catholic church has taught? Does Küng believe the virgin birth in the same sense as a Roman Catholic theologian of the year 1850? To this writer there is not only an uncertainty but a very disturbing ambiguity, for the expositions come through in popular language as double-talk. ("Yes, of course I believe all that you do, but I choose to express it rather differently.")

Can two such theologians grant such authority in their minds to Enlightenment mentality and modern critical conclusions in New Testament studies and still be faithful to historic Christology? We think not. We must all come to terms with the best in modern scholarship and with that which we think has real substance in biblical criticism, but granting crown rights to either crowds fundamental Christian convictions. For the courage which tackles the issues of the times to save Christian faith there can be only admiration. Our complaint is that the pronounced methodology cannot achieve the goal intended.

There are many other Roman Catholic scholars who attempt a critically reconstructed Christology (Raymond Brown, Rudolph Schnackenburg) and who certainly defend something much closer to historic Christology. There are also Protestant New Testament scholars who attempt a critically reconstructed Christology (i.e., who work generally with modern critical methods but come to more historic conclusions). With some variations this would be true of Marshall, Moule, Bruce, and a number of the scholars contributing to Marshall's (editor) *New Testament Interpretation*. Historic Christology can never give an *imprimatur* to either obscurantism in its scholarship or bibliolatry in its doctrine of authority.

CHRISTOLOGY AND MYSTICISM

The main tradition in mysticism has been an encounter with God. But there has been a mysticism in the Christian tradition which centers in Christ. Among the most famous of the Christ-centered mystics is Bernard of Clairvaux (1090-1153), especially for his famous sermons on the Song of Songs. To the Christ of Christian mysticism we may add the Christ of devotional literature in the Protestant tradition, which has similarities to the Christ of mysticism. Both reflect an intense, personal doctrine of *Christus praesens*. A significant dimension of the mystical and devotional Christ has been within the fundamentalism movement; this has not been appreciated because it has not become popularly known.

However a more articulate Christology of mysticism is found in James Stewart's, *A Man in Christ*. It is built upon the Pauline expression, *in Christ*. This Stewart takes to be a mystical expression, for it expresses union with Christ, and it is a union which can only be understood mystically. One of the reasons for a mysticism which centers in Christ is that relentless attention to the rational and theological part of faith divides the Christians. Those who seek mystical unity with Christ find it natural to find unity with their fellow Christians.

The most obvious reference to a mystical experience in Paul's writing is 2 Corinthians 12:1-10. Here are such typical mystical expressions as being caught up to heaven, not knowing whether he was in the body or out, and the experience of ineffable revelations. Paul was showing that in unusual gifts he was not less endowed than any of the charismatics of the Corinthian church. That we all are mystics, as a necessary part of the Christian faith, cannot be denied. It has been rightly said that whoever prays is a mystic. In the more articulate sense of the word most Christians have not been mystic. But that the Christ of the devotional experience should be ever preached and taught, is essential.

REVELATIONAL CHRISTOLOGY

One of the major Christological treatises of the times is Wolfhart Pannenberg's (1968) *Jesus—God and Man*. His system is a complex tapestry of elements from Old Testament scholars, New Testament scholars, and Hegel. He believes that all of history is under the direction of God ("God is the power over all things") and therefore a revelation of God. But it is an indirect revelation which must be deciphered. The clue for deciphering the meaning of history while in transit stems from the eschatological and apocalyptic writing of the Old Testament prophets. Therefore in principle a theologian can discover the revelation of God in history by clues given him by the Old Testament prophets. But as a matter of fact only in Jesus Christ is the Old Testament vision clear enough to be a principle of real interpretative power. Further, only in the resurrection of Jesus Christ is the person of Christ clarified. All that Jesus claimed for himself and taught of the kingdom of God is ambiguous until the resurrection; then all is clarified.

Pannenberg makes a stout defense of the resurrection of Christ. He believes that the evidence of 1 Corinthians 15:1-7 is very substantial, and joined with the independent "empty tomb" tradition of the Gospels it forms a compelling historical case. He discounts the critics of the New Testament for being sceptics rather than historians. He discounts the historicist veto by saying that all historical events are unique and therefore the uniqueness of the resurrection cannot count against it. And he is not hampered by the scientists, for he says not all the laws of science are known, and therefore it is premature to dismiss the resurrection as non-scientific.

He defends the true-man=true-God thesis in the context of a theol-

189

ogy of revelation. He objects to Chalcedon for he says one cannot join two substances—an unbelievable literal interpretation of the Definition. Rather he seems to defend a progressive incarnation. Jesus' will and mind is one with God and this increases more and more in his ministry. Finally it comes to its fulfillment at the resurrection.

There is much to justify high appreciation of Pannenberg's Christology (see Dawe: 1972, 269ff.). However, we experience difficulty with Pannenberg's inconsistent methodology, which is to be found in all of his writings. At times he cites the biblical text; at other times the key thought is from Hegel; and still other times he argues from modern anthropological science. He has written technical materials on the medievalists, and his work on Christology shows much study of patristic Christology. He rejects the virgin birth and accepts the bodily resurrection.

Pannenberg should be classified with Christologies of the future, though he like Moltmann (1974) is also difficult to classify. The latter has been classified as a Word theologian, a futurologist, and a theologian of liberation. Moltmann's method is also perplexing. When Moltmann wants to cite Scripture he does that; or when he wants to dip into the history of theology he does that. To interpret the cross and resurrection in the motifs of liberation is certainly strained exegesis. Moltmann gives the impression of getting the right message for some contemporary issues by using the wrong methods. The passion for social justice we can understand; his Christological method bewilders.

THE RATIONALE FOR HISTORIC CHRISTOLOGY

MODERN DEFENDERS

When *The Myth of God Incarnate* (1977) was published it gave the impression (whether or not endorsed by the authors) that nobody of any theological merit believed in the incarnation. This is an impression not uncommonly found in the critical materials of contemporary Christological writing. The purpose of this section is to counter that impression by reviewing some of the defenders of historic Christology in the twentieth century. The scholars mentioned represent a spectrum of theological positions, but have in common their affirmation of historic Christology.

Before listing these individuals it must be said that there is a large corporate body of believers in historic Christology. This would include all the scholars in the Eastern Orthodox tradition (cf. Meyendorff: 1969) and those Roman Catholic scholars throughout the world who are faithful to the historic stance of their church on Christology. It would also include all the Protestant theologians who remain loyal to the historic Christology in the creeds of their denominations, especially those written from the sixteenth through the eighteenth centuries.

Although B. B. Warfield wrote in the earlier part of this century he is a scholar to be recognized in Christology. His specialized studies on Calvin and Augustine are still read and cited in English literature and in the literature of other European languages. Warfield wrote much on Christology (e.g., *The Lord of Glory* and *Christology and Criticism*). There are also Christological essays in *Biblical and Theological Studies* and extended book reviews in *Critical Reviews*. Although Warfield died in 1921 it is clear in reading his works that the fundamental issues in criticism and two-nature Christology have not essentially changed. Warfield was a scholar who used his massive learning and his sharp intellect to defend vigorously historic Christology.

Dietrich Bonhoeffer's work, *Christology*, comprises lectures given in his unique seminary and recovered from student notebooks. A reading of this book shows how much "pop-Bonhoeffer" is misleading. It is a solid defense of substantially Lutheran Christological thought. There are embellishments to the Lutheran perspective, coming from Bonhoeffer's own studies and thought patterns of the time. One can find in the book strong affinities to Kähler and severe attacks on liberal Christology.

The first edition of Emil Brunner's (1927) *The Mediator (Der Mittler)* did not appear in English translation until 1947. Much of the greatness of this work has been obscured by the debated course of neo-orthodox theology and questions about the orthodoxy of Brunner's view of divine revelation and inspiration. When read today after the impact of Bultmann and his school, Brunner's book stands out as a great defense of historic Christology. Brunner saw very clearly that one's stance in Christology was also one's whole stance towards Christian theology and Christian mentality. Therefore his exposition time and time again spills over the narrow lines of traditional Christology. Granted, Brunner is sceptical about the nice refinements of Chalcedon, for he reasons that an incarnation is a mystery beyond our ability to comprehend. But he develops a total theological enterprise in which he embeds his own version of historic Christology.

Because Barth and Bultmann were close together in the 1920s it is not unusual to find them linked together as if co-founders of neo-orthodoxy, and as if the differences between the two men were trivial. This is unfortunate, for at the end of the 1920s a permanent split occurred. From the 1950s on the differences have been substantial. In *Church Dogmatics* (IV/1, ix) Barth says that he wrote the whole volume in silent conversation with Bultmann. One factor in Barth's great objectification and universalism in theology is precisely his concern to counteract what he thinks is the great subjectivizing of the faith in Bultmann. And to sharpen up his differences with Bultmann he wrote a small booklet on the theme (Karl Barth, *Rudolph Bultmann: Ein Versuch, ihn zu verstehen; Theologische Studien,* Heft 34, 1952).

The thirteen volumes of Barth's *Church Dogmatics* could be called a sustained treatise in Christology. John Thompson (1978) has done a service in attempting to summarize Barth's Christology. There is also a brief but very competent summary of Barth's Christology in Reinhardt's book (1970, 221ff.). Herman Volk has also summarized the Christology of both Barth and Brunner (see Grillmeier: 1975, 3: 613-73).

The Christological materials in Barth's *Church Dogmatics* are so extensive, and the Christological reworking of so many themes (creation, sin, anthropology) is so different, that simple judgments about Barth are difficult. Some scholars, both Protestants and Catholics, suspect that a whole new Christological heresy is smuggled into Barth's Christology (cf. van Til: 1960, 147-66). Others find in him the great restorer of Chalcedon Christology. In the briefest possible way it can be said that Barth has had the following guides in mind in the writing of his Christology: (i) to interact at much depth with the biblical materials; (ii) to maintain historic Christology; (iii) to offer a modern statement of it by attempting to correct the more formalistic and static concepts of the past with more dynamic concepts of the present; and (iv) to give a Christological reinterpretation of every major Christian doctrine. It will be in the wearing of the years that the success of this massive adventure in Christology will be better assessed.

The only competitor to Barth in producing a multi-volumed dogmatics has been G. C. Berkouwer with his *Studies in Dogmatics.* The basic thrust in all his volumes is to present the best possible case for Reformed theology in the context of contemporary theology. His work on Christology, *The Person of Christ*, follows this pattern. Berkouwer is informed of the issues, and each chapter contains a learned and vigorous defense of historic Reformed Christology.

D. M. Baillie's *God Was in Christ* has been one of the most significant books in Christology in the English speaking world. Part of its reputation was due to its unexpectedness. It challenged an unspoken assumption that only New Testament scholars could write anything significant in Christology. It was also a very judicious corrective of some older views in Christology, as well as a stout defense of historic Christology. Baillie was especially strong in his repudiation of docetism in Christology.

Heinrich Vogel's dogmatics is entitled *Gott in Christo* and is similar to Barth in being a theology governed by Christology. It is a massive work of over a thousand pages with no references save biblical ones. His style is a wonderful combination of the academic, theological, homiletical, and the devotional. It is thoroughly on the side of historic Christology but frequently expresses things Christocentrically rather than following accustomed dogmatic formulations.

From the German Roman Catholic side has come Walter Kasper's *Jesus the Christ*. It is a stout defense of historic Roman Catholic Christology, while at the same time interacting with the best of German New Testament scholarship. In a surprising way he does here and there make considerable concessions to criticism, but on the other hand offers some sturdy challenges to the mood of current scholarship, as, for example, when he says that the early church creeds are not strange mixtures of Christian ideas and Greek substance philosophy.

At the end of his career Helmut Thielicke summarized his theology in three volumes which he calls *The Evangelical Faith*. Thielicke claims to have reconciled biblical criticism and the evangelical faith of the Lutheran tradition. He therefore does not assent to all of historic Christology. But the main thread of this though in *The Evangelical Faith* is solidly historic Christology, with the expected Lutheran modifications of it.

Russell Aldwinckle's *More Than Man* is a British-Canadian contribution. It is marked by scholarship, by an attempt to come to terms with the more recent issues in Christology, and it takes its stance in historic Christology. Some topics discussed by Aldwinckle are not found in other works in Christology, and therefore he makes an extra contribution at that point.

J. B. Phillips' *The Ring of Truth* is a small book and does not cover

Christology in any major way. Rather it is a protest against the scepticism in recent New Testament criticism, especially of the Gospels. Phillips' main point stems from his work as a translator over many years. When one is as immersed in translating as he has been, there is a sensitivity to the text, which cannot be obtained any other way. The Gospels have for Phillips *the ring of truth*. He also records in this book two appearances of C. S. Lewis after Lewis' death. The appearances came at times when Phillips was stuck with a difficulty in translation. Lewis appeared as in real life, gave the clue to the translation, and then disappeared.

Otto Weber's *Grundlagen der Dogmatik* (2 Vols.) is an impressive statement of the Barthian theology but with the clear impress of Weber's own scholarship. The book is magisterial in the manner in which it is outlined (hence it borders on the pedantic at times). But nonetheless with great learning in historic theology, it sets out a Barthian version of Reformed theology. In doing so Weber also stands squarely in the tradition of historic Christology.

The annotations need not be extended save to repeat the thesis that the world of theologians and of New Testament scholars have not deserted to modern critical views of Christology. Other theologians could be mentioned, such as Mascal, Thornton, Torrance, Turner, Grillmeier, Rahner, Bromiley, Prenter, Elert, Gollwitzer, and Wingren. Among New Testament scholars one can mention such names as Bruce, Marshall, Moule, Machen, Beasley-Murray, Kallas, Guthrie, Cullmann, Schneider, Ladd, Ellis, Brown, and Schnackenberg. Historic Christology does still have its scholars in the twentieth century, which means that the case for a reconstructed critical Christology is not yet as secure as presumed.

A Savior

The Apostles' Creed has been the object of much research. At root it is the convert's confession (cf. Stead: 1979, 4-8). Hippolytus of Rome sets out the different lines of the creed as questions asked to the baptismal candidate. This means that the creed arose in the context of personal salvation.

The great debate at Alexandria between Arius and Athanasius pivoted on the question of who could really save humankind. Is salvation possible by the second god (*deuteron theon*) of Arius, or could only God save us? In his work, *On the Incarnation*, Athanasius said as clearly as it could be said that humankind could be redeemed only by the incarnation of the Logos. When the bishops met at Nicea and formulated their creed, it affirmed that the incarnation was "for us men and our salvation." If the Symbol or Definition of Chalcedon is but the clarification of Nicea about the nature of the incarnation, then it too has human salvation as its central motive.

Contrary to more that has been written about these creeds, the bishops were not primarily concerned with putting biblical language into the language of Greek substance philosophy. Whatever they did pick up from the Greek language was for the more precise explanation of what they found in Scripture. Their primary concern was to develop a doctrine of a Savior who could really save.

Historic Christology has one overriding passion and that is to have a doctrine of salvation that really saves. And it does not view the debates in the early church as theological wrangling over abstract issues. From Athanasius to Barth, from Anselm to Luther, from Calvin to Torrance, the central concern has been to have a Savior and a gospel which can save men. At the center of the discussion of the incarnation and the atonement is the point, made so clearly by Anselm, that the two were one doctrine.

It is only God who can save us. But for Anselm it is more precisely God-incarnate who must save. It was Anselm who said in so many words that if one faces the true weight of sin there is no other answer to sin but the incarnation. Therefore historic Christology necessarily emphasizes the full humanity of Christ. A dictum from the Patristic period says that that which Christ did not take he cannot save. This means positively that Christ took total humanity in order to save the whole person. Therefore, the full humanity of Christ is as much a passionate concern in historic Christology as in the full deity of Christ.

Van Dusen pokes fun at the Sixth Council of Constantinople (AD 680) because it propounded that Jesus had a human will and a divine will (1963, 33). The issue before the council was whether Jesus had a full humanity or not. True to Chalcedon's Definition it believed that Jesus Christ was fully man and therefore must have a will. As odd as the psychology of the times might appear to us, we must not overlook the fact that they were protecting the full humanity of Christ.

Both the Apostles' Creed and the Nicean Creed speak of the career of Jesus: he was crucified, he was buried, he rose from the dead, he ascended to heaven, and he shall return again for salvation and judgment. This means that Christology is not limited to assertions about

195

the person of Christ but include his saving activity. The person and work of Christ "co-inhere." The person and work of Christ join together to present a Savior to the world. That is the ultimate rationale of historic Christology. Historic Christology claims that its Christology alone presents a Savior who can truly save. Christologies which come short of historic Christology present a Christ who cannot truly save. He may be a spiritual catalyst, a model, a paradigm, or a divine man, but he is not a Savior.

If historic Christology is rejected it does not mean that a theologian abandons Christology. One of the ways of coming to terms with modern criticism and to yet maintain importance for Jesus is to settle for a reduced Christology. A reductionist Christology is any Christology which comes measurably short of historic Christology.

The general formula of reductionist Christology is to point out something unique about Jesus Christ which raises him above other men but does not raise him to deity. It could be said that he had a unique vocation before God, or he was a God-filled man or he was the Agent of the kingdom or he is the existential Model for all men. Or he is the saving picture!! However, the point is that when historic Christology was surrendered, some form of reductionist Christology took its place.

Those who advocated a reductionist Christology imagined that the gains were well above the loses. For one thing there was no longer any need to defend and explain the Greek substance philosophical terms used in the creeds. That in itself was no small gain. Further the supernaturalism of historic Christology proved more of a burden than a help in the modern world. A reductionist Christology greatly reduces the conflict of the Christian faith with the modern world. A reductionist Christology could also be made more relevant to the particular problems of modern people. Thus Bultmann's existential Christology parallels the existential problems of modern minds. Reductionist Christology does not deal with such absolutes as saved or lost, heaven or hell, redeemed or unredeemed, natural humanity or spiritual humanity. It locates the offense of Christianity in its challenge to the "life style" of modern people. Reductionist Christology thus unburdens the church from defending the absurdities bound up with historic Christianity and enables the church to preach a more modern, more relevant, and more believable Jesus.

No doubt those who offer us a reductionist Christology believe that they have made a great gain in making Jesus more credible to the modern person. But before that can be assessed the losses of reductionist Christology must be counted.

(1) J. S. Lawton (1947) argues that modern reductionist Christologies (or paradigm Christologies) are new in the church (except in the general sense that they are revivals of Antiochene or Ebionite Christologies). These Christologies may be more right than the historic Christology but the point of Lawton is that they are not the faith of the prior Christian centuries. They are Christologies that an Augustine, Tertullian, Thomas, Luther, or Gerhard would never recognize. In a word the new Christologies or reductionism represent a major break with the historic Christology of Christendom. But what is reprehensible to followers of historic Christology is the pretension that if Luther were alive today he would really side with Bultmann, or if Calvin were alive today he would agree with Fuchs, Ebelings, or Sölle's Christology.

(2) The Christ of reductionist Christologies was buried and his body corrupted. The claim of the bodily resurrection by the early church is a factual, historical error. If this is the case then a personal relationship with Jesus Christ is impossible. Paul's statements that for him to live is Christ (Phil. 1:21), and that his life in the flesh is lived by the faithfulness of the Son of God (Gal. 2:20) presume a personal relationship of Paul with Jesus Christ. But that presumes the resurrection of Christ. Nor can one meaningfully speak of loving the Lord Jesus Christ as does Peter (1 Pet. 1:8) and Paul (1 Cor. 16:22). In other words the great historic doctrine of *Christus praesens* is gone. If Christ is not risen from the dead he cannot be spiritually present by the Holy Spirit with the believer of the church. The only Christ for the church and the believer is the *remembered* Christ.

(3) Paul presents the greatest conquest of Christ the risen Lord and Victor to be that of death (1 Cor. 15:26). In a reductionist Christology there is no such victory possible. In fact Christ is dead and his dust is somewhere in Palestine. He too is the victim of death. A reductionist Christology may have a message which enables us to face death with courage, but it offers no conquest of death. Modern theologians may take a medical view of death and so naturalize it as one of the events that befall all living things. But again, death is not conquered but neutralized. (Ernest Becker's *The Denial of Death* shows how impossible it is to truly naturalize or neutralize death.)

Again a reductionist Christology may be right. But if the apostle Paul is right, then reductionist Christologies cannot offer the human race the final conquest of death, its greatest enemy.

(4) Reductionist Christologies state directly that the church really did not understand Jesus properly until the nineteenth century or more likely the twentieth. It means that starting with Justin Martyr the church has been wrong in its Christology through the centuries. Christology did rest upon a mistake. Again this may all be true. It may be that the New Testament is infiltrated with mythological ways of thinking that are impossible for us to accept. But before it is granted that modern radical criticism is right on this point it should first be looked at squarely and firmly; namely, for nineteen centuries Christology has been based on an unfortunate error of attributing deity and uniqueness to a man and only a man. One may soften the blow by saying that the real meaning and value of Jesus was maintained in this history regardless of the theological excesses, so it was not all lost time. But it is also a very hard if not cruel statement. Again, the critics may be right, but the full force of their position about the history of the church should be counted before there is consent to their interpretation.

(5) The most serious defect of all reductionist Christologies is that they do not have a Savior who can save. The whole Christian scheme must be retooled. Sin becomes sensuousness, worldliness, or inauthenticity but not an offense to a holy God. Jesus is central, important, and even called the Redeemer, but that is not in virtue of an atoning death and a victorious resurrection. Salvation is a new God-consciousness, a new sense of divine sonship, a new call to authentic living, or a new burden for social justice. But in all of this there is no Savior as offered in Nicea or Chalcedon. If historic Christology is surrendered so is the historic understanding of Jesus Christ as Lord and Savior.

CHRISTUS PRAESENS

Kierkegaard raised an issue very sharply: is there an advantage accruing to those who saw Jesus Christ in the days of his flesh that no other generation of Christians to the end of time may enjoy? Kierkegaard affirmed that there was no such advantage. The encounter with Jesus Christ is the same for all generations. Those of the twentieth century can have the same sense of presence, of immediacy, of directness, and of intimacy with Christ as those who saw him in the flesh in the first century. He stated this in two different expressions: (i) there are no second-hand disciples. If only those who saw Christ in the flesh had the real encounter with Christ then all other believers are disciples at second hand. But if Christ is spiritually the same to all believers of all ages then all disciples are disciples by first hand. (ii) Every person is a contemporary with his own generation and with Jesus Christ. Those of us who live in the twentieth century are as contemporary with Christ as those who knew him in the first century.

This spiritual presence of Christ to every generation of Christians is known as *Christus praesens*. The expression itself is seldom used in theology. Dietrich Ritschl's *Theology of Proclamation* gives it extended treatment and Otto Weber refers to it many times in his *Grundlagen der Dogmatik*. But the concept has a rich place in Christian theology and Christian spirituality.

Christus praesens is at the center of so many doctrines. Conversion: Paul said that his salvation dates from that time in which it pleased God to reveal his Son to Paul (Gal. 1:16). Christian experience: Paul affirms that for him to live is Christ (Phil. 1:21), and that the life he now lives in the flesh he lives by reason of the fidelity of the Son of God to him (Gal. 2:20). Prayer: in time of great affliction of pain Paul prays to the Lord, which in context means Christ (2 Cor. 12:8). The Holy Spirit: the relationship of Christ and the Holy Spirit in the life of the believer and the church is possible only on the grounds of *Christus praesens*. No matter the differences between Lutheran and Reformed Christologies they each assert in their own way *Christus praesens*.

An adherent of historic Christology then believes that to deny *Christus praesens* is to painfully undercut so much New Testament theology; and on the other hand the doctrine of *Christus praesens* is possible only on the grounds of historic Christology.

If historic Christology is denied then there can be no spiritual presence of Christ to the believer or to the church. In what sense is Jesus then present? From Schleiermacher to Bultmann, Jesus can be present only as remembered. There is no real presence of Christ in preaching, prayer, sacrament, or Christian fellowship. Jesus is present only in the sense that his name is mentioned, his words are repeated, or his deeds are recited. Realistically speaking, to the deniers of the historic Christology of the church, Jesus' body corrupted somewhere around Jerusalem. If there is the immortality of the soul then Jesus lives with all the other immortal souls. But he is neither the risen and reigning Lord of the New Testament nor the *Christus praesens* spiritually present in the church. To say with Bultmann and many others that Jesus lives in the kerygma is a highly circumlocutious way of saying that in the kerygma Jesus' name is mentioned.

If the doctrine of *Christus praesens* is denied then certainly the Roman Catholic church as historically understood collapses. For one thing the pope cannot be the earthly vicar of a dead Christ nor the Eucharist be a form of sacrifice if the original victim has become dust in ancient Palestine. Just as certainly the Reformers' version of Christianity collapses. If Jesus Christ is not risen from the dead the doctrine of justification by faith makes no sense, for Paul says that Christ was raised from the dead for our justification (Rom. 4:25). Further, the doctrine of the new birth or regeneration also collapses, for its whole foundation is the crucified and risen Christ.

Part of the doctrine of *Christus praesens* is that manner in which the Holy Spirit is related to Christ, to the gospel, to the believer, and to the church. The Holy Spirit is the person who is the power of God in making Christianity effective. To deny the doctrine of *Christus praesens* is to deny also the doctrine of the Holy Spirit. The question then posed to such a theologian is to explain where the power of Christian preaching is?

One answer is that preaching is directed towards the existential. The existential part of a person is the most powerful part, and so when the existential is aroused the person is transformed. Another answer is that the stories about Jesus have a power in themselves to arouse listeners to discipleship. Both of these solutions fail because they do not face the power of sin in the human life. Only the Holy Spirit is equal to the power of sin in humanity, and therefore a theology without *Christus praesens* is a powerless theology.

THE CHRISTIAN HOPE

The Christian hope is Jesus Christ as crucified, as risen, as reigning, and as coming again. But that hope has been eroded away in the minds of many theologians by modern science and modern philosophy.

That a person has an immortal soul has been attacked by Hume. It is denied that there is empirical evidence for life after death. Modern biology and physiology identify the mind with the brain. Death comes to a person as it does to all animals. A significant number of Christian theologians have been impressed by such arguments and accordingly limit the Christian faith to the quality of life in one's own span of time on this earth. This means that the hope of the Christian contained in historic Christology is surrendered. Jesus Christ is no longer our hope (cf. 1 Tim. 1:1 and TDNT, 2: 530-33 on Christian hope).

To Bultmann hope is openness to the future, which means living a life of radical obedience to love. There is no hope centered in the return of Christ. To Tillich eternal life is the present quality of Christian experience. To process theologians our immortality is to be ever remembered by God, but there is no personal hope.

There are also a number of theologies which can be called theologies of hope. Some input comes from the studies of Old Testament theologians on the eschatological nature of the kingdom of God. Some input comes from Ernst Bloch, the Marxist revisionist, who does not see history as determined but plastic; hence there is hope that the future of humankind may be better. Another source of the new theology of hope is the refusal of younger German theologians to be fixed in everlasting pessimism by the Nazi phenomenon and World War II.

The basic motif of the theologians of hope is that our future is not determined. The course of history is plastic and not rigid cement. The course can be changed. The kingdom of God is here in power and we can cooperate with it. Revolution as a program for all gradations of change is the weapon. Hence we can hope for a world of more justice, of less social and economic evils.

Those who believe in the hope of historic Christology do not demean the necessity of the quality of eternal life in our present existence. John's gospel is clear on that point. Nor is there any less feeling for the great masses of unfortunate people of this earth. A genuine Christian heart is tender to all sufferings and injustices. But these are not the Christian hope itself. Only in historic Christology is there the greatest hope for the human person. This hope has been set out so personally, so existentially, in the *Heidelberg Catechism*:

> *Question 1: What is thy only comfort in life and death?* A. That both in soul and body, whether I live or die, I am not mine own, but belong wholly unto my most faithful Lord and Savior Jesus Christ, who by his precious blood most fully satisfying for all my sins, hath delivered me from all the power of the devil, and so preserveth me, that without the will of my heavenly Father not so much as a hair may fall from my head, yea, all things must serve for my safety. Wherefore by his Spirit also he assureth me of everlasting life, that henceforth I may live to him (Schaff: 1897, I: 539).

It is only in historic Christology that the great hope of the church in the victory, return, and reign of Jesus Christ our Lord is maintained. All modern denials of that hope or alternate versions break with a tradition from the Apostles' Creed to the Barmen Declaration.

Russell Aldwinckle (1972) has complained that the issue of our personal survival after death has been pushed aside in much recent theology, and therefore he thinks it is time to bring it back into focus. It is a balanced book that does not pit against each other (i) serious social concerns now and (ii) hope in the age after this age. But he is resolute that the doctrine of the resurrection of the dead be given its proper hearing.

It is the claim of historic Christology that it alone contains the one real hope of man: the person of Jesus Christ as Lord, as Redeemer, as King of Kings, as Victor. Paul claims that the last great enemy is death (1 Cor. 15:26). In that so many current theologies deny any immortality of the soul or resurrection of the body, they also deny Paul's verdict that death is the final and worst enemy. Instead finite liberation in this life replaces the final liberation from death in the resurrection of the dead. Historic Christology stays with the Christian hope of the ages; namely, the victorious coming of Jesus Christ. He alone has conquered death; he alone entered that eternal, eschatological state in this time span of history, and he therefore alone is our hope in life and in death, in this world and in the world to come.

HOLY SCRIPTURE

The serious attack on the credibility of Holy Scripture had its roots in the seventeenth century (Spinoza and Astruc). The more sustained attack came in the eighteenth century, the century of the Enlightenment. Since then a number of other forces have joined in the attack, such as scientific history and scepticism in philosophy. In the face of such a diversity of attacks, it would seem impossible to defend the integrity of Holy Scripture in the twentieth century.

Efforts to maintain the integrity of Scripture have centered around new and more sophisticated versions of the inerrancy or infallibility of Scripture. But such defenses are only convincing to those who advocate them. The larger critical community in theological education is unimpressed by such a defense. It is our contention that if the Holy Scriptures are to be yet the authoritative Word of God in the church, the first line of defense must be in the content of Scripture and not any theory of inspiration. And that content is the Christological content. In modern times it has been Karl Barth who has relentlessly argued that the basis of accepting Holy Scripture as the Word of God is its Christological content, and in this I think he is right. Christ is the burden, the content, the substance of Holy Scripture, and without him it becomes but another book of religion.

The early church, sometimes wisely and sometimes extravagantly, defended the Christological character of the Old Testament in radical contrast with the Talmudic understanding of the same.

Such a view of Christ and Scripture means that there is a co-penetration, a perichoresis between Holy Scripture and Christology. The reason arguments for the inerrancy of Scripture or the infallibility of Scripture impress only their defenders is that, in making the doctrine of Scripture the primary doctrine of Christian theology, it breaks up the *perichoresis* of Scripture and Christ (or in more formal language it separates the form of Scripture from the content of Scripture).

However three important qualifications are in order lest the above thesis be misunderstood:

(1) The thesis is not intended to undermine the integrity of the Jewish Scriptures as if they did not have a life, a relevance, a substance of their own apart from Christ. If that were done it would in turn undermine the New Testament. The New Testament is grafted onto the Old Testament root.

(2) The thesis is no justification for excessive Christological interpretation of the Old Testament. It does not mean that every paragraph or book carries a hidden Christological substance. The thesis does not support allegorical excesses or fancies of typology. The thesis is concerned with the main highway through the Old Testament.

(3) The thesis does not intend to give a simplified version of an Old Testament theology. To this date no theology of the Old Testament is able to capture all the richness of the Old Testament within one scheme (although the effort goes on).

The church and the synagogue differ at one fundamental point which cannot be masked or abandoned in good Christian conscience; namely, *the provisional character of the Old Testament revelation*. The Old Testament is like a tree trunk which presupposes the rest of the tree. It is filled with anticipations, pointers, future events, and promises which are not complete in Israel's history. Or the Old Testament is like the unfinished ramps of a freeway interchange. They yet await being joined to highways. The prophetic nature of the Old Testament, the apocalyptic passages, and the eschatological overtones are unfulfilled at the end of the Old Testament canon.

It is granted that Scripture is such a varied book that no system of concepts harmonizes it all. That Christ is the burden and substance of Scripture means that he is the center amidst the diversity is such themes as creation, fall, redemption, and consummation; or, the kingdom of God announced, the kingdom of God coming, the kingdom of

203

God here, and the kingdom of God at the end of the human history; or salvation prefigured and anticipated, salvation coming in Christ, salvation as now experienced, and salvation at the end of time.

That Christ is the burden of Scripture saves Scripture from being a gnostic book; that is, it is not a book of specialized knowledge. It is a book of redemption. It attracts and holds the human heart with its message of divine love, divine salvation, and redemption in the name of Jesus Christ. It is a book of divine knowledge, but it is saving or soteric knowledge. It is a book of special revelation but a revelation special in its picture of a Savior and the salvation he profers.

DIVINE REVELATION

It is clear from reading such diverse writers as Prenter, Brunner, Elert, Barth, Kreck, Pannenberg, and Kaspers that if revelation has occurred in our world, its validity hinges on the person of Christ. Whatever revelation occurred in the composition of the Old Testament, it would not be able to hold its own in the modern world if limited to only Old Testament considerations.

The modern developments in science, scientific history, technology, and philosophy subject any claims to a knowledge of God to very sharp scrutiny. The competition is hard and rough. It is our conviction that only a strong doctrine of revelation, centering in the person of Christ, can maintain itself in such a critical atmosphere.

Brunner's claim that we believe in Christ and then the Scriptures is systematically misunderstood by the conservative and fundamentalist writers. His point is that unless we have encountered Christ in our own experience, we would have no inclination to take Holy Scripture seriously. No doubt some of Brunner's views of Scripture and revelation do not please his evangelical critics, but the point he makes cannot be faulted. It is our Christological experience which holds us to Holy Scripture rather than a formal doctrine of revelation or inspiration.

It could also be argued that only a Christological theodicy can maintain itself in the modern world. Human history in the past century is filled with terrible events of injustice, murderous wars, brutality inflicted on the poor and defenseless, senseless acts of murder, etc. Such events of evil have collapsed the traditional theodicies. The only real counterpart to the problem of evil and theodicy is that God's Son took our sins, and burdens, our acts of sadism and brutality, and bore them in his own body to suffer and die on the cross.

SACRAMENTAL THEOLOGY

The Christian church started with three gifts: (i) the gift of the tradition of Jesus Christ from the apostles which eventually produced the New Testament; (ii) the gift of the Holy Spirit; and (iii) the sacraments of baptism and communion. Although there is debate about apostolic succession we may appeal with some confidence to an unbroken tradition of the sacraments in the church.

Certainly there are severe differences in sacramental theology. Christians debate over the number, over the minister of the sacrament, and over the nature of the efficacy of the sacrament. Luther differed from Thomas; Zwingli from Luther; and Calvin from Zwingli. But there is one thing common to all historic sacramental theology: *sacraments of baptism and communion are based upon historic Christology*. It is the vicarious death and bodily resurrection of Jesus Christ which give the meaning and substance to these sacraments. Deny that and the sacraments become ambiguous if not meaningless. It is only in the theology of historic Christology that the sacraments retain their meaning and their substance. Whatever differences the Roman Catholic theologians and the theologians of the Reformation may have had, they both agreed that the sacraments were divinely appointed rituals for the worship of the church.

A unique tribute to the power of the sacraments in the life of the church is the fact that when theologians deny historic Christology, which in principle undermines the sacraments, they nevertheless do not reject the sacraments. They uniformly attempt to save the sacraments by giving them a different interpretation, which still makes them important in the life of the church. Paul Tillich (1963, Vol. 3) gives them the barest of treatment. Rudolph Bultmann (1951) provides an existential interpretation. Gerhard Ebeling (1968) modifies them into "Word occurrences." Others call them enriching symbols necessary to supplement the verbal expression of the faith. Still others convert them into purely part of the depth-fellowship of the church or as symbols of the church as a fellowship and communion. Mellert's (1975, ch. 9) effort to rehabilitate the sacraments within a process philosophy is (in the language of linguistic philosophy) a categorical mistake. Whiteheadian categories and concepts displace the original biblical theology. None of these efforts to rehabilitate sacramental theology within modern reductionist Christologies really harmonize with the theological foundations of the sacraments as set out in the New Testament.

A glance at such sacramental literature as Oliver Chase Quick, *The Christian Sacraments*, Robert S. Paul, *The Atonement and the Sacraments*, Karl Rahner, *The Church and the Sacraments*, or Karl Barth, *Church Dogmatics*, IV/4 reveals that historic Christology is at the root of all such sacramental thinking. A further tribute to the sacraments is how they remain in the church no matter what the shifts are in theology. Theologians who shift radically away from historic Christology and any version of orthodox Christianity nonetheless retain the sacraments. Ministers who deny almost every line of historic Christology nonetheless celebrate the sacraments.

It is common knowledge that Schleiermacher weakened the case for the sacraments. Since he denied historic Christology how could it be otherwise? Currently the effort is made to make them part of the word-event; hence the sacraments are a dramatic or symbolic version of the preached word-event. But sacraments as a word-event, or as the cultic union of believers, or as significant church memorials, or as existential occasions all come far short of the historic understanding of the sacraments. These are trivializations of the sacraments.

It is only within the presuppositions of historic Christology that baptism means anything with its promise of the forgiveness of sins through the cross of Christ and the promise of new life through the resurrection of Christ. And this is also true of holy communion. If the radical critics are right in asserting that there is no vicarious death on the cross and no bodily resurrection from the dead, then they ought to have the courage of their radical convictions and make an end of the sacraments. For to deny the premises of the sacraments in historic Christology is to undermine the meaning of the sacraments in the Christian church for nineteen centuries. To retain them for whatever reason can only be—and we say it sharply—a form of temporizing.

THEORY OF KNOWLEDGE

In philosophy theory of knowledge (or epistemology) is the study of how it is possible to have knowledge or how it is possible to know anything. Or, if a person makes a claim to a certain bit of knowledge, how does such a person claim to know that piece of knowledge and so differentiate it from rumor, gossip, or opinion.

Historic Christology is not only affirmations about the person of Christ but carries with it a theory of knowledge on how Christ is so known. Jesus Christ came as prophet and teacher, which has strong implications for the Christian theory of knowledge. He is also called the Logos who reveals to his followers the intimate secrets of God (John 1:18). High claims in Christology are matched by high claims of knowledge. Hence the church knows what it knows by the divine means of giving and receiving the true knowledge of God. Its theory of knowledge is equal to its claims in Christology.

Of course included in our knowledge of God and of Christ is a large number of ethical materials. And these ethical materials share in the same rootedness of divine revelation as do the Christological materials. Not every ethical issue is to be found in the New Testament, but certainly that is where the Christian conscience finds its orientation and point of departure for ethical issues.

This is precisely what reductionist Christologies cannot do. After the New Testament has been so radically criticized and the supernatural completely eliminated, there is no adequate epistemological base left. When the scholar has used his critical acumen to level down the New Testament Christology, he nonetheless wants to say something normative about Jesus that applies to all human beings. But this is impossible. So much of Christology has been denied that there is no foundation left whereby the universal validity of Jesus Christ and his message can be proclaimed. And whatever critical scholarship may say about historic Christology, it cannot fault it for not having a theory of knowledge equal to the majestic claim it makes about the person of Christ, of whom it has been written: "Jesus Christ the same! Yesterday! Today! Forever!" (Heb. 13:8).

Suggestions for Further Reading

CONTEMPORARY SURVEYS OF CHRISTOLOGY

Bowman, John Wick. *Which Jesus?*

Dawe, Donald G. "Christology in Contemporary Systematic Theology." *Interpretation.*

Grillmeier, Aloys and Henrich Bracht. *Das Konzil von Chalkedon: Chalkedon heute*, Vol. III.

Hendry, George. "Christology," *A Dictionary of Christian Theology.*

McIntyre, John. *The Shape of Christology.*

McDonald, H. D. "The Person of Christ in Contemporary Speculation and Biblical Faith," *Vox Evangelica.*

Macquarrie, John. "Recent Thinking on Christian Beliefs: I. Christology," *The Expository Times.*

Sykes, S. W., and J. P. Clayton, *Christ Faith and History.*

Reinhardt, Klaus. *Der Dogmatische Schriftgebrauch in der katholischen und protestantischen Christolgie von der Aufklarung bis zur Gegenwart.*

HISTORICAL SURVEYS OF CHRISTOLOGY

Duling, Dennis C. *Jesus Christ Through History.*

Franks, Robert S. *A History of the Doctrine of the Work of Christ.*

Grillmeier, Aloys. *Christ in the Christian Tradition*, Vol 1. *From the Apostolic Age to Chalcedon* (451).

Grillmeier, Aloys and Heinrich Bracht, *Das Konzil von Chalkedon: Geschichte und Gegenwart.*

An Evangelical Christology

von Harnack, Adolph. *History of Dogma.*
Meyendorff, John. *Christ in Eastern Christian Thought.*
Schaff, Philip. *Creeds of Christendom.*
Zamoyta, Vincent. *A Theology of Christ: Sources.*

BOOKS ON CURRENT CRITICAL ISSUES
IN NEW TESTAMENT STUDIES

Boers, Hendrikus. "Where Christology is Real: A Survey of Recent Research on New Testament Christology," *Interpretation.*
Braaten, Carl E. and Roy A. Harrisville, *The Historical Jesus and the Kerygmatic Christ.*
Briggs, R. C. *Interpreting the New Testament Today.*
Brown, Colin. Editor. *History, Criticism and Faith.*
Fror, Kurt. *Biblische Hermeneutik.*
Fuller, Reginald. *The New Testament in Current Study.*
_____. *The Foundations of New Testament Christology.*
Guthrie, Donald. *New Testament Introduction.*
Hengel, Martin. *The Son of God.*
_____. *Acts and the History of Earliest Christianity.*
Hoskyns, Edwyn and Noel Davy, *The Riddle of the New Testament.*
Kümmel, Werner Georg. *The New Testament: The History of the Investigation of its Problems.*
Marshall, I Howard. Editor, *New Testament Interpretation: Essays on Principles of Methods.*
Neil, Stephen. *The Interpretation of the New Testament: 1861-1961.*
Reumann, John. *Jesus in the Church's Gospels.*
Soulen, Richard N. *Handbook of Biblical Criticism.*
Stuhlmacher, Peter. *Historical Criticism and Theological Interpretation of Scripture.*

THEOLOGICAL INTRODUCTIONS TO CHRISTOLOGY

Aldwinckle, Russell F. *More Than Man: A Study in Christology.*
Baillie, Donald M. *God Was in Christ: An Essay on Incarnation and Atonement.*
Berkouwer, G. C. *The Person of Christ.*
Bonhoeffer, Dietrich. *Christology.*

210

Suggestions for Further Reading

Brunner, Emil. *The Mediator.*
Kasper, Walter. *Jesus the Christ.*
Mackintosh, H. R. *The Doctrine of the Person of Jesus Christ.*
Pannenberg, Wolfhart. *Jesus–God and Man.*
Vogel, Heinrich. *Gott in Christo.*

General Bibliography

ALDWINCKLE 1972	Russell Aldwinckle, *Death in the Secular City*. Grand Rapids: Eerdmans.
1976	Russell F. Aldwinckle, *More Than Man: A Study in Christology*. Grand Rapids: Eerdmans.
ANDERSON 1972	Charles C. Anderson, *The Historical Jesus: A Continuing Quest*. Grand Rapids: Eerdmans.
ALTHAUS 1966	Paul Althaus, *The Theology of Martin Luther*. Philadelphia: Fortress Press.
BAILLEY 1972	George Bailley, *Germans*. New York: Avon Books.
BAILLIE 1948	Donald M. Baille, *God Was in Christ: An Essay on Incarnation and Atonement*. New York: Charles Scribner's Sons.
BARKER, LANE, MICHAELS 1969	Glenn W. Barker, William L. Lane, and J. Ramsey Michaels, *The New Testament Speaks*. New York: Harper and Row.
BARRETT 1978	C. K. Barrett, *The Gospel According to John*. Second Edition; Philadelphia: Westminster Press.
BARTH 1945	Karl Barth, *Auslegung von Matthaus 23, 16-20*. Basler Missionsstudien Neue Folge, nr. 17. Basel: Basler Missions Buchhandlung.
1952	*Rudolph Bultmann: Ein versuch, ihn zu Verstehen*; Theologische Studien Heft 34. Zollikon-Zurich: Evangelischer Verlag.
1956	*Die Menschlichkeit Gottes*. Theologische Studien. Heft 48. Zollikon-Zurich: Evangelischer Verlag.

1966	*How I Changed My Mind*. Edited by John D. Godsey; Richmond: John Knox Press.
1936-1969	Church Dogmatics. 13 vols. Edinburgh: T. & T. Clark.
BARTSCH 1960	Hans-Werner Bartsch, *Das historische Problem des Lebens Jesu*. München: Chr. Kaiser Verlag.
BECKER 1975	Ernest Becker, *The Denial of Death*. New York: The Free Press.
1975	*Escape From Evil*. New York: Free Press.
BERKOUWER 1954	G. C. Berkouwer, *The Person of Christ*. Grand Rapids: Eerdmans.
1972	*The Return of Christ*. Grand Rapids: Eerdmans.
1975	*Holy Scriptures*. Grand Rapids: Eerdmans.
BERNARD 1867	Thomas Dehany Bernard, *The Progress of Doctrine in the New Testament*. New York: American Tract Society.
BETTENSON 1963	Henry Bettenson, *Documents of the Christian Church*. Second Edition; London: Oxford University Press.
BIETENHARD 1955	Hans Bietenhard, *Das tausend jahrige Reich*. Zürich: Zwingli Verlag.
BOERS 1972	Hendrikus Boers, "Where Christology is Real: A Survey of Recent Research on New Testament Christology," *Interpretation*, 26: 300-327.
BOFF 1978	Leonardo Boff, *Jesus Christ Liberator*. Maryknoll: Orbis Books.
BONHOEFFER 1966	Dietrich Bonhoeffer, *Christology*. London: Fontana Library.
BONINO 1976	Jose Miguez Bonino, *Doing Theology in a Revolutionary Situation*. Philadelphia: Fortress Press.
BORNKAMM 1962	Gunther Bornkamm, *Die Frage nach dem historischen Jesus*. Göttingen: Vandenhoeck & Ruprecht.
BOSLOOPER 1962	Thomas Boslooper, *The Virgin Birth*. Philadelphia: Westminster Press.
BOUSSET 1970	Wilhelm Bousset, *Kyrios Christos*. Nashville: Abingdon Press.

BOWMAN
1970

John Wick Bowman, *Which Jesus*. Philadelphia: Westminster Press.

BRAATEN
1962

Carl E. Braaten, *History and Hermeneutics. New Directions in Theology*, Vol II. Philadelphia: Westminster Press, 1962.

BRAATEN
HARRISVILLE
1964

Carl E. Braaten and Roy A. Harrisville, *The Historical Jesus and the Kerygmatic Christ*. New York: Abingdon Press.

BRIGGS
1914

Charles Augustus Briggs, *Theological Symbolics*. New York: Charles Scribner's Sons.

BRIGGS
1969

R. C. Briggs, *Interpreting the New Testament Today*. Nashville: Abingdon Press.

BROWN
1977

Colin Brown, Editor, *History, Criticism and Faith*. Second edition; Leicester: Inter-Varsity Press.

1984

Colin Brown, *Miracles and the Critical Mind*. Grand Rapids: Wm. B. Eerdmans.

BROWN
1966, 1970

Raymond E. Brown, *The Gospel According to John*. Anchor Bible. 29, 29A. Garden City: Doubleday.

1973

The Virginal Conception and Bodily Resurrection of Jesus. New York: Paulist Press.

1977

The Birth of the Messiah. Garden City: Doubleday.

BRUCE
1881

Alexander Balmain Bruce, *The Humiliation of Christ*. Second Edition; New York: Hodder and Stoughton.

BRUCE
1964

F. F. Bruce, *The Epistle to the Hebrews*. Grand Rapids: Eerdmans.

1970

Tradition, Old and New. Grand Rapids: Zondervan.

1978

"St. John at Ephesus." *Bulletin of the John Rylands University Library* 60: 339-61.

BRUNNER
1947

Emil Brunner, *The Mediator*. Philadelphia: Westminster Press.

BUCHANAN
1962

George Wesley Buchanan, *To the Hebrews*. Anchor Bible, 36. Garden City: Doubleday.

BULTMANN
1934

Rudolph Bultmann, *Jesus and the Word*. New York: Charles Scribner's Sons.

1951   *Theology of the New Testament*, 2 vols. New York: Charles Scribner's Sons.

1962   *History of the Synoptic Tradition*. New York: Harper and Row.

1964   "The Primitive Christian Kerygma and the Historical Jesus," in Carl E. Braaten and Roy A. Harrisville, Editors, *The Historical Jesus and the Kerygmatic Christ*. New York: Abingdon Press, 15-42.

1970   "Foreword," Wilhelm Bousset, *Kyrios Christos*. Nashville: Abingdon Press, 7-9.

BUTTERFIELD
1979   Herbert Butterfield, *Writings on Christianity and History*. C. T. McIntire, Editor; New York: Oxford University Press.

CABESTRERO
1980   Teofilo Cabestrero, *Faith: Conversations with Contemporary Theologians*. Maryknoll, New York: Orbis Books.

CAILLIET
1965   Emile Cailliet, "God Stands Behind the Book," Christianity Today, 9:708-09.

CALVERT
1971-72   D. G. A. Calvert, "An Examination of the Criteria for Distinguishing the Authentic Words of Jesus." *New Testament Studies* 18: 209-18.

CAMPENHAUSEN
1962   Hans Von Campenhausen, *Die Jungfrauengeburt in der Theologie der Alten Kirche*. Heidelberg: Carl Winter Universitätsverlag.

CAUTHEN
1962   Kenneth Cauthen, *The Impact of American Religious Liberalism*. New York: Harper and Row.

CHESTERTON
1925   Gilbert Keith Chesterton, *The Everlasting Man*. London: Hodder and Stoughton.

1973   *Orthodoxy*. New York: Doubleday.

CHILDS
1979   Brevard Childs, *Introduction to the Old Testament as Scripture*. Philadelphia: Fortress Press.

CLARK
1960   Francis Clark, *Eucharistic Sacrifice and the Reformation*. Westminster: Newman Press.

COBB
1975   John B. Cobb, Jr., *Christ in a Pluralistic Age*. Philadelphia: Westminster Press.

CRADDOCK
1968   Fred B. Craddock, *The Pre-existence of Christ in the New Testament*. New York: Abingdon Press.

CRANFIELD
1975, 1979

C. E. B. Cranfield, *The Epistles to the Romans*, 2 vols. International Critical Commentary. Edinburg: T. & T. Clark.

CULLMANN
1949

Oscar Cullmann, *The Earliest Christian Confessions*. London: Lutterworth Press.

1954

Tradition als exegetisches, historisches und Theologisches Problem. Zürich: Zwingli-Verlag.

1959

The Christology of the New Testament. Philadelphia: Westminster Press.

1962

Unsterblichkeit der Seele oder Auferstehung der Toten. Stuttgart: Kreuz-Verlag.

DAVIES
1958

J. G. Davies, *He Ascended into Heaven*. New York: Association Press.

DAWE
1963

Donald G. Dawe, *The Form of a Servant*. Philadelphia: Westminster Press.

1972

"Christology in Contemporary Systematic Theology," *Interpretation* 26:259-77.

DULING
1979

Dennis C. Duling, *Jesus Christ Through History*. New York: Harcourt, Brace, Jovanovich.

DUNN
1978

James D. G. Dunn, *Unity and Diversity in the New Testament*. Philadelphia: Westminster Press.

1980

Christology in the Making: A New Testament Inquiry into the Origins of the Doctrine of the Incarnation. Philadelphia: Westminster.

DURRWELL
1960

F.X. Durrwell, *The Resurrection: A Biblical Study*. New York: Sheed and Ward.

DUSEN
1963

Henry P. Van Dusen, *Vindication of Liberal Theology: A Tract for the Times*. New York: Scribners.

EBELING
1966

Gerhard Ebeling, *The Nature of Faith*. Philadelphia: Fortress Press.

1968

The Word of God and Tradition. Philadelphia: Fortress Press.

EDWARDS
1943

Douglas A. Edwards, *The Virgin Birth in History and Faith*. London: Faber & Faber.

ELERT
1960

Werner Elert, *Der christliche Glaube*. Fifth Edition; Hamburg: Furche-Verlag.

ELLICOTT 1891	C. J. Ellicott, *Christus Comprobator*. Naṣhville: Publishing House of the M. E. Church, South.
ELLIS 1961	E. Earle Ellis, *Paul and his Recent Interpreters*. Grand Rapids: Eerdmans.
EVANS 1979	C. S. Evans, "Mis-using Religious Language: Something about Kierkegaard and the Myth of God Incarnate." *Religious Studies* 15:139-57.
FACKRE 1977	Gabriel Fackre, "Cobb's *Christ in a Pluralistic Age*: A Review Article," Andover Newton Quarterly 17:308-315.
FERRE´ 1951	Nels F. Ferré, *The Christian Understanding of God*. New York: Harper and Brothers.
FISCHER 1970	Hermann Fischer, *Die Christologie des Paradoxes*. Göttingen: Vandenhoeck & Reprecht.
FORSYTH 1909	P. T. Forsyth, *The Person and Place of Jesus Christ*. Boston: Pilgrim Press.
FRANKS	Robert S. Franks, *A History of the Doctrine of the Work of Christ*, 2 vols. London: Hodder and Stoughton.
FROR 1967	Kurt Fror, *Biblische Hermeneutik*. Müchen: Chr. Kaiser Verlag.
FRYE 1979	Roland M. Frye, "Literary Criticism and Gospel Criticism," *Theology Today* 36:207-19.
FUCHS 1964	Ernst Fuchs, *Studies of the Historical Jesus*. London: S. C. M. Press.
FULLER 1962 1965	Reginald Fuller, *The New Testament in Current Study*. New York: Charles Scribner's Sons. *The Foundations of New Testament Christology*. New York: Charles Scribner's Sons.
GALLOWAY 1931	Allan D. Galloway, *The Cosmic Christ*. London: Misbet.
GASQUE, MARTIN 1970	W. Ward Gasque and Ralph Martin, *Apostolic History and the Gospel*. Grand Rapids: Eerdmans.
GERHARDSON 1961	Birger Gerhardson, *Memory and Manuscript*. Lund: C. W. J. C. Gleerup.
GILG 1966	Arnold Gilg, *Weg and Bedeutung der Altkirchlichen Christologie*. München: Chr. Kaiser Verlag.

GORE 1889	Charles Gore, "The Holy Spirit and Inspiration," *Lux Mundi*. Tenth Edition. New York: United States Book Co., 263-302.
GREEN 1977	Michael Green, Editor, *The Truth of God Incarnate*. Grand Rapids: Eerdmans.
GRIFFIN 1973	David R. Griffin, *A Process Christology*. Philadelphia: Westminster Press.
GRILLMEIER 1975	Aloys Grillmeier, *Christ in Christian Tradition* Vol 1: *From the Apostolic Age to Chalcedon (451)*. Second Edition; Atlanta: John Knox Press.
GRILLMEIER, BRACHT 1951-1954	Aloys Grillmeier and Heinrich Bracht, *Das Konzil von Chalkedon: Geschichte und Gegenwart*. 3 vols. Wurzberg. Echter Verlag.
GUNDRY 1967	Robert Horton Gundry, *The Use of the Old Testament in St. Matthew's Gospel*. Leiden: E. J. Brill, 178-85.
GUTHRIE 1971	Donald Guthrie, *New Testament Introduction*. Downers Grove: Inter-Varsity Press.
HAHN	Ferdinand Hahn, *Christologische Hoheitstitel*. Göttingen: Vandenhoeck & Ruprecht.
HAHN, LOHFF, BORNKAMM 1966	Ferdinand Hahn and Wenzel Lohff and Gunther Bornkamm, *Die Frage nach dem historischen Jesus*. Zweite Auflage. Göttingen: Vandenhoeck & Ruprecht.
HARDY 1954	Edward Rochie Hardy, Editor, *Christology of the Later Fathers*. *The Library of Christian Classics*, Vol. 3. Philadelphia: Westminster Press.
von HARNACK 1894 1901	Adolph von Harnack, *History of Dogma*, 7 vols. New York: Dover Publications. *What is Christianity?* Second Edition; New York: G. P. Putnam.
HATCH 1890	Edwin Hatch, *The Influence of Greek Ideas and Usages upon the Christian Church*. The Hibbert Lectures of 1888. London: Williams and Norgate.
HEBBLETHWAITE 1980	Peter Hebblethwaite, *The New Inquisition: The Case of Edward Schillebeeckx and Hans Kung*. Harper and Row: San Francisco.
HEIM 1959	Karl Heim, *Jesus the Lord*. Edinburgh: Oliver and Boyd.

HENDRY 1969	George Hendry, "Christology," *A Dictionary of Christian Theology*, 51-60. Alan Richardson, Editor. London: S. C. M. Press.
HENGEL 1976	Martin Hengel, *The Son of God*. Philadelphia: Fortress Press.
1977	*Crucifixion*. Philadelphia: Fortress Press.
1980	*Acts and the History of Earliest Christianity*. Philadelphia: Fortress Press.
1983	*Between Jesus and Paul. Studies in the Earliest History of Christianity*. Philadelphia: Fortress Press.
HICK 1977	John Hick, Editor, *The Myth of God Incarnate*. Philadelphia: Westminster Press.
HODGSON 1951	Leonard Hodgson, *The Doctrine of the Atonement*. New York: Charles Scribner's Sons.
HOSKYNS, DAVY 1958	Edwyn Hoskyns and Noel Davy, *The Riddle of the New Testament*. Third Edition; London: Faber & Faber.
JEREMIAS 1960	Joachim Jeremias, *Das Problem des historischen Jesus*. Stuttgart: Calwer Verlag.
1963	*The Parables of Jesus*. Second Edition; New York: Charles Scribner's Sons.
JONES 1956	Geraint Vaughn Jones, *Christology and Myth in the New Testament*. Naperville: Allenson.
KÄHLER 1964	Martin Kähler, *The So-Called Historical Jesus and the Historic Biblical Christ*. Carl E. Braaten, Editor and Translator; foreword by Paul Tillich; Philadelphia: Fortress Press.
KALDEWAY 1978	Jens Kaldeway, "Die Geschichte der synoptischen Tradition," *Bible und Gemeinde* 78:34-41.
KALLAS 1961	James Kallas, *The Significance of the Synoptic Miracles*. London: S. P. C. K. Press.
1968	*Jesus and the Power of Satan*. Philadelphia: Westminster Press.
KANT 1969	Immanuel Kant, *The Critique of Pure Reason*. New York: St. Martin's Press.
KÄSEMANN 1954	Ernst Käsemann, "Das Problem des historischen Jesus," *Zeitschrift für Theologie und Kirche* 51:125-253.
1964	*Essays on New Testament Themes*. London S. C. M. Press.

KASPER
1976

Walter Kasper, *Jesus the Christ*. New York: Paulist Press.

KAZANTAZAKIS
1960

Nikos Kazantzakis, *The Last Temptation of Christ*. New York: Bantam Books.

KELLER
1969

Ernst and Marie-Luise Keller, *Miracles in Dispute: A Continuing Debate*. London: S. C. M. Press.

KELLY
1964

1972

J. N. D. Kelly, *The Athanasian Creed*. London: Adam and Charles Black.

Early Christian Creeds. Third Edition; London: Longman, 1972.

KIERKEGAARD
1962

Soren Kierkegaard, *Philosophical Fragments*. Second Edition; Princeton: Princeton University Press.

KINGSTON-
SIGGINS
1970

I. D. Kingston-Siggins, *Martin Luther's Doctrine of Christ*. New Haven: Yale University Press.

KITTEL
1963-76

G. Kittel *et al*, Editor, *Theological Dictionary of the New Testament* (TDNT). 10 vols. Grand Rapids: Eerdmans.

KNOX
1952

1967

John Knox, *Christianity & Criticism*, New York: Abingdon-Cokesbury.

The Humanity and Divinity of Christ. Cambridge; Cambridge University Press.

KOCH
1957

Gerhard Koch, *Die Auferstehung Jesu Christi*. Tübingen: J. C. B. Mohr.

KRAFT
1979

Charles H. Kraft, *Christianity in Culture*. Maryknoll: Orbis Books.

KRAMER
1966

Werner Kramer, *Christ, Lord, Son of God*. Naperville: Allenson.

KRECK
1970

Walter Kreck, *Grundfragen der Dogmatik*. München: Chr. Kaiser Verlag.

KUHN
1970

Thomas S. Kuhn, *The Structure of Scientific Revolutions*. International Encyclopedia of Unified Science, Vol. II, no. 2, Second Edition. Chicago: University of Chicago Press.

KÜMMEL
1973

Werner Georg Kümmel, *The New Testament: The History of the Investigation of its Problems*. London: S. C. M. Press.

KÜNG
1976

Hans Küng, *On Being a Christian*. Garden City: Doubleday.

221

KYSAR 1975	Robert Kysar, *The Fourth Evangelist and His Gospel*. Minneapolis: Augsburg.
LACEY 1976	A. R. Lacey, *A Dictionary of Philosophy*. London: Routledge & Kegan Paul.
LADD 1975	George Eldon Ladd, *I Believe in the Resurrection of Jesus*. Grand Rapids: Eerdmans.
LAWTON 1947	John Stewart Lawton, *Conflict in Christology: A Study of British and American Christology from 1889-1914*. London: S. P. C. K. Press.
LEITH 1973	John Leith, *Creeds of the Church*. Revised Edition; Richmond: John Knox Press.
LESSING 1955	Gotthold Ephraim Lessing, *Nathan the Wise*. New York: Frederich Ungar.
LEWIS 1944	C. S. Lewis *Perelandra*. New York: Macmillan Company.
1967	*Christian Reflections*. Grand Rapids: Eerdmans.
LIDDON 1875	H. P. Liddon, *The Divinity of Our Lord and Savior Jesus Christ*. Seventh Edition; London: Rivingstons.
LITTLE 1934	V. A. Spence Little, *The Christology of the Apologists*. London: Duckworth.
LUBAC 1967	Henri De Lubac, *Teilhard de Chardin: The Man and His Message*. New York: New American Library.
MACHEN 1932	J. Gresham Machen, *The Virgin Birth of Christ*. Second Edition; New York: Harper and Bros.
MACKINTOSH 1931	H. R. Mackintosh, *The Doctrine of the Person of Jesus Christ*. New York: Charles Scribner's Sons.
MACQUARRIE 1979	John Macquarrie, "Foundation Documents of the Faith: III. The Chalcedonian Definition." *The Expository Times* 91:68-72.
MALONEY 1968	George A. Maloney, *The Cosmic Christ from Paul to Teilhard*. New York: Sheed and Ward.
MARSHALL 1976	I. Howard Marshall, *The Origins of New Testament Christology*. Downers Grove: Inter-Varsity Press.
1977	Editor, *New Testament Interpretation: Essays on Principles and Methods*. Grand Rapids: Eerdmans.

General Bibliography

1977   *I Believe in the Historical Jesus.* Grand Rapids:
              Eerdmans.

1978   *Commentary on Luke.* International Greek New
              Testament Commentary. Grand Rapids:
              Eerdmans.

MARTIN   James Martin, *Did Jesus Rise from the Dead?*
1956   New York: Assocation Press.

MARTIN   Ralph P. Martin, *Carmen Christi.* Cambridge:
1967   Cambridge University Press.

MARXSEN   Willi Marxsen, *Die Auferstehung Jesu als his-*
1965a   *torisches und als theologisches Problem.* Gu-
              tersloh: Gutersloher Verlaghaus Gerd Mohn.

1965b   *Der Streit um die Bibel.* Gladbeuk/Westfalen:
              Schriftmission Verlag.

1966   *Die Bedeutung der Auferstehungsbotschaft für den*
              Glauben an Jesus Chrustus. Gutersloh: Gu-
              tersloher Verlag Hause Gern Mohn.

1976   "Christology in the New Testament," *Inter-*
              preter's Dictionary of the Bible: Supplementary
              Volume, 146-56.

McDONALD   H. D. McDonald, "The Person of Christ in
1979   Contemporary Speculation and Biblical
              Faith," *Vox Evangelica* 7:5-17.

McGARRY   Michael B. McGarry, *Christology after Aus-*
1977   *chwitz.* New York: Paulist Press.

McINTYRE   John McIntyre, *The Shape of Christology.* Lon-
1966   don: S. C. M. Press.

MELLERT   Robert B. Mellert, *What is Process Theology?*
1975   New York: Paulist Press.

METZGER   Bruce Metzger, *A Textual Commentary on the*
1970   *Greek New Testament.* Stuttgart: Wurtenberg
              Bible Society.

MEYENDORFF   John Meyendorff, *Christ in Eastern Christian*
1969   *Thought.* Washington: Corpus Books.

MICHAELIS   Wilhelm Michaelis, *Die Erscheinungen des*
1944   *Auferstandenen.* Basel: Verlag von Heinrich
              Majer.

MIGLIORE   B. Migliore, "How Historical is the Resurrec-
1976   tion," *Theology Today* 33:7-14.

MONTEFIORE
1964

H. W. Montefiore, *The Epistle to the Hebrews*. London: Adam and Charles Black.

MONTGOMERY
1964-65

John Montgomery, *History and Christianity*. Downers Grove: Inter-Varsity Press.

MOLTMANN
1974

Jürgen Moltmann, *The Crucified God*, S. C. M. Press.

MOONEY
1968

Christopher F. Mooney, *Teilhard de Chardin and the Mystery of Christ*. Garden City: Image Books.

MORRIS
1965

Leon Morris, *The Cross in the New Testament*. Grand Rapids: Eerdmans.

1971

The Gospel According to John. Grand Rapids: Eerdmans.

MOULE
1977

C. F. D. Moule, *The Origin of Christology*. London: Cambridge University Press.

NEIL
1964

Stephen Neil, *The Interpretation of the New Testament: 1861-1961*. London: Oxford University Press.

NESTLE,
NESTLE,
ALAND
1968

Eberhard Nestle, Erwin Nestle, and Kurt Aland, *Novum Testamentum Graece*. Twenty-fifth Edition; Stuttgart: Wurtenburg Bible Society.

NUEFELD
1963

Vernon H. Neufeld, *The Earliest Christian Confessions*. Grand Rapids: Eerdmans.

NICHOLSON
1971

Henry Nicholson, *Jesus is Dead*. New York: Vantage Press.

NIEBUHR
1948

Reinhold Niebuhr, *The Nature and Destiny of Man*, 2 vols. New York: Charles Scribner's Sons.

OBERMANN
1971

Heiko Obermann, *The Virgin Mary in Evangelical Perspective*. Facet Historical Books. Philadelphia: Fortress Press.

O'GRADY
1981

John F. O'Grady, *Models of Jesus*. New York: Doubleday and Co.

ORR
1907

James Orr, *The Virgin Birth of Christ*. New York: Charles Scribner's Sons.

OTT
1960

Heinrich Ott, *Die Frage nach dem historischen Jesus und die Christologie der Geschichte*. Zürich: EVZ-Verlag.

1972

Die Antwort des Glaubens. Berlin: Kreuz Verlag.

OTTLEY 1896	Robert L. Ottley, *The Doctrine of the Incarnation*, 2 vols. London: Methuen and Co.
PANNENBERG 1968	Wolfart Pannenberg, *Jesus–God and Man*. Philadelphia: Westminster Press.
1976	*Theology and the Philosophy of History*. Philadelphia: Westminster Press.
1977	*Faith and Reality*. Philadelphia: Westminster Press.
PAUL 1960	Robert S. Paul, *The Atonement and the Sacraments*. New York: Abingdon Press.
PELIKAN 1971	Jaroslav Pelikan, *The Christian Tradition: The Emergence of the Catholic Tradition (100-600)*. Vol. 1. Chicago: University of Chicago Press.
PERRIN 1974	Norman Perrin, *A Modern Pilgrimage in New Testament Christology*. Philadelphia: Fortress Press.
1976	*Rediscovering the Teaching of Jesus*. New York: Harper and Row.
1977	*The Resurrection According to Matthew, Mark and Luke*. Philadelphia: Fortress Press.
PHILLIPS 1967	J. B. Phillips, *Ring of Truth: A Translator's Testimony*. London: Hodder and Stoughton.
PITTENGER 1970	Norman Pittenger, *Christology Reconsidered*. London: S. C. M. Press.
PRENTER 1960	Regin Prenter, *Schöpfung and Erlösung: Dogmatik*. Göttingen: Vandenhoeck & Ruprecht.
PUSEY 1876	E. B. Pusey, *On the Clause and the Son*. London: Walter Smith.
QUICK 1932	Oliver Chasea Quick, *The Christian Sacraments*. New Edition; London: Nisbet.
RAHNER 1978	Karl Rahner, *Foundations of Christian Faith*. New York: Seabury Press.
RAMM 1963	Bernard Ramm, *Them He Glorified*. Grand Rapids: Eerdmans.
REINHARDT 1970	Klaus Reinhardt, *Der Dogmatische Schriftgebrauch in der katholischen und protestantischen Christologie von der Aufklärung bis zur Gegenwart*. München: Verlag Ferdinand Schoningen.

RELTON
1917
Herbert M. Relton, *A Study in Christology*. London: S. P. C. K. Press.

REUMANN
1968
John Reumann, *Jesus in the Church's Gospels*. Philadelphia: Fortress Press.

RHINELANDER
1973
Philip H. Rhinelander, *Is Man Comprehensible to Man?* San Francisco: Freeman and Co.

RITSCHL
1960
Dietrich Ritschl, *A Theology of Proclamation*. Richmond: John Knox Press.

ROBERTS
1976
Robert C. Roberts, *Rudolph Bultmann's Theology*. Grand Rapids: Eerdmans.

ROBINSON
1959
James M. Robinson, *A New Quest for the Historical Jesus*. Naperville: Allenson.

1968
The Beginnings of Dialectical Theology, Vol. 1, Richmond: John Knox Press.

SANDAY
1910
William Sanday, *Christologies Ancient and Modern*. New York: Oxford University Press.

SANDERS
1971
Jack T. Sanders, *The New Testament Christological Hymns*. Cambridge: Cambridge University Press.

SAYERS
1943
Dorothy Sayers, *The Man Born to be King*. Grand Rapids: Eerdmans.

1947
Creed or Chaos? London: The Religious Book Club.

1951
The Emperor Constantine: A Chronicle. Grand Rapids: Eerdmans.

SCHAFF
1897
Philip Schaff, *Creeds of Christendom*, 3 vols. New York: Harper and Bros.

SCHILLEBEECKX
1979
Edward Schillebeeckx, *Jesus: An Experiment in Christology*. New York: Seabury Press.

SCHNEIDER
1958
Johannes Schneider, *Die Frage nach dem historischen Jesus in der neutestamentlichen Forschung der Gegenwart*. Berlin: Evangelische Verlagsanstalt.

SCHWEITZER
1910
Albert Schweitzer, *The Quest for the Historical Jesus*. London: Adam and Charles Black.

SKARD
1960
Bjarne Skard, *The Incarnation: A Study of the Christology of the Ecumenical Creeds*. Minneapolis: Augsburg Publishing House.

SMALLEY
1984
Stephen S. Smalley, *John: Evangelist and Interpreter*. Nashville: Thomas Nelson.

SOBRINO 1978	Jon Sobrino, *Christology at the Crossroads*. Maryknoll: Orbis Books.
SOLLE 1967	Dorothee Sölle, *Christ the Representative*. London: S. C. M. Press.
SOULEN 1976	Richard N. Soulen, *Handbook of Biblical Criticism*. Atlanta: John Knox Press.
STANTON 1974	G. N. Stanton, *Jesus of Nazareth in New Testament Preaching*. London: University of Cambridge Press.
STEAD 1979	G. C. Stead, "The Apostles Creed," *The Expository Times* 91:4-8.
STEIN 1979	Robert H. Stein, "Was the Tomb Really Empty?" *Themelios* 5:8-12.
STEWART 1935	James Stewart, *A Man in Christ*. London: Hodder and Stoughten.
STOTT 1979	John Stott. "The 'Mythmakers' Myth." *Christianity Today* 23 (Dec. 7):30.
STROOP 1978	G. W. Stroop, III, "Chalcedon Revisited," *Theology Today* 35:52-64.
STUHLMACHER 1977	Peter Stuhlmacher, *Historical Criticism and Theological Interpretation of Scripture*. Philadelphia: Fortress Press.
TAYLOR 1958	Vincent Taylor, *The Person of Christ*. London: Macmillan.
TDNT	See KITTEL.
THIELICKE 1965	Helmut Thielicke, *How the World Began*. Philadelphia: Muhlenburg.
1974-1982	*Evangelical Theology*. 3 vols. Grand Rapids: Eerdmans.
THOMPSON 1978	John Thompson, *Christ in Perspective: Christological Perspectives in the Theology of Karl Barth*. Grand Rapids: Eerdmans.
THUSING 1970	Wilhelm Thüsing, *Die Erhohung und Verherrlichung Jesus in Johannesevangelium*. Münster: Aschendorffsche Verlagbuchhandlung.
TIL 1960	Cornelius Van Til, "Karl Barth on Chalcedon," *Westminster Theological Journal* 22:147-66.
TILLICH 1951-1963	Paul Tillich, *Systematic Theology*. 3 vols. Chicago: University of Chicago Press.

TOON 1984	Peter Toon, *The Ascension of Our Lord*. Nashville: Thomas Nelson.
TORRANCE 1969	T. F. Torrance, *Space, Time and Incarnation*. London: Oxford University Press.
TURNER 1956	H. E. W. Turner, "The Virgin Birth," *Expository Times* 68:12-17.
VOGEL 1952	Heinrich Vogel, *Gott in Christo*. Berlin: Lettner Verlag.
WAINWRIGHT 1962	Arthur Wainwright, *The Trinity in the New Testament*. London: S.P.C.K. Press.
WALVOORD 1969	John F. Walvoord, *Jesus Christ Our Lord*. Chicago: Moody Press.
WARFIELD 1929	Benjamin Breckenridge Warfield, *Christology and Criticism*. New York: Oxford University Press.
1932	*Critical Reviews*. New York: Oxford University Press.
1952	*Biblical and Theological Studies*. Philadelphia: Presbyterian and Reformed Publishing House.
n.d.	*The Lord of Glory*. New York: American Tract Society.
WEBER 1962	Otto Weber, *Grundlagen der Dogmatik*, 2 vols, Neukirchen-Moers: Neukirchener Verlag.
WELCH 1965	Claude Welch, Editor, *God and Incarnation in Mid-nineteenth Century German Theology*. New York: Oxford University Press.
WELLS 1984	David F. Wells, *The Person of Christ*. Westchester, Ill.: Crossway Books.
WENHAM 1984	John Wenham, *The Easter Enigma*. Grand Rapids: Eerdmans.
WESTERMANN 1974	Claus Westermann, *Creation*. London: S.P.C.K. Press.
WILCKENS 1970	Ulrich Wilckens, *Auferstehung*. Berlin: Kreuz-Verlag.
WILLIAMS 1974	Ronald Williams, "Hebrews 4:15 and the Sinlessness of Jesus." *Expository Times* 86:4-8.
WILLIS 1966	E. David Willis, *Calvin's Catholic Christology*. Leiden: E. J. Brill.

WILSON
1976

Marvin Wilson, "The Jewish Concept of Learning: A Christian Appreciation." *Christian Scholars Review* 5:350-63.

WINGREN
1960

Gustav Wingren, *The Living Word*. Philadelphia: Fortress Press.

WINK
1973

Arthur Wink, *The Bible in Human Transformation*. Philadelphia: Fortress Press.

WOLF
1965

Herbert C. Wolf, *Kierkegaard and Bultmann: The Quest of the Historical Jesus*. Minneapolis: Augsburg Publishing House.

ZAHRNT
1963

Heinz Zahrnt, *The Historical Jesus*. New York: Harper and Row.

ZAMOYTA
1967

Vincent Zamoyta, *A Theology of Christ: Sources*. Milwaukee: Bruce Publishing Co.